☆ ☆ ☆ ☆ ☆ ☆ ☆

PRESIDENTIAL
SEX

☆ ☆ ☆ ☆ ☆

*From the Founding Fathers
to Bill Clinton*

WESLEY O. HAGOOD

A BIRCH LANE PRESS BOOK
Published by Carol Publishing Group

Excerpts from *Past Forgetting: My Affair With Dwight D. Eisenhower,* by Kay Summersby
Morgan, reprinted by permission of Harold Ober Associates Incorporated, copyright ©
1977 by Kay Summersby Morgan

A Birch Lane Press Book
Published by Carol Publishing Group
Birch Lane Press is a registered trademark of Carol Communications, Inc.
Editorial Offices: 600 Madison Avenue, New York, N.Y. 10022
Sales and Distribution Offices: 120 Enterprise Avenue, Secaucus, N.J. 07094
In Canada: Canadian Manda Group, One Atlantic Avenue, Suite 105,
     Toronto, Ontario M6K 3E7
Queries regarding rights and permissions should be addressed to Carol Publishing Group,
600 Madison Avenue, New York, N.Y. 10022

Carol Publishing Group books are available at special discounts for bulk purchases, sales
promotion, fund-raising, or educational purposes. Special editions can be created to
specifications. For details, contact: Special Sales Department, Carol Publishing Group,
120 Enterprise Avenue, Secaucus, N.J. 07094

MANUFACTURED IN THE UNITED STATES OF AMERICA
10 9 8 7 6 5 4 3 2 2 1

Book Design by Robert Freese

Library of Congress Cataloging-in-Publication Data

Hagood, Wesley.
     Presidential sex : from the founding fathers to Bill Clinton /
Wesley Hagood.
          p.   cm.
     ISBN 1-55972-308-4 (hc)
     1. Presidents—United States—Sexual behavior—History.
I. Title.
E176.4H34   1995
973'.099—dc20   95–19925

To my wife, Denise,

who believed in me
and supported me
in all my endeavors
through the years

Contents

Acknowledgments

I would like to thank my editor, Mr. Hillel Black, for making valuable suggestions that greatly improved this book. I'd also like to thank my publicist, Hillary Schupf, for all her assistance in promoting this work.

A special thank-you to Ms. Madeleine Brown for confirming information about her relationship with Lyndon Johnson.

Many thanks to the following individuals for their assistance in helping to obtain the photographs appearing in this book:

- Ann Marie Price of the Virginia Historical Society, Mrs. Bogen-Garrett of the Library of Virginia and Mr. Harrison Baird (for the portrait of Sally Cary Fairfax)
- Jocelyn Clapp of UPI/Bettman News Srevice
- Janice Dockery of the Historical Society of Pennsylvania
- Elvis Brathwaite of AP/Wide World Photos
- Kathy Bratton from the James Buchanan Foundation for the Preservation of Wheatland
- Charles Arp of the Ohio Historical Society
- Joe Sullivan, George Caldwell, Travis Wesley, and Fred Bauman of the Library of Congress
- Bill Loos of the Rare Book Collection of the Buffalo Public Library
- Mark Andries of the New York Public Library
- May Bell of the Buffalo and Erie County Historical Society
- Nancy Young from Princeton University's Mudd Archives
- Stacy Draper of the Renselaer County Historical Society, Troy, New York
- Julie Englander of the Newberry Library
- John Dyer And Debbie Lahanski, of the National Archives and Records Administration, College Park, Maryland

ACKNOWLEDGMENTS

A warm thank-you is extended to all of the librarians at the Eastport Annapolis Neck branch of the Anne Arundel County Public Library for helping to locate obscure books from our nation's libraries.

I would also like to thank Melvin Wulf of Beldock Levine & Hoffman for his legal review of the manuscript.

Finally, I would like to thank authors Oscar Collier, Frances Spatz Leighton, and Richard Balkin, who helped me understand how to turn an idea into a book proposal and finished manuscript.

Author to Reader

Many Americans have come to believe that all U.S. presidents must surely have had dark secrets about extramarital affairs. This perception is not true, or at least there is no written evidence to be found in the historical record. When there was no such evidence available, I just went on to the next president. However, numerous presidents do have a skeleton or two in their closet. A few have so many that there is no room in the closet for their trousers, which coincidentally they did not have much time to wear, except, of course, when they were being received in public.

In *Presidential Sex* I attempt to present an accurate account of what actually occurred. Many U.S. presidents led as colorful lives beneath the bedsheets as they did publicly before millions of Americans. Some may say that this book is patently un-American because it focuses on the darker character traits of some of these men. However, I suggest instead that it will make them seem more human and likable, since we will be better able to relate to them as "real" human beings with the same failings as the rest of us. Perhaps this book will challenge presidential biographers and noted historians to dig deeper to determine what new information the historical record will yield on this intriguing topic. And perhaps in the future presidential biographies will be more comprehensive and contain more information on the sexual behavior of our presidents.

Wesley O. Hagood
Annapolis, Maryland

Presidential Sexual Behavior Quiz

Directions: See if you can answer these questions about the sexual behavior of the U.S. presidents to be described in this book. The answers appear in Appendix B.

1. Which president repeatedly made love to a young girl from his hometown in a White House coat closet when, on at least one occasion, his wife was prevented from beating down the closet door by a Secret Service agent?

2. Which president married a woman who was not yet divorced from her first husband and was later labeled an "adulterer" during his reelection campaign?

3. Which future president wrote love letters to his neighbor's wife while he was engaged to another woman?

4. Which had numerous caustic and politically damaging poems written about his sexual dalliance and published in the major newspapers of the day?

5. Which president called his mistress "Pookie"?

6. Which one smoked marijuana in the nude with a naked, nubile young playgirl and joked about being incapacitated when it came time to push "the button" in the event of a nuclear attack?

7. Which two presidents had their former lovers die under mysterious circumstances? (Name the lovers, too.)

8. Which president said, "What a way to end the day!" when anticipating a rendezvous that was about to take place with a young playgirl?

9. Which presidents allegedly fathered illegitimate children?

10. Which vice president became angry because he felt that his record of actual sexual conquests was far greater than the then existing president's reputation for such conquests?

11. Which presidents called upon visits from young women in the White House secretarial pool for recreational sex?

12. Which had an alleged affair that lasted for decades with a slave who was also his wife's half sister?

13. Which president had a torrid love affair with the first lady's personal secretary?

14. Which president had sex with one of his secretaries stretched out on top of a desk in the White House?

15. Which two presidents had rendezvous with their mistresses at the Mayflower Hotel in Washington, D.C.?

16. Which future president never married because his fiancée broke off their engagement because of his reputation as a "man about town" and her death (which was rumored to be a suicide) occurred shortly thereafter?

17. Which president allegedly had an affair with one winner and one finalist in the Miss America Pageant?

18. Which president's wife was labeled an adulteress during his election campaign?

19. Which one had an affair with his driver?

20. Which president had a song written about his alleged illegitimate child that was often chanted at parades and political rallies?

21. Which president's campaign train made a layover so he could visit his mistress?

22. Which president lined up all the women willing to sleep with him at a private party on the eve of his inauguration and selected two with whom he would have sex?

23. Which president hid in his mistress's wardrobe when he thought a police raid was occurring?

24. Which two presidents allegedly asked their mistresses to participate in a ménage-à-trois sexual encounter?

25. Which one made love in a closet while telling his lover about a former president who made love in a White House coat closet?

PRESIDENTIAL
SEX

1

GEORGE WASHINGTON

Thou Shalt Not Covet Thy Neighbor's Wife

☆

At age fifty-one George Washington wrote, "When once the woman has tempted us and we have tasted the forbidden fruit, there is no such thing as checking our appetites, whatever the consequences may be." When he mentioned the *forbidden fruit*, was he talking about sex or simply the type of passion that can develop between a man and a woman but can never be legitimately fulfilled? Although a few historians believe that George Washington was a womanizer and some of his friends called him the "Stallion of the Potomac," there is little evidence that this was the case.

As a young man George was awkward, shy, and rather clumsy with women. When he was sixteen years old, a good friend wrote to a woman, "George Washington is beginning to feel the sap rising, being in the spring of life, and is getting ready to be the prey of your sex, wherfor may the Lord help him."

In his early twenties George was over six feet tall, bony, and broad-shouldered; he weighed 175 pounds. His feet and hands were huge. He had dark chestnut-colored hair, pale skin, penetrating blue-gray eyes, high cheekbones, and a broad, round face. He was passionate but re-

George Washington
First President of the United States (1789–97)

Biographical Information

Born: February 22, 1732
Died: December 14, 1799
Wife: Martha Dandridge Custis
Children: Two stepchildren; two adopted

Extramarital Affairs

Known and Suspected Sexual Partners:	Dates:	Locations:
Sarah ("Sally") Cary Fairfax	1748–59	Virginia

Illegitimate Children: None

---

strained, respectful and strong-tempered. He enjoyed dancing and wearing the latest fashions and loved horse racing. In 1759 he married the widow Martha Dandridge Custis. George was twenty-six; Martha, twenty-seven.

Martha was described as plump, pretty, and good-natured. She had a pert face, with almond-shaped hazel eyes, and was amiable and self-reliant. George himself said she was a "quiet wife" with a "quiet soul."

George married Martha more out of a need for companionship and an improved financial condition than for love. Martha was a young widow with two children when he married her. She was also the richest widow in Williamsburg. She had an estate valued at over £20,000 ($100,000), which belonged to George after their marriage. He admitted that he pursued judgment rather than passion and favored domestic felicity and tranquillity to excitement. He signed one letter shortly after their engagement "Your ever faithful and affectionate friend."

Years later, a flirtatious female acquaintance of Washington's admitted she had found a package of love letters written by him to a young woman. When she finally revealed that the young woman was his own wife, George said, commenting about the letters, "They would, I am per-

2

suaded, have been found to be more fraught with expressions of friendship than of enamoured love." He also added, referring to his sexual relationship with Martha, "To give the sheets warmth, one would have to
set them on fire." George and Martha seemed to be affectionate friends,
but their relationship and love lacked passion.

Years later, George wrote the following advice about marriage to one
of Martha's granddaughters:

> Love is a mighty pretty thing but like all other delicious things, it is cloy-
> ing; and when the first transports of the passion begin to subside, too
> dainty a food to live on alone . . . and ought not to be considered farther
> than a necessary ingredient for that matrimonial happiness which results
> from a combination of causes, none of which are of greater importance
> than that the object on whom it is placed should possess good sense, good
> dispositions, and the means of supporting you in the way you have been
> brought up. . . . There is no truth more certain than that all our enjoy-
> ments fall short of our expectations; and to none does it apply with more
> force, than to the gratification of the passions.[1]

Later, he penned the following passage about love and marriage in a letter to his granddaughter Nellie:

> Men and women feel the same inclination toward each other now that
> they always have done and which they will continue to do until there is
> a new order of things and you, as others have done, may find perhaps that
> the passions of your sex are easier raised than allayed. Do not therefore
> boast too soon or too strongly of your insensibility to or resistance of its
> powers. In the composition of the human frame there is a good deal of
> inflammable matter, however dormant it may lie for a time, and like an
> intimate acquaintance of yours, when the torch is put to it, that which is
> within you may burst into a blaze.[2]

Certainly George was drawing this advice from his personal experi-
ences. He didn't find these words of advice to Nellie in some dusty, old
commentary on love and passion. He was not referring to any passion
felt for his wife, Martha. He apparently was writing about an earlier instance in his life when he struggled with his passions. George was then
in his early twenties and discovered himself hopelessly in love with an
intimate acquaintance who was also his best friend's wife. There was no

legitimate way George could consummate this passion he discovered within himself. It likely had been fanned by some innocent event that could have ended with disastrous consequences.

Although George and Martha's relationship can at best be characterized as that of affectionate friends, he was romantically interested in several women during his lifetime, among them Frances Alexander, Betsy Fauntleroy, Mary Philipse, and Sally Fairfax—the one great passion of his life.

☆ ☆ ☆

George's first love was Frances Alexander. He wrote this acrostic poem to her in 1748 when he was just sixteen. The first letter of each line spells her name.

> *From your bright sparkling eyes, I was undone;*
> *Rays, you have more transparent than the sun,*
> *Amidst its glory in the rising Day,*
> *None can you equal in your bright array;*
> *Constant in your calm and unspotted Mind;*
> *Equal to all, but will to none prove kind;*
> *So, knowing, seldom one so young, you'll find*
>
> *Ah! woe's me, that I should love and conceal,*
> *Long have I wish'd, but never dare reveal,*
> *Even though severely love's pains I feel;*
> *Xerses that great, was't free from Cupid's Dart,*
> *And all the greatest Heros, felt the smart.*[3]

Later that same year he also wrote this sonnet for her.

> *Oh Ye Gods why should my poor heart*
> *Stand to oppose thy might and power*
> *At last surrender to cupid's feathered dart*
> *And now lays bleeding every hour*
> *For her that's pitiless of grief and woes*
> *And will not on me pity take*
> *I'll sleep amongst my most inveterate foes*
> *And with gladness never (wish) to wake*
> *In deluding sleepings let my eyelids close*

That in an enraptured dream I may
In a soft lulling sleep and gentle repose
Possess those joys denied by Day.[4]

Apparently she was not moved by either poem, and George gave up his pursuit when he became convinced that "were I ever to attempt anything, I should only get a denial which could be only adding grief to uneasiness."

☆ ☆ ☆

Betsy Fauntleroy was just sixteen, George twenty, when he began to show interest in her. Betsy was described as a small girl, with a round, petite face, a turned-up nose, and brown hair and eyes. The daughter of one of George's neighbors, one of the richest men in the area, she was charming, lively, and spirited. It is not clear whether George was interested in her romantically or whether he saw her primarily as a path to wealth and an exalted social standing in the colony. He proposed, and she turned him down. He decided to propose marriage a second time in a letter to her father, William, in 1752, but neither of them thought George a suitable husband, and Betsy rejected him once more. Again, George gave up his pursuit of a young woman.

☆ ☆ ☆

During a trip to Boston in February 1756 to settle a dispute over who was the senior ranking officer at Fort Cumberland, George spent several days on a side trip to New York visiting a wealthy young woman named Mary Eliza Philipse. She was twenty-six years old, two years his senior. Mary was described as deep-bosomed, slim and beautiful, with brown eyes and hair, a rather large nose, and a sensuous mouth. She was said to be gay and intelligent but also intimidating and strong-willed. Although George was very interested in Mary, little happened on this trip. Perhaps he saw in her some of the same undesirable traits that he could not abide in his own mother. For Mary was also notoriously strong-willed, dominating, and intimidating. He wrote a friend over a year later inquiring if his favor with Mary had changed. The friend recommended that he march to New York and "storm the works." Before he could decide whether to propose marriage, Mary announced her engagement to another gentleman.

☆ ☆ ☆

George first met the great love of his life in 1748, eight years before his trip to Boston, while living at the Mount Vernon home of his half brother, Lawrence. Her name was Sarah Cary Fairfax, and she was known as Sally. George was only sixteen; Sally, eighteen. Flirtatious and tantalizing, Sally was also worldly and well educated and was married to George's neighbor and best friend, George William Fairfax. One of Sally's descendants said that George experienced a "spontaneous combustion" after he met her. Sally was the most passionate love of his life. She had great influence in educating and molding this future president of the United States. It appears that George controlled his affections and behaved toward her in a very dignified and respectable manner. However, he was so openly affectionate that some thought they were having an affair. Unlike many modern politicians who often take advantage of their power and fame, it appears that George carried on a proper relationship with Sally. The only duplicity in his behavior occurred when he wrote this married woman a love letter six months after becoming engaged to marry Martha Custis.

George had been corresponding with Sally for some time before meeting Martha. He eventually destroyed all of Sally's letters, but she saved his. This is how we know about their relationship and of his fondness for her. But it was not until after her death—and his letters were found and returned from England to America—that this secret romance was discovered.

Although George was busy fighting the French from his wilderness post at Fort Cumberland during the late 1750s, he managed to find time to write Sally letters and even to slip away from the battlefield occasionally to visit her for a day. Sally acted in an ambivalent manner toward George, drawing him closer while pushing him away. This behavior intrigued and flabbergasted young George. Finally, after she jokingly wrote suggesting that he was impatiently trying to end the war sooner than he should because of his desire to hurry back and marry Martha, he wrote her this passionate letter. In it he openly declared his love for her. He then waited for her reply.

George Washington

Camp at Fort Cumberland,
12th September 1758.

Dear Madam,

Yesterday I was honourd with your short, but very agreable favor of the first Inst. How joyfully I catch at the happy occasion of renewing a corrispondance which I fear'd was disrelish'd on you part. . . .

If you allow that any honour can be derivd from my opposition to our present System of management, you destroy the merit of it entirely in me by attributing my anxiety to the animating prospect of possessing Mrs. Custis, when—I need not name it, guess yourself—should not my Honour and Country's welfare be the ex[in]citement? 'Tis true, I profess myself a Votary to Love. I acknowledge that a Lady is in the case; and, further, I confess that this Lady is known to you. Yes, Madam, as well as she is to one who is too sensible of her Charms to deny the Power whose influence he feels and must ever submit to. I feel the force of her amiable beauties in the recollection of a thousand tender passages that I could wish to obliterate till I am bid to revive them; but Experience alas! sadly reminds me how impossible this is, and evinces an Opinion, which I have long entertained, that there is a Destiny which has the sovereign controul of our actions, not to be resisted by the strongest efforts of Human Nature.

You have drawn me my dear Madam, or rather have I drawn myself, into an honest confession of a Simple Fact. Misconstrue not my meaning, 'tis obvious; doubt it not, nor expose it. The world has no business to know the object of my Love, declared in this matter to—you, when I want to conceal it. I do not believe you are happy as you say. Mirth, good humor, ease of mind—what else?—cannot fail to render you so and consummate your wishes. . . . One thing, above all things in this World I wish to know, and only one person of your acquaintance can solve me that, or guess my meaning.—but adieu to this, till happier times, if ever I shall see them; the hours at present are melancholy dull. . . .

Be assur'd that I am D Madam, with the most unfeigned regard

Yr. most obedient
most obligd Hble. Servt.
G. Washington.[5]

She responded quickly, within two weeks. Although we do not have a copy, since Washington destroyed all of her letters, the reply must have been disheartening, as we can see by reading this excerpt from the follow-up letter he wrote to Sally:

Camp at Rays Town
25th Sept'r., 1758

Dear Madam:

Do we still misunderstand the true meaning of each other's Letters? I think it must appear so, tho' I would feign hope the contrary, as I cannot speak plainer without—But I'll say no more and leave you to guess the rest.[6]

Although these actions may seem reasonable in a frustrated young man in love, we must remember he was engaged to marry Martha Custis at the time. Perhaps George was throwing caution to the winds in the hopes of satisfying the passion that burned within him. It appears he decided to make one last attempt to draw a straightforward confession of love from Sally. He might have even considered ending his engagement to Martha if Sally had responded to his letter in kind, but this we shall never know. Sally failed to acknowledge his open confession of love, thus provoking the follow-up letter. George and Martha were wed just four months later, on January 6, 1759.

But what of Sally's true feelings for George? Perhaps she realized just how dangerous it would have been for her to reciprocate and admit her love for him. Perhaps she did not love him at all but merely enjoyed toying with him. The best evidence we have of her love for him is that she saved all of his letters throughout her life. Some biographers have speculated that she spent far too much time at Mount Vernon nursing him back to health, which has given risen to the speculation that they were having an affair. Wilson Miles Cary, her biographer and descendant, said, "Sally and George loved each other in the fullest sense of the word because they were human."[7] Cary's conclusion is not shared by most Washington biographers.

George last saw Sally in 1773, when she left with her husband for England. They went to settle what they thought would be a minor legal matter but were prevented from returning to America after war broke out, since Fairfax was a loyalist. George collected the rents on the Fairfax plantation for them, and after it was clear that they would remain in England, he sold off their furnishings for them. He bought the bolster and pillows from Sally's bed himself. Sally's husband died in 1787. When a Fairfax relative mentioned that he would soon be leaving on a ship for

England and offered to take a letter to Sally, George penned this last missive to her:

>   Mt. Vernon
>   16 May, 1798.
>
> My dear Madam:
>   Five and twenty years have nearly passed away since I have considered myself as the permanent resident at this place, or have been in a situation to indulge myself in a familiar intercourse with my friends by letter or otherwise. During this period so many important events have occurred and such changes in men and things have taken place as the compass of a letter would give you but an inadequate idea of. None of which events, however, nor all of them together, have been able to eradicate from my mind the recollection of those happy moments, the happiest in my life, which I have enjoyed in your company . . . it is a matter of sore regret, when I cast my eyes towards Belvoir, which I often do, to reflect, the former inhabitants of it with whom we lived in such harmony and friendship no longer reside there and that the ruins can only be viewed as the memento of former pleasures. Permit me to add that I have wondered often, your nearest relations being in this country, that you should not prefer spending the evening of your life among them, rather than close the sublunary scene in a foreign country, numerous as your acquaintances may be and sincere as the friendships you may have formed. . . .
>   G. Washington[8]

George admitted that in spite of all of the amazing events that took place during his lifetime, he never forgot her and thought of her often. He adds that the happiest moments of his life were enjoyed in Sally's company and then suggests that she could return to Virginia to live out the final years of her life nearby at the Belvoir estate. Surely he hoped to rekindle their relationship and relive those happy moments once again. She never returned to America. George died eighteen months later, in December 1799. Sally died in Bath, England, in 1811, at the age of eighty-one.

☆ ☆ ☆

Although several other rumors have circulated about George's sexual misbehavior, there is little evidence that any of them were true. For example, many people mistakenly believe that he debauched his female slaves, who had many children by him. There is no evidence that this was the case. George treated his slaves with compassion and behaved toward them in a dignified manner. It is also very likely that he was unable to have children. Although he and Martha wanted them, they never had any. She had four children by her first husband, the last child just two years before her marriage to George. Since we know she was fertile, it is likely that George was sterile.

During the Revolutionary War, the British circulated a manufactured letter (purportedly written by Washington himself) to undermine his broad public support and weaken the rebellion. In the letter George supposedly disclosed that he had an affair with "pretty little Kate, the Washer-Woman's daughter." Undoubtedly, this propaganda is one of the factors contributing to the persistent rumors of Washington's debauchery.

There was another rumor, which stills persists to this day, that George caught a cold and died of pneumonia after a secret assignation on a freezing, wet winter night with one of his female slaves. Although he did die from pneumonia after catching a cold, it was contracted while riding for hours on his horse in cold, drizzly weather and remaining too long in his rain-soaked clothes, not from a forbidden liaison.

Although George Washington was a passionate man, he may have lived his entire life never having fulfilled his sexual passion for a woman.

2

THOMAS JEFFERSON

A Man of Passion

☆

Betsey had excused herself along with the other women, for it was getting late and time to retire for the evening. After thanking her host, Colonel Coles, she went upstairs to bed. This was the moment Thomas Jefferson had been waiting for. He pretended he was sick, complained of a headache, and excused himself for the evening as well. But instead of going to his room, Tom sneaked into Betsey's room, the wife of his best friend, John Walker.

Tom may have been hoping to indulge in a little promiscuous love, for days earlier he had slipped a note into her sleeve when she and her husband had arrived for a visit. He did this to convince Betsey that there would be nothing wrong with a little innocent lovemaking.

Betsey was still undressing, or may have just slipped into bed, when Tom arrived. She allegedly rebuffed his advances with righteous anger and threatened him with a pair of sharp scissors until he ran off. But Betsey did not tell her husband about the incident until many years later, when they were reported in the press by a newspaperman named Callender who was bent on ruining President Jefferson's reputation on the eve of his reelection campaign. There is some speculation that Tom and Betsey had a long-term affair, but Betsey maintained publicly that she

Thomas Jefferson
Third President of the United States (1801–9)

Biographical Information

Born: April 13, 1743
Died: July 4, 1826
Wife: Martha Wayles Skelton
Children: One boy; five girls

Extramarital Affairs

Known and Suspected Sexual Partners:	Dates:	Locations:
Betsey Walker	1768–79	Virginia
Sally Hemings	1787–1826	Virginia; Paris
Maria Cosway	1786–87	Paris
Angelica Schuyler Church	1788	Paris
Dolley Madison	1808	Washington, D.C.

Alleged Illegitimate Children: Sally Hemings's seven children

resisted Tom's advances for over ten years so that her husband, a philanderer himself, could save face.

We know for certain that Jefferson became enamored of Betsey (Moore) Walker, the wife of John Walker, his neighbor and boyhood friend. Walker trusted Jefferson so completely that he named him primary executor of his estate in his will. He left his wife and young daughter in Jefferson's care when he was away on a trip that lasted more than four months. Jefferson had been a bridesman in John and Betsey's wedding party in June 1764, so we know he was on good terms with his friend at the time.

Tom made advances toward Betsey in the summer of 1768, while John Walker was attending an Indian conference in Albany, helping to negotiate a treaty. Jefferson had just been elected to the Virginia House of Burgesses. According to John Walker, Tom wrote Betsey a love letter and implied, or suggested, that there would be nothing wrong with some lovemaking between the two of them. Betsey allegedly destroyed this little note about "the innocence of promiscuous love."[1] It seems fairly certain that Tom forced his way into her room at Colonel Coles's that night and on another occasion, dressed only in his nightshirt, may have tried to grab her just outside her bedchamber.

When asked about this affair many year's later, Jefferson acknowledged only "that when young and single I offered love to a handsome lady. I acknolege its incorrectness."[2] In a letter to his presidential secretary, Jefferson indicated that the affair was well known, was a onetime event, and had occurred without premeditation on his part and was the result of an accidental visit.[3]

Betsey did not tell her husband about Jefferson's advances until 1784, nearly twenty years after they took place. She waited until after Tom left for France to succeed Benjamin Franklin as the U.S. minister and was safely out of her husband's reach. With his honor sullied, John challenged Tom to a duel. After Jefferson returned from France, he arranged privately to meet with Walker at James Madison's home and narrowly escaped settling the matter with pistols. However, when John Walker wrote a letter to Light-Horse Harry Lee, the Revolutionary War hero, in 1805, his rendition of the facts was very different from Jefferson's, whose own correspondence made this matter sound as if it were a one-time event. Walker's letter indicated that Jefferson had attempted unsuccessfully to seduce his wife over a period of eleven years, from 1768 to 1779, and that she had defended her honor and rebuked Jefferson's advances each and every time. The actual letter is reproduced in its entirety so that readers can make their own judgment about whose version was most accurate. The truth was probably somewhere between the two accounts. Several historians consider Walker's account highly improbable and believe it to be exaggerated and the events aggrandized to some degree.

I was married at Chelsea the seat of my wifes father on the 6th of June 64. I was educated at Wm & Mary where was also educated Mr. J.

We had previously grown up together at a private school & our boys acquaintance was strengthened at college. We loved (at least I did sincerely) each other.

My father was one of his fathers exr & his own guardian & advanced money for his education, for which part of an unsettled act my father gave me an order on him returning from France & is the act to which he refers in our correspondence—

I took Mr. J. with me the friend of my heart to my wedding. He was one of my (bridegrooms) bridemen.

This as I said above took place in 64.

In 68 I was called to Fort Stanwix being secretary or clerk to the Virginia commission at the treaty with the Indians there held by Sir W Johnson which was composed of Gen'l A Lewis & my father.

I left my wife & infant daughter at home, relying on Mr. Jefferson as my neighbor & fast friend having in my will made before my departure, named him first among my executors.

I returned in Novr. having been absent more than 4 months.

During my absence Mr J conduct to Mrs W was improper so much so as to have laid the foundation for her constant objection to my leaving Mr J my exct telling me that she wondered why I could place such confidence in him.

At Shadwell his own house in 69 or 70 on a visit common to us being neighbors & as I felt true frds. he renewed his caresses placed in Mrs W! gown sleeve cuff a paper tending to convince her of the innocence of promiscuous love.

This Mrs W on the first glance tore to pieces.

After this we went on a visit to Col. Coles a mutual acquaintance & distant neighbor. Mr. Jefferson was there. On the ladys retiring to bed he pretended to be sick, complained of a headache & left the gentlemen among whom I was.

Instead of going to bed as his sickness authorized a belief he stole into my room where my wife was undressing or in bed.

He was repulsed with indignation & menaces of alarm & ran off.

In 71 Mr J was married and yet continued his efforts to destroy my peace until the latter end of the year 79.

One particular instance I remember.

My old house had a passage upstairs with a room on each side & opposite doors.

Mr J and his wife slept in one. I & my wife in the other.

At the end of the passage was a small room used by my wife as her private apartment.

She visited it early & late. On this morning Mr. J's knowing her custom was found in his shirt ready to seize her on her way from her chamber—indecent in manner.

In 83 Mr J went to France his wife died previously.

From 79 Mr J desisted in his attempts on my peace.

At this time I believed him to be my best frd & so felt & acted toward him.

All this time I held him first named in my will, as exct. ignorant of every thing which had passed.

Soon after his sailing for France was known Mrs W then recurred to my will & being as before asked her objections, she related to me these base transactions apologizing for her past silence from her fear of its consequence which might have been fatal to me.

I constantly wrote to him. You have our correspondence & you go now to Mr. J. My injury is before you. Let my redress be commensurate. It cannot be complete & therefore ought to be as full as possible.[4]

It does indeed seem difficult to believe that Thomas Jefferson attempted to seduce Betsey over a period of eleven years. Perhaps Thomas Paine captured this skepticism best when he wrote, "We have heard of a ten year siege of Troy, but who ever heard of a ten year siege to seduce?"[5] It also seems unlikely that Betsey would rebuff Tom's advances every time he tried to make love to her over such an extended period of time. Perhaps she fancied the attention from such a handsome man. Perhaps she did not rebuff him at all or was just ambivalent enough to cause him to continue. Perhaps she yielded to Tom's solicitations and her husband wrote this letter to try to salvage her reputation and his honor. Some historians feel it would have been out of character for Jefferson to pursue a woman after she had repeatedly rebuffed him. It also seems unlikely that Jefferson would have continued his efforts to pursue Betsey after his own marriage on New Year's Day, 1772, but according to John Walker's letter, Jefferson attempted to "disturb his peace" until 1779, nearly eight years after Tom had married Martha Wayles Skelton. We will never know exactly what did occur. It is clear, however, through Jefferson's own admission, that as a young bachelor he did incorrectly offer his love to a handsome lady who happened to be the wife of his neighbor and his best friend, John Walker.

☆ ☆ ☆

But now let us return to the very beginning of young Thomas Jefferson's struggles with love and the story of his first known passion. He was nineteen; she, only sixteen. Her name was Rebecca Burwell. She was described as pious and beautiful. She gave Jefferson a silhouette of her profile, which was later ruined by water from a leaky roof. He wrote multiple letters about her to one of his friends, John Page, but devised various codes for her name to prevent the letters from "being a cause for a great deal of lighthearted laughter, jest, and ridicule." Clearly, Jefferson was afraid these letters might be revealed or discovered by others at some future time. Page warned him in January 1763 that he had competition and encouraged Tom to go to Rebecca immediately and "lay siege," but Jefferson put it off, reminding Page that he had to travel to Britain first to visit relatives. Instead, he asked Page to intercede on his behalf and ask her to wait to marry him until after he returned from abroad. Jefferson was building a boat for the planned trip to Europe and named it *Rebecca*, but the trip never took place. He tried to propose to Rebecca at a dance in the Apollo Room of the Raleigh Tavern in Williamsburg on October 6, 1763, but he couldn't get the words out in an intelligible fashion. He wrote in another letter to Page the following description of his performance that evening:

> I had dressed up in my own mind such thoughts as occurred to me, in as moving language as I knew how, and expected to have performed them in a tolerably credible manner. But, good God! When I had an opportunity of venting them, a few broken sentences, uttered in great disorder, and interrupted with pauses of uncommon length, were the too visible marks of my strange confusion![6]

Later, in 1764, he was saddened to learn that Rebecca had become engaged to marry a man named Jacquelin Ambler. Although Tom lamented the loss, in time the pain and embarrassment subsided, and he was again ready for love.

That same year, Jefferson served as one of the bridesmen at John and Betsey Walker's wedding. This led to his first entanglement with a married woman. All of his remaining love affairs would be with women who were "forbidden."

☆ ☆ ☆

In 1785, while Jefferson, age forty-two, first served as minister to France, he found himself involved in more mischief. These incidents involved a young slave girl from back home on his plantation in Virginia, and two young, refined ladies he would meet in France. His wife had died two and a half years earlier, and although one could assume he would be free to pursue women and find another wife, Jefferson became entangled in a series of affairs with women he could never marry.

Let's begin with the young slave girl. Her name was Sally Hemings. Sally was the mulatto daughter of slave Elizabeth (Betty) Hemings. Sally's white father was rumored to be her master, John Wayles. Wayles made Betty his mistress after his own wife died. Betty herself was also a mulatto. This made Sally a quadroon, a person of only one quarter Negro ancestry. John Wayles was also Martha Jefferson's father and became Jefferson's father-in-law when they married. This made Jefferson's wife, Martha, and Sally half sisters. Jefferson had acquired Sally as part of his wife's inheritance when John Wayles died, approximately a year and a half after his marriage to Martha.

Sally was born around 1773 and was about nine years old when Jefferson's wife, Martha, died on September 6, 1782. One story handed down among the slaves at Monticello and by other Jefferson relatives was that both Sally and her mother, Betty, were in the room when Martha Jefferson died. It was an emotionally gripping scene. Martha was moved to tears while discussing the details of her children's care after her death. She admitted to Tom that she could not bear the thought of some other stepmother taking her place after she was gone and then made Tom promise he would never remarry. Jefferson kept his promise. However, since he was still a relatively young man, at age thirty-nine, and believed by some historians to have been a man of great sexual vitality, this sacred vow may have left him with few choices. To keep his promise he may have been looking, knowingly or unknowingly, for women who were "off limits" and for love that could not end in marriage.

Within two months of Martha's death Jefferson had reentered the world of public service. He served Congress when it was located in both Princeton and, later, Annapolis. He left as minister to France in July 1785 and did not return to Virginia again until 1789. He took with him his oldest daughter, Martha, or Patsy, as she was called, then twelve years old. He also took along James Hemings, Sally's older brother, a light mulatto slave, to drive his horse-drawn carriage. In 1785, after an outbreak of whooping cough took the life of Jefferson's youngest daughter, Lucy Elizabeth, Jefferson decided to have his younger surviving daughter, Maria, or Polly, as she was called, join him in France. However, she did not arrive until more than two years later, because the caretakers to whom Jefferson had entrusted her, the Eppes, sought to delay her departure. Sally Hemings was selected to accompany Polly on the voyage. When they arrived, Polly was nine years old, and Sally was fourteen but easily mistaken for a young woman of fifteen or sixteen years of age.

Abigail Adams was not pleased when she first saw Sally. Abigail wrote Jefferson a letter in which she quoted the sea captain of the vessel that brought Sally to France: She "will be of so little service that he had better carry her back with him." Sally was described by a number of different people using the following terms: "decidedly good looking, very handsome, beautiful, radiant, lovely, and intelligent with long straight hair down her back."[7] She was easily mistaken for a Caucasian and described by another slave as "mighty near white"[8] and by another Jefferson relative as "light colored."[9] Since Sally was Martha Jefferson's half sister, she may have resembled Tom's deceased wife and reminded him of Martha. Perhaps Abigail was more worried that Sally would become Jefferson's mistress and therefore attempted to end this potentially disastrous affair before it began, which apparently took place while Sally and Jefferson were in France.

Sally's affair with Tom probably did not start until late that summer or early the next year. However, when she returned home to Virginia, she was visibly pregnant with a child who was born in late 1789 or early 1790, when Sally was nearly seventeen years old. Sally's third child, Madison Hemings, claimed that Sally had become Mr. Jefferson's mistress when she was in Paris and that he had fathered all seven of her children.

Tom purchased fine clothes for Sally and made arrangements for a French tutor so that she could learn the language. He paid a small fortune for her medical care and gave her spending money each month. Biographer Fawn Brodie in *Thomas Jefferson: An Intimate History* claims this as evidence that Sally was more than a slave to Jefferson and considered this type of spending an indication that Sally was his lover. But many historians take issue with Brodie's theories.

Jefferson returned home to Monticello in early 1789, but Sally and Polly may have stayed behind in Paris for a few additional months. In Paris, Sally was legally a free woman. In Virginia she would be returning to slavery. Tom intended for Sally to accompany him on the return voyage and made provision for her passage on his same ship. However, according to her son Madison, she objected and was not willing to accompany him until he promised her special privileges and agreed to free all of her children at age twenty-one through manumission, the practice of formally emancipating a slave.

Tom's alleged affair with "Dashing Sally," as she was known at Monticello, remained secret for many years, until it was revealed through a news story by an alcoholic newspaperman and political muckraker named James Thomson Callender. Jefferson, as vice president, had praised and supported Callender when he was criticizing then president John Adams. Callender wrote a political pamphlet in 1799 which earned him a $200 fine and landed him in jail for sedition. After Jefferson was elected president, he gave Callender an official pardon just days following his inauguration in March 1801. Although Jefferson agreed to repay his fine, Callender wanted to be appointed postmaster of Richmond, which provided an annual salary of $1,500. After he was refused, Callender vowed to get revenge. He published the following news story in the *Richmond Recorder* on September 1, 1802:

> It is well known that the man, whom it delighteth the people to honor, keeps and for many years has kept, as his concubine, one of his slaves. Her name is Sally. The name of her eldest son is Tom. His features are said to bear a striking though sable resemblance to those of the president himself. The boy is ten or twelve years of age. His mother went to France in the same vessel with Mr. Jefferson and his two daughters. The delicacy of this arrangement must strike every portion of common sensibility. What a sublime pattern for an American ambassador to place before the eyes of two young ladies! . . .
>
> By this wench Sally, our president has had several children. There is not an individual in the neighbourhood of Charlottesville who does not believe the story, and not a few who know it. . . . Mute! Mute! Mute! Yes very Mute! will all those republican printers of biographical information be upon this point.

A careful reader of this chapter will already have spotted at least one inaccuracy in the newsman's facts, but that did not stop Callender from going to print with this scandalous story. Sally did not accompany Jefferson on his voyage to France. Three weeks later, Callender published another article and corrected this mistake. However, he used the correction as an opportunity to rub more salt into the wound, calling Sally Tom's black wench.

As you can imagine, this story unleashed a flurry of other newspaper articles both denouncing and supporting the Callender story. Many editors called for Jefferson to deny the story, but he remained silent. As a result, journalists conducted their own investigation, and several newspapers (among them *Gazette of the United States*, *Frederick-Town Herald*, and the Lynchburg *Virginia Gazette*) reported that they were able to corroborate the basic accuracy of Callender's account. One of the more memorable items, published in October 1802, was a poem written by Joseph Dennie, the editor of the Philadelphia *Port Folio*. It was intended that this verse be sung to the tune of the popular song "Yankee Doodle." The poem is written in the first person, as if Jefferson is singing the tune himself.

Yankee Doodle

Of All the damsels on the green,
On mountain, or in valley,
A lass so luscious ne'er was seen,
As Monticellian Sally.

Yankee doodle, who's the noodle?
What wife were half so handy?
To breed a flock of slaves for stock,
A blackamoor's the dandy.

Search every town and city through,
Search market, street and alley:
No dame at dusk shall meet your view,
So yielding as my Sally.
Yankee doodle, etc.

When press'd by loads of state affairs
I seek to sport and dally

THOMAS JEFFERSON

The sweetest solace of my cares
  Is in the lap of Sally.
    Yankee doodle, etc.

Yet Yankee parsons preach their worst—
  Let Tory Wittling's rally!
You men of morals! and be curst,
  You would snap like sharks for Sally.
    Yankee doodle, etc.

She's black you tell me—grant she be—
  Must colour always tally?
Black is love's proper hue for me—
  And white's the hue for Sally.

What though she by the glands secretes;
  Must I stand shil-I shall-I?
Tuck'd up between a pair of sheets
  There's no perfume like Sally.

You call her slave—and pray were slaves
  Made only for the galley?
Try for yourselves, ye witless knaves—
  Take each to bed your Sally.

Yankee doodle, whose the noodle?
  Wine's vapid, tope me brandy—
For still I find to breed my kind
  A negro-wench the dandy!

Jefferson once said, "When a man assumes a public trust, he should consider himself public property." After these stories were published, he was probably ready to retract his words. He might have agreed that "silence is the best policy," since he refused to answer any of the scandalous charges. The American people reelected him two years later in spite of the press reports.

If Jefferson continued his intimate love affair with Sally Hemings for approximately thirty-eight years (as some historians allege), then she must have been a source of immense pleasure to him.

☆ ☆ ☆

21

Thomas Jefferson was despondent after Martha died. He supposedly said, "I wish to die." After a brief but intense period of mourning, he immersed himself in politics once again. He understood that activity would help ease the pain and otherwise divert his attention from this sorrow. During Martha's final months, Tom cut himself off from all others socially and rarely left Monticello. He was constantly near Martha, in her bedroom or in a small room nearby, where he could write. However, with the passage of time, the changing of seasons, and new surroundings, he again experienced romantic love.

Jefferson had accepted the assignment to be the next minister to France in May 1784 and, at age forty-two, sailed for Paris in July of the next year. He was in a state of near shock after arriving in this decadent city where many aristocratic gentlemen were pursuing sexual liaisons with young women. His friend and the former minister to France Benjamin Franklin was among them.

As ambassador, Jefferson became friends with Col. John Trumbull, the famous American painter and Revolutionary War veteran. Trumbull was commissioned to create a series of paintings illustrating great moments in the American Revolution, beginning with the Declaration of Independence. He stayed with Jefferson in his expensive house on the Champs Elysées while he painted. One Sunday afternoon in August 1786, while accompanying Trumbull and several other friends on an outing to the Halle aux Bleds, an upscale grain market in Paris, Trumbull introduced Tom to a young artist and musician named Maria Louisa Catherine Cecelia Hadfield Cosway. The attraction was instant and mutual.

Born in Florence and imprisoned in an unhappy marriage to Englishman Richard Cosway, Maria was described as beautiful, modest, and well educated, with deep blue eyes, a coquettish Italian accent, and great blond curls.[10] She was a devout Catholic and had even once considered becoming a nun.

Richard Cosway was a miniaturist, painted for many rich socialites, and became involved in numerous hetero- and homosexual relationships. Certainly his behavior contributed to an unhappy marriage. Richard seemed unconcerned about the close relationship developing between Maria and Tom. In fact, on the very first day they met, Tom became almost obsessed with Maria. He did not want to leave her side, immediately dropped his plans for the rest of the day, and insisted everyone else do the same so that he could prolong his time with her. Her husband, Richard, did not protest. When Tom came to visit Maria, Richard would leave the two alone.

By 1786, Tom and Maria were involved in a brief, torrid, on-again, off-again love affair. Tom was forty-three; Maria, only twenty-seven. Maria revived the fire that had lain dormant for four long years.

One month later, in mid-September, Jefferson injured his right wrist, purportedly when attempting to jump over a fence while trying to impress Maria.

In early October, Maria and her husband left for London. This left poor Tom "more dead than alive." On October 12, within a week of Maria's departure, Tom wrote her an unusual twelve-page letter (or dialogue) with his left hand. It was a conversation he supposedly overheard between his head and heart on the day when Maria left him. It is known as the famous "My Head and My Heart" letter.

His HEART, which represented *emotion* talked of the happiness he had found in Maria. His HEAD, which represented *reason*, warned the heart from becoming too fond and attached to someone he must lose so soon and would eventually cause him so much sorrow. A portion follows:

My Head and My Heart

Madam:

Having performed the last sad office of handling you into your carriage at the Pavillion de St. Denis, and seen the wheels get actually into motion, I turned on my heel and walked, more dead than alive, to the opposite door, where my own was awaiting me. Mr. Danquerville was missing. He was sought for, found, and dragged down stairs. We were crammed into the carriage, like recruits for the Bastille, and not having soul enough to give orders to the coachman, he presumed Paris our destination, and drove off. After a considerable interval, silence was broke with a "je suis vraiment affligé du depart de ces bons gens." This was the signal for a mutual confession of distress. We began immediately to talk of Mr. and Mrs. Cosway, of their goodness, their talents, their amiability, and tho we spoke of nothing else, we seemed hardly to have entered into the matter when the coachman announced the rue St. Denis, and that we were opposite Mr. Danquerville's. He insisted on descending there and traversing a short passage to his lodgings. I was carried home. Seated by my fire side, solitary and sad, the following dialogue took place between my Head and my Heart.

HEAD.　Well, friend, you seem to be in a pretty trim.

HEART.　I am indeed the most wretched of all earthly beings. Over-whelmed with grief, every fibre of my flame distended beyond it's natural powers to bear, I would willingly meet whatever catastrophe should leave me no more to feel or to fear.

HEAD.　These are the eternal consequences of your warmth and pre-cipitation. This is one of the scrapes into which you are ever leading us. You confess your follies indeed: but still you hug and cherish them, and no reformation can be hoped, where there is no repentance.

HEART.　Oh my friend! This is no moment to upbraid my foibles. I am rent into fragments by the force of my grief! If you have any balm, pour it into my wounds: if none, do not harrow them by new torments. Spare me in this awful moment! At any other I will attend with patience to your admonitions. . . .

HEAD.　Thou are the most incorrigible of all beings that ever sinned! I reminded you of the follies of the first day, intending to deduce from thence some useful lessons for you, but instead of listening to these, you kindle at the recollection, you retrace the whole series with a fondness which shews you want nothing but the opportunity to act it over again. I often told you during it's course that you were imprudently engaging your affections under circumstances that must cost you a great deal of pain: that the persons indeed were of the greatest merit, possessing good sense, good humour, honest hearts, honest manners, and eminence in a lovely art: that the lady had moreover qualities and accomplishments, belong-ing to her sex, which might form a chapter apart for her: such as music, modesty, beauty, and that softness of disposition, which is the ornament of her sex and charm of ours. But that all these considerations would in-crease the pang of separation: that their stay here was to be short: that you rack our whole system when you are parted from those you love, com-plaining that such a separation is worse than death, inasmuch as this ends our sufferings, whereas that only begins them: and that the separation would in this instance be the more severe as you would probably never see them again.

HEART.　But they told me they would come back again the next year.

HEAD.　But in the meantime see what you suffer: and their return too depends on so many circumstances that if you had a grain of prudence you would not count upon it. Upon the whole it is improbable and therefore you should abandon the idea of ever seeing them again.

HEART.   May heaven abandon me if I do!

TH:JEFFERSON[11]

Maria left her husband behind in England, arrived alone in Paris in August 1787, and spent four months seeing Tom in what would turn into a lukewarm relationship. Why her husband did not accompany her we do not know. Nor was the purpose of her trip entirely clear. We also do not know what went wrong in her relationship with Tom. Certainly his letters to her indicate the trip was anxiously anticipated. However, love did not blossom this time. Maria did not show up for their final breakfast together on the day of her departure for London, as she had promised her former lover, and although they continued to write letters for the rest of their lives, Tom would never see her again.

☆ ☆ ☆

Shortly after Maria left Tom again in the winter of 1787, Trumbull quickly introduced him to another one of Maria's married friends. Her name was Angelica Schuyler Church. She was Alexander Hamilton's sister-in-law. A romantic attachment quickly developed, although not as intense as the one with Maria. Tom and Angelica spent a great deal of time together, and he began writing her letters, some of which were nearly identical to the ones he was still writing to Maria. Within two months Angelica departed for England, leaving Tom alone once again.

☆ ☆ ☆

In 1808 the Federalist-controlled newspapers printed even more scurrilous stories about Jefferson. According to one story, Dolley Madison had agreed to service the aging ex-president in exchange for his endorsement and support of her husband, James Madison, who was running for president. Although Tom asserted that this scenario was implausible and Dolley said she would never let any man into her bedroom "unless entitled by age and long acquaintance," neither of them actually denied that the story was true.

Jefferson was the first U.S. president to become involved in numerous extramarital affairs and, with the possible exceptions of John F. Kennedy and Bill Clinton, was the most active.

3

Andrew Jackson

The Adulterer

☆

Some Americans think that dirty political campaigns were a creation of the twentieth century. Nothing could be further from the truth. Many of our presidential elections, dating as far back as the late 1700s, touched upon sexual scandal and included dirty political maneuvering. The presidential election of 1828 was just another example of such sordid campaigns.

During this election, America's beloved hero of both the Revolutionary War and the War of 1812, Andrew Jackson, was branded an adulterer; his wife, Rachel, was labeled a bigamist. The first volley had been fired by Jackson's political opponents, who were working in the campaign of the incumbent president, John Quincy Adams, who was seeking reelection.

Another opposition candidate, Thomas D. Arnold, criticized Jackson and said that he "spent the prime of his life in gambling, in cock-fighting, in horse racing . . . and to cap all tore from a husband the wife of his bosom." A political pamphlet declared, "Anyone approving of Andrew Jackson must therefore declare in favor of the philosophy that any man wanting anyone else's pretty wife has nothing to do but take his pistol in one hand and a horsewhip in another and possess her." A political banner read: ABC's of Democracy . . . The Adulteress. The Bully.

Andrew Jackson
Seventh President of the United States (1829–37)

Biographical Information

Born: March 15, 1767
Died: June 8, 1845
Wife: Rachel Donelson Robards
Children: One adopted son

Extramarital Affairs

Known and Suspected Sexual Partners:	Dates:	Locations:
Wife only	NA	NA

Illegitimate Children: None

The Cuckold, referring to Rachel, Andrew, and Rachel's first husband, respectively.

One newspaper asked the question: "Ought a convicted adulteress and her paramour husband be placed in the highest offices of this free and Christian nation?" The editor of the Cincinnati *Gazette* wrote, "In the summer of 1790, Gen. Jackson prevailed upon the wife of Lewis Robards of Mercer County, Kentucky, to desert her husband, and live with himself, in the character of a wife." The Cincinnati *Advertiser,* a pro-Jackson paper, denied the *Gazette* story, labeling it a "base, wanton, and malignant falsehood," and demanded proof of these false accusations.

The Jackson camp lashed back at Adams's wife with volleys of its own. They condemned any administration that would lavishly expend money to introduce corrupt "gambling tables and gambling furniture" to the President's House (as the White House was called at the time), referring to Louisa Adams's fondness for playing billiards. The *United States Telegraph* accused John Quincy Adams and his wife of having engaged in premarital sex. And Isaac Hill, author of a Jackson campaign biography, claimed President Adams had pimped for Czar Alexander I of Russia while he served as the U.S. ambassador there and had "procured" an American girl for the czar.

Andrew Jackson distanced himself personally from all the mudslinging toward Mrs. Adams and said, "I never war against females, it is only the base and cowardly that do." However, he tacitly approved of this type of dirty political warfare as long as it was delivered in retaliation for slander uttered against his wife and was justly deserved.

But what about these accusations? Were they slanderous, or were any of them true? Did Andrew Jackson really marry a bigamist? Did he steal his wife from her first husband? How much did Jackson know about Rachel's past when he married her? To answer these questions and others we need to review the events leading up to this acrimonious presidential election and also understand something about the background and personal qualities of Andrew Jackson.

☆ ☆ ☆

Andrew was no doubt a complicated and passionate man. Two different pictures of him emerge. Some considered him a crass, uneducated backwoodsman who had unwittingly stumbled into a position of great power and prestige. Others saw him as a rugged American hero who represented the common man and not the rich, corrupt aristocracy that ruled Washington. Jackson has been described as intelligent, generous, and sincere but also as coarse and rash. Henry Clay, the famous statesman, characterized Andrew as "ignorant, passionate, hypocritical, corrupt, and easily swayed by the base men who surround him." However, one female visitor from abroad noted, "Jackson, unlike most of his countrymen, was a gentleman." In truth, Jackson was a combination of the qualities attributed to him.

When Andrew was thirteen years old, he joined the Continental army. He was a mounted messenger under the command of Col. William Davis. He participated in the Battle of Hanging Rock in August 1780 and was taken prisoner the following year, in April 1781, by the British, along with his brother. Andrew sustained a deep gash on his hand and another on his forehead, delivered by the sword of a British officer after he refused to polish the officer's boots. Afterward, Andrew was led on a forty-mile forced march to a prisoner-of-war camp in Camden, South

Carolina, with untreated wounds and without food or water. He was released approximately two weeks later after the war had ended.

He studied law at Salisbury, North Carolina. He was apparently very popular with the young woman in this college town. One woman described him as "most captivating" and said, "There was something about him I cannot describe except to say that it was a presence."[1] Similar statements were made by women about President John Kennedy. Kennedy's secret was his ability to listen carefully. It made the women he conversed with feel very special. Apparently, that was Andrew's secret, too. One acquaintance said that he much preferred the company of woman to men, "was easy and graceful in his attentions," and "had great powers of attention and concentration."

Andrew was six feet tall, thin, and lanky. His hair was coarse and straight and would be considered long by today's standards. It was combed straight back and had a tendency to stick straight up and out. His nose was long and broad. He had pronounced cheekbones and a firm mouth. The romanticized paintings (like the portrait on the twenty-dollar bill) of a handsome and noble-looking man with a long, thin face, wild, flowing hair, burning eyes, and a hawk nose bear little resemblance to the only surviving daguerreotype of Jackson.

After being admitted to the bar, Andrew served as a prosecuting attorney on behalf of the federal government in Tennessee Territory. It was there he met his future wife, Rachel Donelson Robards.

Rachel Donelson was born on June 15, 1767, in Halifax County, Virginia, to Rachel Stockley and Col. John Donelson, a member of the Virginia House of Burgesses. Named after her mother, Rachel had dark brown hair and warm, sensitive eyes. She was gracious, witty, and vivacious. Her family moved from Virginia to Tennessee and later to Kentucky

She met Capt. Lewis Robards in Kentucky, and they married in 1784, when she was just seventeen years old. An insanely jealous husband, guilty of many adulteries, Robards repeatedly accused Rachel of numerous extramarital affairs. He once accused her of having an affair with a man to whom she had only provided a drink of cool water. Although she pleaded innocent, he sent her to live with her widowed mother, who had returned to Tennessee.

After rejoining her mother in 1788, Rachel met Andrew Jackson after Mrs. Donelson took in the young traveling attorney general as a boarder.

Andrew and Rachel fell in love and wanted to marry, but when Robards returned to fetch her, she accompanied him to Kentucky. His fits of jealous rage continued, however, and Andrew rushed to Kentucky to rescue Rachel and take her back to Tennessee. At first, Robards tried to have Andrew arrested for taking liberties with his wife, but eventually he gave up and returned to Kentucky Territory alone. In 1790 he threatened to come back to Tennessee to take Rachel home with him, this time by force, if necessary. In January 1791, to escape her imminent abduction, Rachel fled to Natchez, Mississippi, with Andrew and another man. Robards sued Rachel for divorce in Kentucky, saying she had "eloped with another man." In December 1790, Robards had persuaded the Kentucky legislature to pass an act that allowed him to sue Rachel for divorce. However, his petition was only a preliminary legal action and not a final divorce decree. After learning about the divorce petition, Rachel and Andrew believed they were free to marry. However, the petition was dismissed after the court discovered that Robard's charges were untrue and found no grounds for divorce.

Andrew Jackson and Rachel Donelson Robards were married in August 1791 in Natchez, Mississippi. They were both twenty-four. Afterward, they returned to Nashville, Tennessee, to live. Although Robards had tried to divorce Rachel, he did not fulfill all of the legal requirements. As a result, Rachel and Andrew were not legally married when they wed. Rachel was still legally married to Lewis Robards. Andrew should have ensured Rachel's divorce was final before going forward with his plans to marry her. As a practicing attorney, he should have known better. He also married Rachel in Mississippi, then a Spanish territory, where Protestants needed to obtain permission from the Roman Catholic church to marry legally. But he failed to obtain the needed permission and instead rushed impulsively to wed a woman who was still legally married to someone else. Technically, this made him an adulterer, her a bigamist, and her legal husband a cuckold.

When Robards learned that his wife had married Andrew and was living with him, he sued her for divorce on the grounds of adultery. After Rachel's divorce became final in September 27, 1793, she and Andrew remarried on January 18, 1794, in Nashville, Tennessee.

More than thirty-five year later, Jackson's political opponents decided to rake up news of this unfortunate situation and raise doubts about

Rachel's moral values on the eve of Andrew's first presidential campaign. Andrew tried to hide news of this attack from his wife, who had a weak heart, but one day, while shopping in Nashville, she saw a political pamphlet defending her against the charges of bigamy leveled by her husband's political opponents and was mortified. Soon afterward, she became ill with pleurisy and died of a heart attack in late December 1828, three months before Andrew's inauguration. She was buried in the satin evening gown that she would have worn to his inaugural ball if she had lived to see it. Approximately ten thousand people attended her funeral (twice the population of Nashville). It is probable that the shocking and slanderous news spread by the political pamphlets and newspapers had triggered her illness and subsequent heart attack. Andrew had the following inscription placed on Rachel's tombstone: "A being so gentle, so virtuous, slander might wound but could not dishonor."[2]

He made the following vow at Rachel's funeral: "In the presence of this dear saint, I can and do forgive all my enemies. But those vile wretches who have slandered her must look to God for mercy."[3] This was no cavalier threat, either. Earlier in 1806, Jackson defended Rachel's honor in a duel after a lawyer named Charles Dickinson made offensive remarks about Rachel's "adultery" while drunk at a local tavern. Andrew faced almost certain death in the duel, since Dickinson was an excellent marksman, but challenged him nonetheless. During the duel, Andrew was hit first, as he imagined he would be, but managed to stand on his feet long enough to calmly and coldly gun down his opponent. This earned him a reputation of being cruel, violent, and vengeful.

Andrew wore a black armband during his inauguration, reminding the nation of his recent sorrow. But it also reminded his political enemies, especially Adams and Henry Clay, that he blamed them for the death of his beloved Rachel and that he would visit vengeance on them when the opportunity arose. In a letter to his old friend and wartime comrade Sam Houston, Andrew referred to Clay and his other political opponents when he wrote, "You know me, I will curb my feelings until it becomes proper to act, when retributive Justice will visit him and his pander heads."

Although charges of sexual impropriety did not ruin Jackson's presidential campaign, these charges may have had a devastating effect upon his wife's health and sent Andrew Jackson to the White House a widower.

4

JAMES BUCHANAN
A Dark Secret

☆

His mind was numb and in utter confusion. Anne, his ex-fiancée, had quite possibly committed suicide after a simple misunderstanding of his intentions. Had he been thoughtless and insensitive? Why did he stop to see another woman and her unmarried sister after returning to Lancaster from Philadelphia instead of going directly to see Anne? Thoughts of Anne's death, of the ugly scandal, and of his public humiliation must have swirled around in his head. He remembered little about the long coach ride from Lancaster to Mercersburg, where he had grown up and where he was now going to remain in seclusion for several weeks.

This was the condition James Buchanan found himself in during the winter of 1819. Buchanan's ex-fiancee, Anne Coleman, may have committed suicide in December of that same year when she was only twenty-three years old. There was some mystery surrounding her death.

Knowledge of Buchanan's behavior and personal relationships will also help us discover whether Buchanan held an even darker secret than complicity in a young woman's suicide.

☆ ☆ ☆

James Buchanan
Fifteenth President of the United States (1857–61)

Biographical Information

Born: April 23, 1791
Died: June 1, 1868
Wife: None
Children: None

Extramarital Affairs

Known and Suspected Sexual Partners:	Dates:	Locations:
William Rufus King	1830–53	Washington, D.C.

Sexual Deviancy: Homosexuality

Illegitimate Children: None

James Buchanan was born on April 23, 1791, in a log cabin at Cove Gap, near Mercersburg, Pennsylvania. He had four brothers and six sisters. His father, James Buchanan Sr., had emigrated to the United States in 1783 from County Donegal, Ireland. He worked as a clerk in a trading post in Stony Batter, Pennsylvania, and then started his own mercantile business, eventually relocating his store to Mercersburg, where he prospered greatly. James's mother, Elizabeth Speer Buchanan, was born in Lancaster County, Pennsylvania. Although she had no formal education, she regularly read the Bible and memorized the poetry of John Milton, Alexander Pope, William Cowper, James Thomson, and others. She was very active in her Presbyterian church and made sure James and his siblings were indoctrinated in matters of her faith.

More fortunate than most youngsters, James studied the three Rs as well as Latin and Greek at the Old Stone Academy in Mercersburg. At age sixteen, he was admitted to Dickinson College in Carlisle, Pennsylvania, as a junior. Immediately, he realized that Dickinson was a bad choice, since the professors there didn't appreciate his antics or point of view. He was in trouble from the start. During the first summer break, after completing a year of studies, a letter came to his father indicating that if it were not for their respect for him, James would have been booted out for "disorderly conduct." But, it also added, in spite of their respect for Mr. Buchanan Sr., James was not welcome back at the college. James's father read the letter, developed an anguished look on his face, handed the letter to James, and then left the room. They never discussed its contents. But James also understood he was on his own. James enlisted the support of a family friend and trustee at the college. The trustee vouched for him, and James pledged to behave if they would take him back. They did, and there were no more complaints. James graduated in 1809.

In December 1809, James began work as a law clerk for James Hopkins in Lancaster. He applied himself to the study of the law and was admitted to the bar in November 1812. Soon James became the most eligible bachelor in Lancaster.

Buchanan was six feet tall. He was slender, strong, and athletic. His eyes were light blue, and he had a good complexion. He was described as high-spirited, even-tempered, and rustic.

James's first serious romantic feelings of which we are aware involved a young woman named Anne Caroline Coleman. Anne had dark black hair, dark brown eyes, a long, slender face, a classic Roman nose, and delicate lips. She was very beautiful, introspective, sensitive, and shy. But she could also be giddy, proud, and self-willed. She may also have been emotionally unstable.

Anne was the daughter of Lancaster, Pennsylvania, millionaire Robert Coleman, the richest man in the state. Coleman made his fortune in the manufacture of iron. Anne's father had emigrated to the United States from the same county in Ireland as had James's father. Anne had five brothers and three sisters.

James's good friend Molton Rogers was courting Eliza Jacobs, the daughter of another wealthy man who lived in Pool Forge, near Lancaster. In 1818, Molton suggested that James join him on a date with Eliza's cousin, Anne Caroline Coleman. Thereafter, James would often visit Anne at one of her father's numerous mansions and was always invited to stay for a few days. They spent many nights together, enjoyed

romantic candlelight dinners, and attended the theater and poetry read-
ings. He and Anne continued to date with Molton and Eliza, often taking a sleigh ride together during the winter of 1818–19. James became
engaged to marry Anne during the summer of 1819. He was twenty-
eight. Anne was twenty-three. Molton asked Eliza to marry him during
this same time period. There was even talk of a double wedding. At first,
Anne's father may have been somewhat wary, wondering if James was
marrying Anne for love or for money. Eventually, however, he whole-
heartedly approved of their union.

At first, things went smoothly. But by the end of that summer James
and Anne were quarreling. Soon after their engagement, James had become immersed in an important legal case on behalf of the Columbia
Bridge Company. Many of the leading citizens of Lancaster had invested
in the company. The lawsuit would decide whether the company would
continue to be solvent. It was a must-win case. It forced James to work
late at night and travel frequently to nearby Philadelphia. The case left
him little time to spend with Anne. She became annoyed and thought
that James was showing more interest in his profession than in her. Rumors started which suggested that perhaps James was more interested in
Anne's wealth than in Anne. Certainly she had heard these rumors. One
that circulated indicated that James had been seen in the company of
another young woman.

Several reasons were suggested for the quarrel. One may have been
an innocent, but thoughtless, social visit James had made. After returning from one of his frequent business trips to Philadelphia and instead of going to see Anne first, he made a side trip to call on an
associate's wife. Although she was married and the purpose of his visit
had been innocent, the woman's attractive, charming, and single younger
sister, Miss Grace Hubley, was also present. This visit may have been the
source of the ugly rumors which began to circulate. Anne may have become jealous of this other woman. She confronted James with the rumors. It was partially true, he admitted. He had been in the company of
another woman, but, he indicated, "it was neither a loving nor a lasting
relationship."[1]

Another reason has also been suggested for their quarrel. Anne had
come to believe that James was marrying her for her father's money. Certainly the rumors and James's admission he had been seen in the com-

pany of another woman might have led her to believe he was after her fortune and not her love.

Whatever the reason for the argument, Anne hastily sent James a note asking him to release her from the engagement. The note was delivered to him while he was in the courthouse. Witnesses said he turned pale when they saw him reading it. James's feelings toward her had not changed, but sadly, he replied that if it was her desire to put an end to their engagement, he would comply. James tried to visit Anne again, but she refused to see him. Her father banished James from his house. He continued to write Anne throughout the autumn of 1819, hoping she would change her mind. His letters were returned unopened.

Ann became depressed after breaking off their engagement. She decided to visit her older sister, Margaret Hemphill, in Philadelphia to cheer herself up. She left Lancaster on Saturday and died the following Thursday on December 9, 1819. Her remains were brought back to her father's home on Saturday, just one week after she had left. Anne was in fine health when she left for Philadelphia but soon fell ill. The following description from Judge Thomas Kittera of Philadelphia describes what happened:

> At noon yesterday I met this young lady on the street, in the vigour of health, and but a few hours after[,] her friends were mourning her death She had been engaged to be married, and some unpleasant misunderstanding occurring, the match was broken off. This circumstance was preying on her mind. In the afternoon she was laboring under a fit of hysterics; in the evening she was so little indisposed that her sister visited the theatre. After night she was attacked with strong hysterical convulsions, which induced the family to send for physicians, who thought this would soon go off, as it did; but her pulse gradually weakened until midnight, when she died. Dr. Chapman, . . . says it is the first instance he ever knew of hysteria producing death. . . .[2]

At first, word was received that Ann had died of an overdose of medicine. Later, her death was rumored to be suicide. Certainly her passing could have been caused by taking an overdose of medicine, but it also could have also been caused by a brain hemorrhage. It is not clear what caused Anne's death or whether it was self-inflicted. But still the ugly rumors circulated. One woman in Lancaster wrote that Anne's friends "may now look upon him [Buchanan] as her Murderer." After James learned of Anne's death, he was overcome with grief. He quickly wrote her father the following letter:

[James Buchanan to Robert Coleman, Esq.]

Lancaster,
December 10, 1819.

My Dear Sir:

You have lost a child, a dear, dear child. I have lost the only earthly object of my affections, without whom life now presents to me a dreary blank. My prospects are all cut off, and I feel that my happiness will be buried with her in the grave. It is now no time for explanation, but the time will come when you will discover that she, as well as I, have been much abused. God forgive the authors of it. My feelings of resentment against them, whoever they may be, are buried in the dust. I have now one request to make, and, for the love of God and of your dear, departed daughter whom I loved infinitely more than any other human being could love, deny me not. Afford me the melancholy pleasure of seeing her body before its interment. I would not for the world be denied this request.

I might make another, but, from the misrepresentations which must have been made to you, I am almost afraid. I would like to follow her remains to the grave as a mourner. I would like to convince the world, and I hope yet to convince you, that she was infinitely dearer to me than life. I may sustain the shock of her death, but I feel that happiness has fled from me forever. The prayer which I make to God without ceasing is, that I yet may be able to show my veneration for the memory of my dear departed saint, by my respect and attachment for her surviving friends.

May Heaven bless you, and enable you to bear the shock with the fortitude of a Christian.

I am, forever, your sincere and grateful friend.

James Buchanan.[3]

The letter was returned to James unopened, as were all of the others he had written since Anne had broken off the engagement. The next day, an obituary notice appeared in the *Lancaster Journal* newspaper. Purportedly penned by James Buchanan, it was actually written by a friend, Judge Walter Franklin, because James was too overcome with grief and confused to write it. It read:

JAMES BUCHANAN

December 11, 1819

Departed this life, on Thursday morning last, in the twenty-third year of her age, while on a visit to her friends in the city of Philadelphia, Miss Anne C. Coleman, daughter of Robert Coleman, Esquire, of this city. It rarely falls to our lot to shed a tear over the mortal remains of one so much and so deservedly beloved as was the deceased. She was everything which the fondest parent or fondest friend could have wished her to be. Although she was young and beautiful, and accomplished, and the smiles of fortune shone upon her, yet her native modesty and worth made her unconscious of her own attractions. Her heart was the seat of all the softer virtues which ennoble and dignify the character of woman. She has now gone to a world where in the bosom of her God she will be happy with congenial spirits. May the memory of her virtues be ever green in the hearts of her surviving friends. May her mild spirit, which on earth still breathes peace and good-will, be their guardian angel to preserve them from the faults to which she was ever a stranger—

The spider's most attenuated thread
Is cord, is cable, to man's tender tie
On earthly bliss—it breaks at every breeze.[4]

James disappeared for several weeks after Anne's death. He did not tell anyone where he had gone. He spent the time traipsing through the woods in Mercersburg near his boyhood home, as he had done so often as a boy. He seriously considered leaving the Lancaster area for the rest of his life but decided to return. Having no direction in his life after Anne's death, he reluctantly agreed to have his name placed in consideration as a congressional candidate, primarily as a "distraction from his great grief." He knew that if he won the election he would leave Lancaster for Washington.

He was elected to the House of Representatives in October 1820 to represent Lancaster, York, and Dauphin counties. He held the seat for ten years. President Andrew Jackson appointed him ambassador to Russia, and he served in that post for two years, from 1832 to 1834. In 1834, Buchanan was elected to the Senate. He served in this national office for ten years. In 1844, Buchanan was appointed secretary of state by President James K. Polk. In 1852 he reluctantly accepted a post as minister to Great Britain under President Franklin Pierce. In June 1856 the Democrats selected Buchanan as their nominee for the upcoming presidential election at their national convention in Cincinnati. He managed to hold together the angry northern and southern factions of the country that were threatening civil war during his single term as president. When leaving the White House, he made the following comment to incoming president Abraham Lincoln:

> "If you are as happy, my dear sir, on entering this house as I am in leaving it and returning home, you are the happiest man in this country!"[5]

Many years later, James delivered sealed materials to a bank in New York, to be opened after his death, and indicated they would explain the trivial matter over which he and Anne had argued decades earlier. However, when the materials were discovered after his death, a note was attached ordering that they be destroyed unopened. His executors did just that. We will never know for certain what caused the quarrel that led to the breakup of their engagement. However, his letter to Anne's father after her death may give us a clue. First, he said, "It is now no time for explanation," most likely referring to whatever caused the end of their engagement. James also talked about how he and Anne were "much abused." He most likely was referring to some type of mental abuse or anguish they both had experienced. It was likely caused by the vicious gossip that had troubled their relationship. He goes on to ask for forgiveness for the authors of this abuse, "whoever they may be," indicating he did not know who they were. Gossip is almost always anonymous, the source rarely known. Writing about these matters in the context of her death seems to indicate that they had caused, or contributed to, her death in some way. These references also lend credence to the belief that Anne's death was not coincidental but that she may have committed suicide.

James mourned Anne's passing for the rest of his life. Several historians indicate that this trauma may have caused Buchanan to remain a bachelor for the rest of his days. One author said that Buchanan took a vow never to marry soon after Anne's death. However, there may have been another reason for his perpetual bachelorhood. It involved a darker side of Buchanan, one that until now he had denied and even suppressed. And it involved not a woman but a man.

JAMES BUCHANAN

☆ ☆ ☆

William Rufus King was a longtime friend of James Buchanan's. He was elected to the House of Representatives from Alabama in 1819, during the same period as Buchanan, and moved to the Senate in 1834. He was eventually selected as the Democratic party's running mate for Franklin Pierce, at Buchanan's urging, and was elected vice president in 1852. Just as Buchanan was the only bachelor president, King was the only bachelor vice president.

King and Buchanan were roommates and best friends for twenty-three years. Some think they shared more than a room. There is some evidence that both King and Buchanan were homosexuals. They had a very intimate relationship and were nearly inseparable. They spent so much time together in Washington, they were called "the Siamese twins." Historian Elbert B. Smith, wrote: "Whatever the effects of bachelorhood upon his personality, the lack of a wife and family obviously affected his personal associations and emotional attitudes."[6]

In a letter written to Mrs. James K. Polk and marked *Confidential*, Tennessee representative Aaron Brown referred to King when he wrote:

> Washington
> January 14th 1844
>
> Dear Madam
> . . . Mr. Buchanan looks gloomy & dissatisfied & so did *his better half* until a little private flattery & a certain newspaper puff which you doubtless noticed, excited hopes that by getting *a divorce* she might set up again in the world to some tolerable advantage. Since which *casual* events, which she has taken for real and permanent overtures, *Aunt Fancy* may now be seen every day, triged out in her best clothes & smirking about in hopes of securing better terms than with her former companion.
> . . . But I have done with metaphor & in words. . . .[7]

Notice that Brown refers to King as Buchanan's "better half" and later as "Aunt Fancy." It would appear from this brief excerpt that the relationship between Buchanan and King was breaking up and King was looking for a new companion. In other places in the letter Brown refers to King as "Mrs. B" and as Buchanan's "wife."

King may have also left a clue that he was a homosexual when as minister to France, in a letter to Buchanan in 1844, he wrote:

> I am selfish enough to hope you will not be able to procure an associate who will cause you to feel no regret at our separation. For myself, I shall feel lonely in the midst of Paris, for here I shall have no Friend with whom I can commune as with my own thoughts.[8]

In another letter to Buchanan, King said that the United States would be better represented in France "by someone who has more the spirit of a man" than he.

King had the shortest tenure of any vice president. He died within one month of the inauguration from tuberculosis.

Fortunately for James Buchanan, neither the untimely death of his fiancée nor his strange relationship with King troubled his political career, though both of these relationships must have been the source of much private pain.

5

JAMES GARFIELD

Forever Fickle

One day James Garfield confessed to his future wife that he had engaged in a sexual relationship with a mutual acquaintance. James had been carrying on a steamy love affair in an upstairs room he called "the prophet's chamber" with an affable and passionate young woman named Rebecca J. Selleck. When his wife-to-be, Lucretia Rudolph, heard Garfield's confession, she became doubly depressed, for this young woman had often requested that she and Lucretia form a close relationship and become "sisters." Strangely, however, Lucretia felt betrayed, not by her fiancé but by his lover. Not only had Rebecca taken Lucretia's place in her fiancé's arms; she had also tried to draw Lucretia to her breast as well.

To understand the details of this affair and how James became involved, we must examine Garfield's early upbringing, his religious affiliations, and his relationship with his fiancée and future wife, Lucretia Rudolph, whom he called Crete.

☆ ☆ ☆

James Abram Garfield received his early education at a local school in Orange township, Ohio. He was enrolled in Geauga Academy, a sem-

James A. Garfield
Twentieth President of the United States (1881)

Biographical Information

Born: November 19, 1831
Died: September 19, 1881
Wife: Lucretia ("Crete") Rudolph
Children: Four boys; one girl

Extramarital Affairs

Known and Suspected Sexual Partners:	Dates:	Locations:
Mary Louisa Hubbell	1861–62	Warrensville and Hiram, Ohio
Rebecca J. Selleck	1855–58	Williamstown, Mass.
Mrs. Lucia Gilbert Calhoun	1862 (?)	New York City

Illegitimate Children: None

---

inary in Chester, Ohio, from 1849 to 1850. He supported himself as a schoolteacher and carpenter while attending the academy.

James had bright blue-gray eyes, dark brown hair with red patches, and a dark beard. When he was twenty-eight years old, a reporter described James as "robust and healthy; about six feet high, light hair and whiskers, which latter are inclined to be curly. His head is unusually large; his forehead is very prominent." James was eloquent, persistent, and spiritual. But he was also brooding, fickle, and impulsive.

He was moved spiritually by the preaching of Disciples of Christ minister W. A. Lillie and joined this religious denomination after being baptized into the faith in 1850. James appears to have had a true religious conversion. He believed in the literal truth of the Bible, the deity of Christ, and life after death. He became a lay preacher and often spoke at the Disciples' meetings in the vicinity of the old Dutch village of Poestenkill, New York.

In 1851, James attended the Western Reserve Eclectic Institute in Hiram, Ohio. It was a Disciples school. He spent three years there before matriculating in 1854 as a junior at Williams College in Williamstown, Massachusetts. He was a member of the Equitable fraternity, editor of the *Williams Quarterly*, and president of both the Philologian Literary Society and Mills Theological Society. He graduated with honors in 1856.

☆ ☆ ☆

James's first love affair occurred with one of his young students, Mary Louisa Hubbell. He met her in 1851 while teaching at the district school in Warrensville, Ohio, to support himself while attending the Eclectic Institute. James was twenty-nine; Mary, in her twenties. She was intelligent, seductive, and possessive. They were so familiar with each other and their relationship was so open and well known by all the local townsfolk that everyone assumed they were engaged to marry, but James never formally proposed. Their affair spawned gossip, and James was very embarrassed by all of the stinging barbs from the wagging tongues in this small town. Although he was a man of high moral principle, he did not think it improper to cultivate a romantic relationship with one of his pupils at the time. Today it would certainly be considered inappropriate by a large number of people.

Mary joined James as a fellow student at the Eclectic Institute in 1852, and their affair resumed. She chose to enroll in the institute no doubt to be near him and to continue the serious love affair they had begun in Warrensville, without all the scrutiny from the small-town folk. James told her brother-in-law that he had fallen in love with Mary and presumably indicated that he intended to marry her. It was probably at this time that their physical relationship began. She was determined to marry him, but as their relationship cooled, he became ambivalent and did not want to make a commitment when he had so much schooling still ahead of him. He tried to talk Mary out of marriage, but she became insistent. He became concerned that he had trifled with her emotions and may have led her to believe that a proposal of marriage was imminent—an implied promise which he had no intention of fulfilling. In 1853 he wrote these words in a letter to make his intentions clear: "Shall the inconsiderate words and actions and affections of thoughtless youth fasten their sad consequences upon the whole after life? Or is it right to shake them off . . . ?"[1] Mary was heartbroken. This rejection had a profound and lasting effect on her. First, she became sad and depressed, then angry and vindictive, and finally anxious and restless. Many on the Eclectic campus rallied around her and turned against James. He consoled himself in the fact that he had never made a formal proposal of marriage to her, but he felt guilty nonetheless. He eventually sought to obtain the love letters he wrote Mary, which likely proved that his guilt was warranted, and at some point after January 1855 she returned them to him. Mary's mother later indicated that there was enough in the letters to "prove all they wanted."[2]

Mary eventually married William Taylor in 1858 but evidently never forgave James for his actions. She died five years later, on January 1, 1863. When James learned of her death, he wrote the following in a letter to his cousin:

> It seems very strange and sad that Mary Hubbell is dead. It is a most sad and painful thought to me that one has gone down to the grave with feeling in her heart that I have wronged her. God knows I never intended to do her any wrong. . . .[3]

Although several of Garfield's biographers believe he had a physical relationship with Mary, no hard evidence exists. Their speculation is largely based on gossip, innuendo, and circumstance. None of Mary's letters to James have ever been discovered; they were probably destroyed after he retrieved them. Several of the letters he wrote her have survived. He kept them in a little bundle with a cryptic Latin notation on the envelope which contained them indicating they represented to him a sad, mournful memory.

☆ ☆ ☆

James first met Lucretia "Crete" Rudolph in 1849 at the Geauga Academy, where both were students. Crete was rather plain, small, and delicate. She had dark black eyes and dark brown hair that she kept braided tightly and piled upon her head. Crete was intelligent, demure, and dignified. But she was also sensitive and shy and had difficulty showing her affection in a demonstrative way. These qualities would eventually lead to difficulty in her relationship with Garfield.

Lucretia Rudolph was born in Hiram, Ohio, on April 19, 1832, to Zebulon Rudolph and Arabella Mason Rudolph. They were caring parents, but both were also stoic Christians who rarely showed their affection to Crete. Her mother kissed her only on rare occasions. She could never remember her father having kissed her at all.

In the spring of 1853, James became drawn to Crete, who was one of the top students in his Greek and Latin classes. James found himself more and more interested in her. The Eclectic campus buzzed with gossip again, this time suggesting that James was in love with Crete. She dismissed all the chatter as so much idle talk, since James had not yet tipped his hand. He began corresponding with her in November 1853 during a break from school, and even though he hoped to provoke a response from her indicating that she had similar feelings toward him, her letters were very proper and revealed nothing.

Their first private conversation occurred in February 1854. During this meeting James held her in his arms, kissed her, and professed his love. She reciprocated and enjoyed resting her head upon the "holy calm" of his breast. He must have been pleased by the outcome of this meeting and recorded the following understated account of these events in his diary: ". . .[we had] found a mutual desire to become better acquainted and agreed to cultivate a more intimate acquaintance. . . ."4 For the balance of the year they met for pleasant chats or to recite verse. They also attended concerts and lectures together. James often visited Crete at her parents' home, where the young couple were allowed to visit alone in the privacy of her tiny bedroom.

However, James soon became ambivalent and was unsure he could finish the course of action he had started. He was not sure their affection would withstand the test of time. Although she treated him kindly, her physical embraces were holy and chaste and did not arouse in him a "delirium of passion." Perhaps he compared her with Mary Hubbell, his first love, who undoubtedly had been more seductive and accommodating. James moved cautiously toward the topic of marriage. He wanted both of them to be convinced in their own minds that the relationship would endure. Perhaps he was also troubled by his own impulsive actions at their first private meeting, or he may have become unclear about his own intentions as time progressed. Then again, he may have been unsure because his heart was divided. He always seemed to cultivate romantic attachments with more than one women at a time.

Soon rumors spread throughout the student body at the Eclectic Institute that James was becoming fickle again about another amorous relationship. Crete was wounded by the gossip and considered it to be "false, base lies." Yet the gossip proved to be well founded. James met with her the morning of the Eclectic commencement exercises and talked openly with her about his concerns. Although she pretended to have the same concerns, she was hurt deeply by his ambivalence. But she managed to hold back her tears until after he left that day to resume his studies at Williams College.

Although James and Crete originally intended to marry in 1854, after he graduated from the Eclectic Institute, they postponed the wedding for two more years, ostensibly to allow James more time to earn a larger salary. His mother persuaded him that the near poverty of his juvenile years would continue if he did not give himself time to earn a good income before he married. However, this postponement may have been due more to his own ambivalence about marrying Crete than his mother's financial concerns.

In the fall of 1854 he proposed to Crete in a letter. She responded favorably and confidently. However, Crete soon developed some misgivings of her own when James seemed to ignore her by failing to write for long periods of time and gave only weak explanations when he resumed his correspondence.

After completing his junior year in 1855, James visited Crete in Hiram during summer vacation. Although she longed for a warm reception, James seemed distant and preoccupied. In his estimation she seemed shy and impassionate. Two days after he left, a friend informed him that Crete was deeply depressed, and when James realized he was the cause of her unhappiness, he came quickly to apologize but instead chided her, saying she had been cold and unemotional. Perhaps out of desperation after realizing that this moment would be the watershed of their relationship, she opened her diary and let him read her entries over the last several months. James was deeply touched by the passionate comments he read in these pages. For example, he discovered that Crete feared she might love him more than God himself. Later, he described the insight he gained after reading her journal entries:

> When my letters did not reach her, her heart was tortured with fear lest I might be suffering with sickness and pain. From that journal I read depths of affection that I had never before known that she possessed. A new light between our hearts . . .[5]

This experience created a deep bond between them and provoked a heightened sense of passion. After this meeting, when he returned to Williams College that fall to complete his senior year, Crete's letters openly expressed her love for James. She was finally convinced to leave her "doubt and cold distrust" behind. James also expressed his love in the letters he wrote her that fall. One contains this passage: "How inexpressibly blissful would it be could I but take you to my arms tonight and feel the throbbing of your own heart against mine, and the thrill of your ardent kisses."[6] If all seemed right with the world, the bliss this happily engaged couple experienced would soon be disrupted by two other women. They were Maria Learned and Rebecca J. Selleck.

☆ ☆ ☆

James first met Rebecca Jane ("Rancie" or "Ranca") Selleck at a Thanksgiving dinner in 1855, when he visited the home of a mutual friend, Mrs. Maria Learned, in Poestenkill, New York. Maria had a spare bedroom known as the prophet's chamber where James would stay whenever he traveled during the weekends and summers to preach at the Disciples' church meetings in this quaint Dutch village. Insatiable and bored with her unsympathetic husband, Maria knew she loved James the first time they met. She missed James terribly when he returned to college after each visit home, would cry over him, and kissed the letters to wrote to her.

After James became engaged to Lucretia, it appears that Maria purposefully encouraged Rebecca and James to develop a deeper relationship. Perhaps she thought this new relationship would cause him to end his engagement to Crete. In this way she could keep James unattached and accessible a little while longer. James and Rebecca would spend hours in the prophet's chamber reading Tennyson and Charles Kingsley. She would often recline her head on his breast and twirl her finger in his beard. She once said, "Very early in our day, you gave it to me as a plaything," referring to his beard.

Rebecca Selleck was twenty-four years old. She was petite and had delicate features, a fair complexion, and dark hair. She was described as elegant, sensuous, and witty.

Maria, Rebecca, and James formed a love triad of sorts. They even referred to themselves as the "triangle" and the "holy trinity." It consisted of the two Christian "sisters" and one brother and was limited to a platonic or spiritual dimension at first. However, this relationship changed rapidly. Maria never consummated her love for James physically, but she encouraged Rebecca to do so. In fact, she gave Rebecca her blessing. Rebecca described the night in December 1855 that James and she spent alone together in the prophet's chamber this way:

> When the good-night hour came our beloved sister dismissed us with her blessed smile of approval. . . . Had we never met afterwards, I should have thought that I had caught up the whole of love and garnered it in my heart in those few passing hours.[7]

This physical relationship suddenly complicated matters. James was betrothed to marry Crete but was now sleeping with "sister Rebecca." This hypocrisy on his part opposed everything he believed, stood for, and preached. But instead of sinking into a deep depression, as one might expect based on his past behavior, James gained a renewed vigor from this duplicitous activity. His letters written during this period indicate a confident college senior who thought things couldn't be going better.

James decided to encourage Rebecca and Crete to become good friends. Perhaps he thought they could form a new love triangle. But it is unclear whether James asked Rebecca to initiate this sisterly friendship with his fiancée or whether it was her own idea. The two did become close through a frequent exchange of letters. In her letters to Rebecca, Crete often bared her heart and confided she had a feeling of trepidation about seeing James again after so long a period of time. She was afraid that the disaster of the previous summer might be repeated.

Crete even invited Rebecca to spend the winter with James and her in Hiram. She suspected nothing.

In March 1856, while engaged in this sexual affair with Rebecca, James wrote Crete these words in a letter to her: "I am already, in spirit, your husband and you are my darling wife."[8] However, when spring vacation arrived, James did not visit Crete; instead, he spent the time with Rebecca. They stayed in what Rebecca referred to as "our room" at her parents' house for three weeks. Although James wrote Crete describing his friendship with Rebecca, he made it sound as if all Rebecca talked about was meeting Crete. Rebecca even kept a thank-you note she had received from Crete and a memorable letter from James in the "snowy cradle" of the cleavage between her breasts. James even promised Rebecca that her home would be the location of his reunion with his fiancée.

In June 1856, James wrote Crete another letter to assure her of his love. "The love that fills my soul is not a wild, delirious passion—a momentary effervescence of feeling—but a calm, strong, deep, and resistless current that bears my whole being toward its object.[9] But, again, James did not honor his written promises. From the moment he met Crete at the train station at Troy, New York, until he took her back nearly three weeks later, he was cold, reserved, and close-mouthed. Like the last visit, he seemed otherwise preoccupied and silent about what had caused this fickle change of heart. Certainly he must have compared the two women, consciously or unconsciously, and decided that the serious and impassive Crete did not compare with the passionate and yielding Rebecca. Perhaps James was also feeling guilty over his affair with Rebecca and this was his way of coping. Whatever the reason, Crete went away wounded and heartbroken again. She must have suspected something was awry by this time, for she wrote the following in her next letter to James after she had returned to Ohio:

> How many times have I felt that if you would only love me just enough to come and tell me all, I could endure to know the worst; but to see you shrink away from me as though you could not endure my presence, and hide from me the truth, was almost more than I could bear.[10]

After the graduation exercise at Williams College in July 1856, James dutifully boarded the train with Crete for Hiram. He was deeply depressed, appeared dazed, and must have looked like a man being led away by his executioner. Crete knew something was not right but couldn't figure out exactly what was wrong. It was not until James told her of the affair that she finally understood. Ironically, she became resentful not toward James, because he finally was totally open with her, but toward Rebecca, because at the same time she had been pledging her love and fidelity to Crete, Rebecca was sleeping with her fiancée.

After arriving in Hiram, James became embroiled in a battle over the leadership of the Eclectic Institute. He eventually won and was elected president of the school's five-member board of education. He visited Crete infrequently, and she took a teaching job in nearby Cleveland. James would visit her on weekends, and they would walk together or play chess. He talked with her openly about his inner conflict over the two women. She was patient and tried to give him the time and space he needed to make up his mind as to which of the two women he wanted, but she still felt bound to uphold her end of their engagement.

In 1857, James spent two weeks alone with Rebecca and then spent another two weeks with Maria Learned and Rebecca in Poestenkill in July. The unholy triangle was together again. It appears that James resumed his sexual relations with Rebecca during this time and even confessed that he feared he could not honor his wedding vows to Crete. But when his vacation ended and it was time for him to return to his duties at the Eclectic Institute, he returned to Hiram. He continued to visit Crete, and she released him from his wedding vow so he could marry Rebecca if he wanted. But he had decided to either marry Crete or live as a bachelor for the rest of his life. He eventually told her that he wanted to marry her but was doing so out of a sense of duty. Although she told him she would not marry him without love, she eventually relented.

James and Crete were finally married at the home of the bride's parents on November 11, 1858, just three years before the Civil War began. They were both twenty-six. James had reluctantly agreed to the marriage but appeared uninterested in the preparations for the wedding, which he left to Crete. They did not even go on a honeymoon. Unlike Rebecca, Crete seemed stifled and was cold and unresponsive in bed.[11] Both of them were unhappy. James even told his new wife that he considered their marriage "a great mistake."[12]

James Garfield

☆ ☆ ☆

Friends who were happy with Garfield's stand against the spread of slavery asked if he would allow his name to be placed in consideration for a state senate seat at the Ohio Republican convention. Though James regarded most politicians as scoundrels and drunkards, he agreed to run. He said he was not seeking this office personally but was asked by others to serve his state. He was nominated as the Republican candidate at the convention for this seat and won the election in 1860. He moved to Columbus and roomed with Jacob Cox, another Republican state senator.

☆ ☆ ☆

James joined the Union army in August 1861 and was commissioned as a lieutenant colonel with Ohio's Forty-second Regiment. Three weeks later, he was promoted to full colonel. He saw action in the Battle of Middle Creek as a brigade commander, defeating a superior force of rebel soldiers and halting the advance of Confederate forces into eastern Kentucky. This military victory earned him a second promotion to brigadier general in 1862. He also fought in the Battle of Shiloh in April 1862 and the Battle Chickamauga in September 1863. He was then promoted to the rank of major general—the highest rank he earned until he was elected president and became the commander in chief of all U.S. military forces.

When James returned home after the war, he was ill with jaundice and diarrhea. He had lost over forty pounds in his last month in the army and had to be carried into court on a stretcher to perform his duties. Crete nursed him back to health and, perhaps because she knew how close she had come to losing him, threw restraint to the wind and began to act toward him in a very affectionate and passionate manner. After four years of an unhappy marriage, James Garfield fell in love with his wife.

☆ ☆ ☆

Around October 1862, James had an affair with Mrs. Lucia Gilbert Calhoun. James was in New York City and still a philanderer. Lucia was approximately eighteen years old. She was a young writer and reporter for the *New York Times*. Little is known about the affair except that it did occur. James told his wife, and she eventually forgave him. If the affair did take place after Garfield's marriage in 1856, this would make him the first future president known to have cheated on his wife. Although Thomas Jefferson had an affair and it's possible that George Washington did as well, in both cases they were bachelors at the time they became involved with married women.

In 1867, James made a trip to New York and visited Lucia to retrieve certain papers (probably several love letters) which she had in her possession and which he feared could hurt him. Although James had already confessed this affair to his wife, Crete was still unsure whether he could be trusted to be alone with this former lover. Her letter revealed this lack of trust when she said:

> Somehow I cannot but feel that to her at least you would compromise your love for me were you voluntarily to go into her presence. And for her too I believe it would be better to let the fire of such lawless passion burn itself out unfed and unnoticed.[13]

> James, I should not blame my own heart if it lost all faith in you. I hope it may not . . . but I shall not be forever telling you I love you when there is evidently no more desire for it on your part than present manifestations indicate.[14]

James returned from New York after successfully retrieving the love letters. It is likely he destroyed them, since they have never been found among his personal papers. We only know about this affair because James referred to it in letters to Crete.

☆ ☆ ☆

There were also rumors that after he was elected president in 1876, James visited a prostitute in a New Orleans brothel. However, this has never been confirmed. Other rumors of his philandering continued to circulate for many years after his death. Crete, who became very distressed after hearing such rumors, said they were "nothing more nor less than an infamous lie."

JAMES GARFIELD

☆ ☆ ☆

One month after moving to the White House, Crete became sick with malaria and nearly died. James curtailed some of his official duties to help nurse her back to health.

James Garfield was shot on July 2, 1881, in the Baltimore and Potomac railroad station in Washington, D.C. The assassin was Charles Julius Guiteau, a failed office seeker. James did not die immediately but lingered on for several months. Crete stayed at his bedside, meeting his every need until he died on September 19, 1881. He had been president for only six months.

Crete died while spending the winter in Pasadena, California, in March 1914. She is buried next to James in the Lake View Cemetery in Cleveland.

6

GROVER CLEVELAND

"Ma! Ma! Where's My Pa?" . . . "Gone to the White House, Ha! Ha! Ha!"

☆

It was their turn now! They had enough of the malicious attacks against the upright moral character of their candidate, James G. Blaine, the Republican nominee for president of the United States. It was time for them to get even. They made their final preparations. It took a lot of work to round up all of the equipment and props needed for the publicity stunt they were about to unveil. Revenge would be sweet. The men had all reached the rallying point. The leader blew the mouth harp to sound a distinct note that could be heard throughout the room. All of the men began to hum in unison. The doors of the building were flung open.

The smartly dressed businessmen, adorned in their top hats, vested suits, ties, and polished shoes paraded into the darkness carrying burning torches. They marched down Main Street pushing tiny baby carriages while singing, "Ma! Ma! Where's My Pa?" in voices of high diminuendo. They were mimicking the voices of the small children supposedly coming from within the carriages. All the children were crying out for their "Pa," Grover Cleveland, the Democratic party's nominee for president

Grover Cleveland
Twenty-second President of the United States (1885–89)
Twenty-fourth President of the United States (1893–97)

Biographical Information

Born: March 18, 1837
Died: June 24, 1908
Wife: Frances Folsom
Children: Two boys; three girls

Extramarital Affairs

Known and Suspected Sexual Partners:	Dates:	Locations:
Maria Crofts Halpin	1873–74	Buffalo, N.Y.

Alleged Illegitimate Children: Oscar Folsom Cleveland

---

of the United States. Some angry Democrats began shouting out, "Gone to the White House, Ha! Ha! Ha!" after each Republican chorus.

The election of 1884 is often considered one of the dirtiest in American political history. Grover Cleveland's political fortune had taken him from the obscurity of mayor of Buffalo, New York, to governor of that state to democratic candidate for president in less than three years. The Republicans were "pulling out all stops" trying to exploit a recently discovered sex scandal soon after Cleveland was selected as his party's nominee.

☆ ☆ ☆

Stephen Grover Cleveland, the fifth of nine children, was born on March 18, 1837, in Caldwell, New Jersey. He was named after his paternal grandfather. His father, a Congregational-Presbyterian minister, earned a meager annual salary of $600 to support his large family. Eventually, he became district secretary for the American Home Missionary Society, which provided a little more income. On Sundays he was expected to attend church twice, both in the morning and early evening, as well as Sunday school. He also went to regular midweek prayer meetings with his father. As he grew older, he became less observant of church, and no longer attended until he became president.

After his father's death, Grover, at age sixteen, was on his own. Too poor to attend nearby Hamilton College in Clinton, New York, he traveled to New York City in search of work and found a job assisting his brother, a teacher in the New York Institution for the Blind. Later, Grover's uncle helped him get a job as a law clerk in the Buffalo law offices of Rogers, Bowen, and Rogers. He clerked during the day and began studying Blackstone's *Commentaries* about the law at night, often going without any sleep. Grover was admitted to the New York bar in May 1858 at the age of twenty-two. He was drafted in 1863 during the Civil War but selected a legal option available to him under the Conscription Act of 1863 and paid $150 to a young Polish immigrant, George Benninsky, to fight in his place.

In 1870, Grover ran for sheriff of Erie County, New York, and won by a margin of only 303 votes. He served for three years, then joined Bass and Bissel, to practice law full-time again. He became a partner in 1878.

Grover established a reputation as one of the most respected attorneys in Buffalo. He would often work through the night until early the next morning memorizing the legal arguments he would present during trial. He was very thrifty and considered extravagance sinful. By 1881 he had amassed nearly $75,000 in a savings account.

He sought solace from the monotonous practice of the law in male companionship, poker games, and ribaldry he found in several of Buffalo's local saloon-restaurants and German beer gardens, especially the Shades, Bass's Saloon, Louis Goetz's restaurant, and Schenkelberger's. He loved to eat German food—beer, sausages, and sauerkraut—and soon his weight doubled to 250 pounds. Relatives began to call him "Uncle Jumbo."

Grover was a short, stocky man with a portly figure. He had a prominent nose, a bushy walrus mustache, and steely blue eyes. A wisp of gray hair adorned his balding pate. His official presidential portraits show a stout, fleshy man with great jowls. Two different pictures of his character emerge. Some thought Grover to be a coarse, humorless, and uneducated roisterer. Others considered him an honest and responsible lawyer.

In 1881, "Big Steve," as he was known to his close friends, ran for mayor of Buffalo as a reformer against Republican corruption and won. A year later, he was elected governor of New York. He was selected as the presidential nominee in 1884 when the Democrats were looking for some new blood to invigorate their national campaign.

Occasionally, he paid a visit to a brothel, but his love life remained relatively lackluster. It was in Buffalo, during 1873, that he met and had a brief affair with a young widow named Maria Crofts Halpin. Although there was some talk about his scurrilous behavior at the time, the local scandal soon died down.

Maria was a thirty-five-year-old widow who had left her two children behind in New Jersey to start a new life in Buffalo. She was described as attractive and amusing. She "never swore" and "seldom drank except at meals."[1] First, she found work as a collar maker; later, as a clerk in a local department store. She worked hard and eventually became the director of the cloak and lace department.

In 1884, ten days after Grover Cleveland won the Democratic party's nomination for the presidency, Maria Crofts Halpin made newspaper headlines when she declared that Grover was the father of her illegitimate ten-year-old son, Oscar Folsom Cleveland. On July 21, 1884, the *Buffalo Evening Telegraph* printed a front-page news article about Grover's past liaison with Halpin headlined by: "A Terrible Tale—A Dark Chapter in a Public Man's History." The article said in part:

> A child was born out of holy wedlock. Now ten years of age, this sturdy lad is named Oscar Folsom Cleveland. He and his mother have been supported in part by our ex-mayor who now aspires to the White House. Astute readers may put the facts together and draw their own conclusions.[2]

The chief source of this sensational journalism was Rev. George H. Ball, pastor of the Hudson Street Baptist Church and a loyal Republican. He characterized the story as the sexual liaison of "Grover the Good" and Mrs. Maria Halpin. Since Cleveland was running against Blaine as a spotless reformer, this juicy bit of salacious gossip emboldened the Republicans. Reverend Ball characterized Grover's bachelor quarters as "a harem" and said he sought out victims "in the city and surrounding villages."

The paper also published a political cartoon showing a disheveled Grover Cleveland attempting to cover his ears while a young baby with outstretched arms held by a crying woman wails, "I WANT MY PA!" The baby in the cartoon is reaching out toward Cleveland. The cartoon is captioned; "Another voice for Cleveland."

Soon other newspapers jumped on the bandwagon. Charles Dana, editor and publisher of the *New York Sun*, wrote: "We do not believe the American people will knowingly elect to the Presidency a coarse debauchee who would bring his harlots with him to Washington and hire lodgings for them convenient to the White House."[3]

The Republicans had a field day. They also subsidized the mass distribution of a song published by the National Music Company of Chicago entitled: "Ma! Ma! Where's My Pa?"

Other clergy rallied around Cleveland after the shock of the story died down. Rev. Kinsley Twining, a highly respected minister at the time, was sent to Buffalo to investigate the reports of the local clergymen. He wrote the following words in Cleveland's defense, published in the *New York Times* on August 12, 1884:

> The kernel of truth in the various charges against Mr. Cleveland is this, that when he was younger . . . he was guilty of an illicit connection; but the charge brought against him, lacks the elements of truth in these substantial points; there was no seduction, no adultery, no breach of promise, no obligation of marriage . . . his conduct was singularly honorable, showing no attempt to evade responsibility, and doing all he could to meet his duties involved, of which marriage was certainly not one. . . .[4]

Another clergyman, the Reverend Henry Ward Beecher, who was having his own struggle with moral probity and adultery, said: "If every New Yorker who had broken the Seventh Commandment were to vote for Cleveland, he would carry the state by a large majority."[5]

The issue had been raised by the Republican opposition. After this story was revealed in the newspapers and his panicked campaign staff wired him for instructions, Grover advised them by telegraph, "Above all, tell the truth." Although Grover heard similar smutty accusations against his Republican opponent, James G. Blaine, he chose not to use them. For example, the Democratic camp learned that Mrs. Blaine had given birth to their first child just three months after their wedding, technically making Blaine a fornicator, too. Instead of using this bit of sensitive information, Cleveland tore up the report and burned it in the fireplace. He said, "The other side can have a monopoly on all the dirt in this campaign." However, word did leak out, and the *Democratic Sentinel* published an account of Blaine's shotgun wedding. Instead of admitting the truth, Blaine concocted a story about having had two wedding ceremonies six months a part. His explanation was sketchy and had few details. No witnesses to the earlier ceremony were ever identified. Needless to say, no one believed him.

Grover did admit that as a bachelor he, and some of his friends, had kept company with Mrs. Halpin. "The boy could be mine, I do not know," he confessed. This young widow had given birth to a son in September 1874, claimed Cleveland was the father, and tried to pressure him into marrying her. When Grover refused, Maria began to drink heavily. Fearing for the child's safety, Grover had his friend, Judge Roswell L. Burrows, commit Maria to an asylum for five days and place the child in an orphanage until suitable parents could be found. Grover regularly paid the orphanage's costs of five dollars a week. After Maria was released from the asylum, Grover gave her enough money to start a small business in Niagara Falls, New York. Eventually, she became angry and pursued legal custody of her child. After getting nowhere with the courts, Maria kidnapped Oscar in 1876. The boy was quickly found and brought back to the orphanage three months later. Grover paid her $500 to leave town, drop the lawsuit, and allow the boy to be placed for adoption. Eventually, Grover found a prominent, wealthy New York couple living in the western part of the state to adopt young Oscar. He received a good education and eventually become a respected medical doctor. Maria moved to New Rochelle, New York, and later married.

Grover never denied he was the child's father. But he couldn't be sure, since Maria also shared her pleasures with many men. Grover could have easily pushed Maria aside, claiming he was but one of many men who had slept with her. However, he reasoned that since he was a bachelor and all of his other friends and her suitors were married, it would be the least damaging for him to respond to her claims of paternity and agreed to give the child his last name. Maria named the boy Oscar Folsom Cleveland after Grover and Oscar Folsom, his friend and law-firm partner. Perhaps Maria was trying to imply that his partner was twice as likely to be the child's father, since the boy's first and middle name pointed not to Grover but to his friend.

Grover decided to do the responsible thing. He placed young Oscar in a orphanage until he found suitable parents and provided assistance to the couple. The presidential campaign of 1884 could have devolved into mudslinging, but he refused to yield to this temptation. Grover may also have felt his chances of being elected would be greater if he were candid with the American people rather than trying to cover up his past mistakes. He told his close friends and campaign workers that there should be absolutely "no cringing" from the truth.

Grover's chances of winning the presidential election soon looked bleak. The Democrats knew that capturing New York State was pivotal to winning the national election, but Cleveland's scandal threatened to destroy any victory they had hoped for there. But a last-minute attempt by Republican presidential nominee Blaine to milk this scandal one last time apparently backfired and very probably cost him the election. Just a week before the election, on October 29, 1884, at the Fifth Avenue Hotel in New York City, Blaine met with a group of five hundred clergyman who were upset that someone with such loose morals as Cleveland could possibly become the next president. Members of the press were present at this meeting and were jotting down notes from this lively discussion for another feature story. The Reverend S. D. Burchard, pastor of the Murray Hill Presbyterian Church, a good Republican, and spokesman for the group of clergymen, referred to Cleveland's Democrats as "the party of Rum, Romanism, and Rebellion." Blaine did not object to this description. Irish Catholics, deeply offended by the religious slur, turned out at the polls in record numbers to vote against Blaine. They helped Cleveland carry New York State by a mere 1,150 popular votes and, consequently, win the presidential election.

Cleveland's gambit paid off. The electorate decided to forgive his philandering, or rather fornicating, since he was not married at the time of his sexual indiscretion, and elected him twenty-second president of the United States. The Democrats had the last laugh. After their victory they responded to the Republican-backed song "Ma! Ma! Where's My Pa?" with "Gone to the White House, Ha! Ha! Ha!"

☆ ☆ ☆

In 1885–86, two years after the election, Grover married Frances Folsom. She was the daughter of Grover's law partner, Oscar Folsom. He had been her unofficial guardian and looked after her since her father's untimely death when she was only eleven years old. Frances was only twenty-one at the time of their marriage. Grover was forty-nine. Grover first met Frances soon after her birth when he was twenty-seven and she just an infant. A regular visitor at the Folsoms' house, Grover bought Frances toys, her first baby carriage, and even a pet terrier.

Tall, charming, and graceful, Frances was very beautiful. She had dark brown hair and delicate features. She graduated from Buffalo's Central High School and then attended Wells College in Aurora, New York. Grover once confessed to his sister that he was "waiting for his wife to grow up," referring to young Frances. During her college days, Grover's interest took on a more romantic quality. Her dorm room was often decorated with flowers sent by her ever-so-considerate "Uncle Cleve." Soon after Frances graduated, in August 1885, Grover proposed by letter. One can imagine what this young woman must have thought when she received a marriage proposal by letter from the president of the United States. She immediately accepted. Their engagement was kept secret until just five days before the wedding, no doubt to prevent gossip and to spare her from the media's curiosity and prying.

The wedding ceremony took place in the flower-filled Blue Room of the White House on June 2, 1886, at 7:00 P.M. Their wedding was attended by thirty-one close friends, relatives, and cabinet members and their wives. Theirs was the first wedding to take place inside the White House. As president, Cleveland had to work on their wedding day but managed to set aside five days for their honeymoon. The location of the honeymoon cottage was a heavily guarded secret. The press, however, discovered its location in the Cumberland Mountains near Deer Park, Maryland. The new couple awoke to find their cabin surrounded by reporters equipped with high-powered binoculars, ready to snap photographs when the happy couple emerged. Infuriated, Cleveland called the press "professional gossips" and accused them of "doing their utmost to make American journalism contemptible." Subsequent newspaper reports conjectured about the dangers slim young Frances faced on her honeymoon because of the president's size and weight.

Frances enlivened the dreary atmosphere that prevailed at many official White House events during the first two years of Grover's term as president. She liked parties, and her receptions brought youth and culture into the White House. Happily married, she was Grover's constant companion. She convinced him to work a little less hard, to take longer vacations, and in general to enjoy life more.

Their first child was born between Cleveland's two terms. Their second child, Esther, arriving during Cleveland's second term, was the first baby to be born in the White House.

After the Republican's muckraking strategy failed to doom Grover's first presidential campaign, one might think they would have developed a new plan of attack. But his Republican opponents did not change their tack. They continued to spread rumors, saying Cleveland often flew into drunken rages and beat his young wife. William A. White, presidential biographer and newspaperman, interviewed Cleveland and asked him, "Is it true what the papers say about your kicking your wife downstairs?" "I never laid a hand on her" was Cleveland's reply. Although Frances repeatedly denied such rumors, they persisted nonetheless. Both Grover and Frances were wounded by the baseless accusations, but for the most part they suffered together in silence.

Grover lost his bid for reelection in 1888 to Benjamin Harrison. Frances told the back-stairs staff at the White House not to worry; she and Grover would be returning in four years. Her forecast proved to be correct. Cleveland was elected to a second term in 1892, the only president to serve two nonconsecutive terms. After his second term ended in 1897, Grover and Frances moved to Princeton. Grover lectured at the university there and eventually became a trustee. They had two more children, born in Princeton. The Clevelands lived in Princeton until Grover's death in June 1908.

After Grover's death, Frances married a professor of archaeology at Princeton University, Thomas J. Preston, making her the first presidential widow ever to remarry. Frances died in October 1947. She was buried in Princeton, next to her beloved Grover.

7

WOODROW WILSON

A Discreet Man's Indiscretion

☆

Woodrow was tormented. He was in agony. But why was he so troubled? His wife had died the previous winter. And although he felt like dying himself at that time, her passing no longer was the source of his pain.

To make matters even worse, he had just secretly become engaged to an attractive widow who lived in Washington. She made him so happy and gay that he was acting boyish, like a man half his fifty-eight years. He had practically danced all the way back to the White House that evening from her home after a discreet dinner. She had finally agreed to marry him. Woodrow was so excited, he was planning to send a press release to the newspapers, only a year after his beloved wife's untimely death, announcing that he was engaged to marry another woman. Although his cabinet and political handlers had thought such a public declaration would endanger his chances of reelection, he was unwilling to listen to them. He wanted to tell the world his "good news."

Just a few days later one of his trusted political advisers, a close relative, had come to pay him a solemn visit. He had horrifying news. His enemies were planning to publish some of the ardent love letters Woodrow had written to another man's wife while his own wife was still alive. According to the adviser, it seems this woman was offering to sell some of Woodrow's letters to the newspapers. Woodrow was aghast.

Woodrow Wilson
Twenty-eighth President of the United States (1913–21)

Biographical Information
Born: December 28, 1856
Died: February 3, 1924
Wife: Ellen Louise Axson; Edith Bolling Galt
Children: Three girls

Extramarital Affairs
Known and Suspected Sexual Partners:	Dates:	Locations:
Mary Allen Hulbert Peck	1907–8	Bermuda; New York City

Illegitimate Children: None

How could she do this to him. It seemed so out of character for this virtuous woman.

Not only did this indiscreet behavior of years ago now jeopardize his reelection; it also threatened his love and personal happiness, which meant more to him at this time than the nation's problems, which made him weary and despondent.

In great haste he jotted down a note to his new fiancée, releasing her from her vow to marry him. He could not ask her to endure the public scandal that was sure to come. He could not have her noble named dragged through the mud along with his own.

What Woodrow did not know is that his trusted adviser had fabricated the story about political enemies publishing his love letters. The adviser was simple trying to prevent Woodrow from announcing his upcoming engagement until after the elections.

☆ ☆ ☆

U.S. presidents have difficulty knowing whom to trust. Even the most trusted adviser may lie to protect his own self-interest. It seems that this one was trying to prevent Woodrow Wilson from doing anything that might hurt his chances of reelection and prematurely end the adviser's budding political career. However, the ruse had the opposite of its intended effect. It drove Woodrow and his fiancée even closer together and did not prevent the announcement of their engagement.

But who was the other woman? What was in the letters that threatened to ruin Wilson's political career? Did Woodrow cheat on his wife? How did she die? What could he have done or said that made him think he had to release his new fiancée from her wedding vow?

☆ ☆ ☆

Woodrow Wilson was born in Staunton, Virginia, on December 28, 1856, just five years before the beginning of the Civil War. His father, Joseph Wilson, was a Presbyterian minister with strong southern sympathies, and his mother, Jessie Wilson, was a refined and self-effacing woman with great inner strength.

A lanky young man with a plain, rugged face, he was brilliant, courageous, and reserved. But he could also be cold and critical. People loved to hear him speak, even those that might disagree with his point of view.

He attended the University of Virginia at Charlottesville but had to leave during his sophomore year due to health problems. He continued to study the law on his own and was admitted to the bar in Georgia in October 1882 and began practicing in Atlanta. While attending the University of Virginia, Woodrow became president of the Jefferson Literary Society debate club. He also sang tenor in the college quartet and the glee club. He did not enjoy practicing law and decided to teach, attending the Johns Hopkins University graduate school, where he earned a doctorate in political science in 1886. He was the only U.S. president to earn a Ph.D. He taught young women at Bryn Mawr but became restless and secured a position at Wesleyan College in Connecticut teaching young men. He eventually became a professor and then president of Princeton University.

After a failed romance with his cousin Hattie Woodrow while still in college, he was introduced to a young woman named Ellen Axson. She was born on May 15, 1860, to a Presbyterian minister, the Rev. Samuel E. Axson, and his wife, Margaret Hoyt Axson. Ellen was a refined and talented young woman who loved the arts. She had brown curls and a "bright, pretty face." She was charming, warm, and funny. She first met Woodrow at his cousin's home in Rome, Georgia, in 1883. After a brief courtship they became engaged to be married five months later.

Woodrow and Ellen wed in June 1885 at the home of the bride's grandparents in Savannah, Georgia. He was twenty-eight, and she was twenty-five. The ministers officiating at the nuptial service were Woodrow's father, the Rev. Joseph R. Wilson, and Ellen's grandfather, the Rev. I. S. K. Axson. After honeymooning at a mountain resort in Waynesville, North Carolina, and a brief trip to Columbia, South Carolina, they spent the rest of the summer in a cottage in Arden, North Carolina, a small town near Asheville.

In June 1910 one of the New Jersey Democratic political bosses, Jim Smith, visited Woodrow in his Princeton office and encouraged him to run for governor of New Jersey. Smith told Wilson that he would also be positioning himself to run for president of the United States two years later. Wilson agreed to run on the condition that he would be beholden to no man. He won the gubernatorial race handily and was soon traveling around the country giving speeches. Ellen helped him prepare his campaign speeches, and he discovered that her ideas were very popular with the voters. She proved to be an astute political adviser as well. She encouraged her husband to support the popular William Jennings Bryan for president in 1912, and when the Democratic convention could not agree that Bryan should be their candidate that year, Bryan reciprocated and threw his support behind Wilson, helping him win the nomination. Because the Republican party was split, Wilson won the presidential election easily, defeating his Republican opponent, William H. Taft and Theodore Roosevelt, who was running for a second term.

As first lady, Ellen asked Congress to appropriate the funds to clear the slums from Washington. She sketched and painted and had an art studio in the family's private living quarters on the third floor of the White House. She donated the proceeds from the sale of her artwork to charity.

Ellen was afflicted with Bright's disease (acute inflammation of the kidneys). She died in the White House in August 1914. Woodrow was stunned and depressed by her death, so much so that he said he "hoped to be assassinated." Perhaps his sense of despondency was deepened by feelings of guilt about the extramarital affair he may have conducted seven years earlier on the pink sandy shores of Bermuda.

☆ ☆ ☆

At age fifty, while still president of Princeton University, Woodrow vacationed alone in Bermuda for three weeks in 1907 when his wife was ill and suffering from acute depression. Although he begged her to accompany him on the trip, she refused, saying she must stay in her home, "like the fixtures." Woodrow had promised his doctors he would take several vacations to Bermuda for a much-needed rest. A year earlier he awoke one morning and could not see out of his left eye. He also felt pain on the left side of his body and when using his right hand to write.

Woodrow relaxed in Bermuda, watching the carriages roll by, reading poetry, playing croquet with other vacationers, among them Mark Twain, and attending social events. He also preached several times at a local church. While vacationing there, he met an attractive young woman named Mary Peck.

Born Mary Allen, she first married Thomas Hulbert in Duluth, Minnesota, on October 31, 1883, at 8:00 A.M. Since the town's railroad station was holding the only train leaving Duluth for the newlywed couple, Mary was married in her traveling clothes, a gray dress trimmed in brown velvet ribbon, a brown topcoat, and a brown hat that sported the feathers of a bird of paradise. Tom was a mining engineer and explorer who searched the Canadian wilderness for new mother lodes of copper ore. The Hulberts had one son, Allen S. Hulbert. Then tragedy struck. Tom was involved in an accident, probably some type of fall while in the woods, from which he never fully recovered. Lingering effects from the accident, coupled with too much work, led to his untimely death. The doctors said Tom's death resulted from a blood clot reaching his brain. Mary discovered the sad news when a telegram printed on a yellow sheet of paper was mistakenly delivered to her house instead of to her father-in-law. He was supposed to break the bad news to her gently. The telegram read starkly: "Hulbert died at nine o'clock this morning. Break the sad news to Mrs. Hulbert."[1]

The young widow married Thomas D. Peck. But her second marriage ended in divorce. Tom Peck was an industrialist who had a factory in

Pittsfield, Massachusetts. Mary was a manic depressive and wintered in Bermuda to find relief from her depression. She attended social events, danced in the ballroom of the Hamilton Hotel with high-ranking military officers, played golf with the governor, and ate lunch with members of high society. Mary lived at Inwood, one of the original old homes constructed during the colonial era from the coral blocks and cedarwood which were Bermuda's customary building material.

Mary was charming, flirtatious, and spirited. Woodrow found her intellectually stimulating. They would take long walks together along the South Shore while Woodrow read her poetry from the *Oxford Book of Verse*. He found himself hopelessly enamored of Mary.

Woodrow, now fifty-two, returned to Bermuda in January 1908 for a second vacation that lasted a few weeks. He went straight to Mary's home at Inwood, only to discover she had moved to a new residence known as Shoreby. He had injured his leg during the rough sea voyage to Bermuda, so he went to Mary's house daily to lie aimlessly in her hammock, take tea, and recover. They would take long strolls together along the beach, becoming intimate friends and sharing their hurts and dreams. Mary sensed that Woodrow seemed as if he were trying to make up for all those fun times he had been denied by his parents as a young boy (like skating and swimming) because they thought them too dangerous. However, one day as they strolled along the beach, he became somber and very serious and sought Mary's advice—about a political opportunity that had been offered to him—with the following question:

> My friends tell me that if I will enter the contest and can be nominated and elected Governor of New Jersey, I stand a very good chance of being the next President of the United States. Shall I, or shall I not, accept the opportunity they offer?[2]

When Mary encouraged him to accept this offer, he stood up, took off his hat, and responded with: "Very well, so be it!"

In September 1909, Woodrow wrote Mary the following letter, in which he said:

> It is easy on a day like this to think of you, and to realize what you would think and say, were I near enough to hear and share what was passing through your thoughts. You love nature so genuinely and so simply, re-

spond to it so eagerly and entirely, grow so gay and excited, so like a delightful girl, when it is at its best, its most poignant phases of beauty, that a day like this, so sweet and yet so vivid, so still and yet so quick with life, seems as if it were meant to contain you and to draw out in you all that is sweetest and happiest. . . . There is an air about you like the air of the open, a directness, a simplicity, a free movement that link you with wild things that are meant to be taken into one's confidence and loved. And so you have seemed part of the day to me ever since morning.[3]

Before long, Woodrow and Mary were engaged in an intense love affair. It is not clear exactly when it began. Most likely it was during this second vacation to Bermuda in 1908 or possibly during his frequent trips to New York City from Princeton in late 1909, after Mary had separated from her second husband and had moved into an eleventh-floor apartment just north of Madison Square Garden, at 39 East Twenty-seventh Street. It was like a miniature country home. It contained some of her antiques, and the balconies were covered with green plants. In her book *The Story of Mrs. Peck*, Mary admits that business "frequently called Mr. Wilson to New York" but indicates that "they," referring to Woodrow and Ellen Wilson, often came to see her. It seems doubtful that Ellen would have accompanied Woodrow on all of his trips to New York City, so Mary and Woodrow had the opportunity to be alone in her apartment. Woodrow's letters to Mary became more and more ardent in the period leading up to her move to New York City; curiously, however, no letters exist from late November 1909 to February 1910, the time that they most likely would have had their affair. Some historians believe that Woodrow's letters written during this period were destroyed before his papers were turned over to his biographer.

Woodrow considered New York City a place of dangerous temptation. Back in 1892, during a two-month separation from his wife while she visited relatives in the South with their children, his letters to her indicate he was afraid to stay overnight in this city after delivering his lectures and quivered at the thought of what he might do if he yielded to his "imperious passion." He added that if he were unfaithful to her in his thoughts it would not mean "one wit of real infidelity to you—[it] is anatomical and not of the heart."

Wilson's political career looked promising. In 1910, Woodrow had been elected governor of New Jersey with the assistance of the conservative wing of the Democratic party. He was a reformer who quickly set the state in order.

Soon after Wilson's announcement of his candidacy for president, Mary Peck and her husband filed for divorce. A rumor circulated that Wilson was going to be identified in the lawsuit. Supposedly, the judge had been shown some of Woodrow's letters to Mary. Needless to say, this type of notoriety would have seriously damaged his credibility and might have dashed his hopes of obtaining the Democratic nomination. Although Wilson and his political handlers were greatly troubled by this disturbing news, he finally claimed he had not written one word to Mrs. Peck that he would be uncomfortable reading to his wife, Ellen. This analysis was no doubt rendered in resignation, since he could do little to prevent news of his affair from being revealed to the voters. Had he known what his chief democratic opponent, Teddy Roosevelt, thought of this matter, he would have thanked him profusely. Roosevelt refused to sling mud at Wilson, even though his political advisers urged him to use this potentially damning evidence to his advantage. But Roosevelt didn't think the story would sound credible even if it were true. He told his handlers, "It won't work! You can't cast a man as a Romeo who looks and acts so much like an apothecary's clerk."

In 1912, Woodrow was nominated as the Democratic candidate for president on the forty-sixth ballot. He won the general election handily, defeating his Republican opponent by more than 2 million popular votes, and received 435 of the 513 possible votes in the electoral college. With his reputation as a reformer, he cleaned up the federal government with the same zeal he had demonstrated in New Jersey.

President Wilson wrote Mary Peck approximately thirty letters a year between 1912 and 1914. Their correspondence stopped in 1915 and never resumed.

In an unpublished press release that Woodrow was preparing in case the story of his affair become known, Wilson admitted to ". . . 'a passage of folly and gross impertinence' . . . during which he had forgotten 'standards of honourable behavior.' "[4] To his fiancée, and second wife, he would eventually confess to a " 'folly long ago loathed and repented of' one bringing him 'stained and unworthy' to plead his love. It had been, he told her, 'the contemptible error and madness of a few months.' "[5]

Ellen discovered the affair, although it is not clear how she learned about her husband's philandering. Perhaps he told her, or perhaps, like a subsequent president's wife, Eleanor Roosevelt, she discovered the affair on her own after reading the letters exchanged between her husband and his lover. However, unlike Eleanor, who never slept with Franklin again after her discovery of his infidelity, Ellen forgave Woodrow, and they became full marital partner again as well as lovers. Woodrow said of Ellen, "She, too, knew and understood and has forgiven."[6] Ellen's trust in Woodrow was so great that she allowed him to entertain Mary Peck at Princeton years later. Mary even invited Ellen and Woodrow to visit her home in Bermuda in 1912 after he was elected president, and they accepted. Woodrow visited Mary unexpectedly in 1912, and they went about New York City alone together doing things "light and frivolous in the way of amusement." The Wilsons invited Mary to visit the White House, and she came in 1913. Mary's last visit to the White House occurred in 1915, after Ellen's death, when Woodrow helped her through a series of financial troubles.

Although Mary wrote her book to set the record straight, she never specifically denied having an affair with Woodrow Wilson. Her account of the story was very discreet. When describing her divorce from her second husband, she would not even list the reason for which she sought it. In the introduction to the book she added:

> It was not the lies nor the persecutions that hurt the real Mrs. Peck. It was that any of her countrymen (and the countrywomen, alas!) would stoop to throw mud and stones at the sorely tried man in the highest position of trust our country can bestow. She was ashamed, not for the part for which she was cast, but for those who did the casting.[7]

Wilson was reelected in 1916 after defeating Republican challenger Charles Evans Hughes. He was voted into office, riding all the way on the slogan He Kept Us Out of War. However, after he was elected, this "peace president" proceeded to involve America in World War I by supplying munitions and troops to the Allies soon after the sinking of the *Lusitania*. The German's had torpedoed the ship, which had American civilians aboard.

His biggest dream was establishing the League of Nations, the forerunner of today's United Nations. Although Woodrow supported the creation of this international league, the United States never joined; an isolationist Congress voted against it. Wilson had just started a cross-country speaking tour to gather support for the League of Nations in 1919 when he collapsed, suffering from a cerebral thrombosis that left him paralyzed on his left side.

Wilson lowered trade tariffs, lobbied for the Federal Reserve Act, established the Federal Trade Commission, and signed the Child Labor Law. We also have Wilson to thank for the federal income tax deduction made every time we receive a paycheck. He was the president that introduced the graduated income tax system. Federal income tax was never supposed to exceed 3 percent of income.

Religion played an important role in Woodrow's life. He said, "My life would not be worth living if it were not for the driving power of religion, for faith, pure and simple."[8] He believed that he had been ordained by God to become president. As president he prayed every morning and evening on bended knees, said grace before every meal, read the Scriptures daily, and often attended midweek evening prayer meetings at the Central Presbyterian Church in Washington, where he was also an elder.

☆ ☆ ☆

Woodrow Wilson's second wife, Edith Bolling, was born on October 15, 1872, in Wytheville, Virginia, to a circuit court judge, William Bolling, and his wife, Sallie White Bolling. Like Woodrow's first wife, Edith was educated at private girls schools and had refined tastes. She married Norman Galt, her first husband and a jeweler in Washington, D.C., in 1896. But Galt died in 1908, leaving her an attractive middle-aged widow.

Edith was a tall woman with dark hair and gray eyes. Funny, romantic, and sophisticated, she spoke in a soft, melodious voice and possessed a cheerful smile.

Edith first met Woodrow in the White House in April 1915. They were introduced by Woodrow's cousin, Helen Bones, who played matchmaker. Helen asked her if she wanted to tour the White House, and she refused, saying that her boots were too muddy. But Helen assured her that Woodrow was not at home and that she would not run into him, so she consented. But Helen was wrong (or was not entirely honest) about Woodrow's whereabouts, and Edith ran into him during her tour. He asked her to stay for tea, and she agreed. Within a few weeks Woodrow began writing Edith letters daily. His first letter was written on April 28, 1915. Within a week, Woodrow took her out on the south portico of the White House after dinner and asked her to marry him. She told him she was shocked that he would breach customary protocol and request her hand in marriage after such a brief acquaintance, but he was not deterred. The following day, he wrote her:

> God has indeed been good to me to bring such a creature as you into my life. Here stands your friend, a longing man, in the midst of a world's affairs—a world that knows nothing of the heart he has shown you and which would as lief break it as not. . . . Will you come to him some time, without reserve and make his strength complete?[9]

The president, now fifty-eight, was in love with a forty-two-year-old widow. He would go for long walks with Edith in Rock Creek Park and behave amorously and foolishly, like a man half his age. He leaped over rock walls and hugged Edith under the privacy of the tall trees. All the while the couple would be followed by tense Secret Service agents, who felt somewhat embarrassed by the president's behavior.

In September 1915, Wilson's cabinet met in unofficial session to discuss the president's courtship. They liked Edith and supported his desire to marry but were afraid a marriage so soon after his first wife's death would upset the electorate, ruin his chances of being reelected, and quite possibly throw the Democratic party out of power. They did not want to lose their jobs and all the perks that went with them or harm the budding political careers they had been nurturing for some time. The cabinet selected the secretary of the navy, Josephus Daniels, Woodrow's closest friend and adviser, to tell the president they did not want him to marry again so soon, but Daniels was unwilling and refused to be the "Envoy Extraordinary to the Court of Cupid on a mission in which neither my heart nor head was enlisted and in the performance of which my official head might suffer decapitation." In the end, none of the cabinet members had the courage to approach the president about this affair. However, another matter arose that soon made a public pronouncement of the president's engagement look trivial by comparison.

Soon after their engagement, rumors began to circulate around Washington that Woodrow had an extramarital affair with Mary Peck while married to his first wife, Ellen. Additionally, it was rumored that Woodrow had allegedly paid Mary $15,000 not to reveal their extramarital affair. Since Woodrow would soon run again, his campaign handlers feared that this information would be used either to embarrass or blackmail him before the next election.

Learning about these rumors and knowing that any public announcement about Woodrow's engagement to Edith so soon after Ellen's death could shock the electorate, Wilson's treasury secretary and son-in-law, William G. McAdoo, devised a plan to prevent him from doing anything that would hurt his chances for reelection. McAdoo informed Wilson and another of his close advisers, Colonel House, that he had received an anonymous letter from Los Angeles (where Mary Peck Hulbert was now living) indicating that she was going to sell some of the love letters Woodrow had sent her. These letters would incriminate him as her former lover. In truth, McAdoo had not received any such letter, but he had heard that Woodrow had sent Mary a large check and was hoping to discover if he had anything to hide that could threaten his chances of reelection. Woodrow was not overly concerned about the content of his letters to Mary, but he couldn't believe that someone as principled as she would resort to such behavior. He knew, however, that his unscrupulous political opponents were capable of distorting the substance of their letters to harm him.

Knowing that this information could wreak havoc on his fragile engagement, Woodrow decided it was best to explain this matter to Edith personally, before it hit the newsstands, so he hastily penned the following note to her:

Dearest,
    There is something, personal to myself, that I feel I must tell you about at once, and I am going to take the extraordinary liberty of asking you if I may come to your house this evening at 8, instead of your coming here to dinner. You will understand when I have a chance to explain, and will,

I believe, think even this extraordinary request justified and yourself jus-tified in granting it. I love you with the full, pure passion of my whole heart and because I love you beg this supreme favor.

With a heart too full for words,

Your own,
Woodrow[10]

Fearing that the story would soon hit the streets in the newspapers, Woodrow panicked, told Edith all about Mary Peck, and offered to re-lease her from the promise to marry him. But, in the same breath, he begged her, "Stand by me—don't desert me!" Instead of giving him the response he hoped for instantly, Edith hesitated, wanting some time to think things over. She told Woodrow she would give him her answer in the morning. She stayed up all night, thinking the matter over. Instead of choosing to run away from this potentially humiliating and scan-dalous controversy, Edith decided to stand by her man. She wrote Woodrow the next morning:

1308 Twentieth Street
Sept 19, 1915

Dearest:

The dawn has come—and the hideous dark of the hour before the dawn has been lost in the gracious gift of light.

I have been in the big chair by the window, where I have fought out so many problems, and all the hurt, selfish feeling has gone with the dark-ness—and I now see straight—straight into the heart of things and am ready to follow the road "where love leads."

How many times I have told you I wanted to help—and now when the first test has come I faltered—But the faltering was for love—not lack of love. I am not afraid of any gossip or threat, with your love as my shield—even now this room aches with your voice—as you plead, 'Stand by me—don't desert me!'

This is my pledge, dearest one, I will stand by you—not for duty, not for pity, not for honour—but for love—trusting, protecting, compre-hending love. And no matter whether the wine be bitter or sweet we will share it together and find happiness in the comradeship.

Forgive my unreasonableness tonight (I mean last night, for it is already Sunday morning), and be willing to trust me.

I have not thought out what course we will follow for the immediate present for I promised we would do that together.

I am so tired I could put my head down on the desk and go to sleep—but nothing could bring me real rest until I had pledged you my love and my allegiance.

Your own
Edith[11]

Although the letter came to Woodrow on Sunday morning—later, according to Edith—he was afraid to open it. Perhaps Edith's initial hesitancy caused him to fear that her response would be one of rejection. He became consumed with worry and soon found himself sick and in bed. Meanwhile, Edith must have wondered what was happening, since she heard no reply from Woodrow until Wednesday, when his trusted doctor, Grayson, summoned her to the White House to see the president, who was very ill. She found Woodrow lying in bed in a darkened room with a tormented look on his face. When she asked if he had received her letter, he responded with a solitary "Yes." She did not know that he had been too afraid to open her letter, but her affection and care for him assured him that things would be fine between them. Months later he told her about the letter, and they opened it together. He thought it was a lovely letter and finally realized he had nothing to fear from this courageous woman. She promised to preserve the letter and never destroy it. But there is some evidence to suggest that Edith's account of this crisis is overly romanticized, since some of Woodrow's letters to her written that same week make references to the letter she wrote him that Sunday morning. Some of the facts seem to contradict her story that Woodrow pocketed her letter without opening it for several months.

Before Woodrow announced his engagement publicly, he sought the advice of another of his advisers, Colonel House. When McAdoo discovered that the colonel was scheduled to meet with the president on September 22, he expressed great concern over the imminent announcement. Woodrow met Colonel House and told him the full story of his affair with Mrs. Peck. He admitted writing letters to her but didn't believe they contained any compromising information. But to be safe Woodrow had prepared a written statement to issue as a response if his

George Washington, our first president, wrote a love letter to his neighbor, Sally Cary Fairfax, while he was engaged to Martha Custis. LIBRARY OF CONGRESS

Martha Washington was loved by her husband but did not arouse a great romantic passion within him. LIBRARY OF CONGRESS

Sally Cary Fairfax, probably the greatest love of George Washington's life, was the wife of Washington's best friend. VIRGINIA HISTORICAL SOCIETY

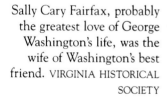

Thomas Jefferson, alleged philanderer, may have had several affairs in Paris and a long-term affair with one of his slaves, Sally Hemings. LIBRARY OF CONGRESS

Maria Cosway enchanted Thomas Jefferson in Paris when he was minister to France. LIBRARY OF CONGRESS

Andrew Jackson was accused of being an adulterer during his presidential election campaign since his wife was still legally wed to another man when Jackson married her. LIBRARY OF CONGRESS

Rachel Donelson Jackson died of a heart condition that may have been brought on by charges of adultery and bigamy during her husband's presidential campaign. She was buried in the dress she would have worn to her husband's inauguration. LIBRARY OF CONGRESS

James Buchanan is the only bachelor president whose fiancée may have committed suicide. LIBRARY OF CONGRESS

Ann Coleman may have committed suicide over her failed engagement with James Buchanan because she thought he was seeing another young woman. HISTORICAL SOCIETY OF PENNSYLVANIA

Vice President William Rufus King and James Buchanan were roommates for twenty-three years. There is some evidence they may have had a homosexual relationship. LIBRARY OF CONGRESS

James Garfield is the first president known to have had an extramarital affair. LIBRARY OF CONGRESS

Lucretia Rudolph married James Garfield out of a sense of duty but learned to love him passionately. LIBRARY OF CONGRESS

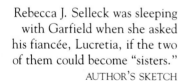

Rebecca J. Selleck was sleeping with Garfield when she asked his fiancée, Lucretia, if the two of them could become "sisters." AUTHOR'S SKETCH

Grover Cleveland had an affair with Maria Halpin, a woman of questionable morals. LIBRARY OF CONGRESS

Cleveland planned to marry Frances Folsom since she was a young child and once told a relative he was waiting for his wife to grow up. LIBRARY OF CONGRESS

Maria Halpin leveled charges that Cleveland had fathered her illegitimate son, Oscar Folsom Cleveland. NEW YORK PUBLIC LIBRARY

Political cartoon showing Maria Halpin, Cleveland, and his illegitimate son, Oscar Folsom Cleveland. LIBRARY OF CONGRESS

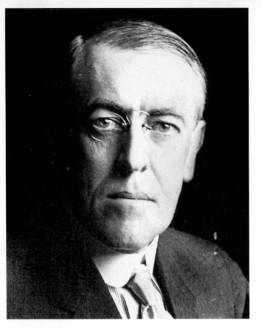

Woodrow Wilson shocked the electorate during his reelection campaign by announcing he was engaged to marry soon after his first wife's death. LIBRARY OF CONGRESS

Rumors circulated that Wilson had plotted the demise of his first wife, Ellen Axson Wilson, because he wanted to marry another woman. LIBRARY OF CONGRESS

Edith Boling Galt Wilson, his wife, was nicknamed the "Lady President" because she oversaw many of the president's affairs while he was bedridden during much of his last term. LIBRARY OF CONGRESS

Mary Allen Hulbert Peck, shown here later in life, may have had an affair with Woodrow Wilson in Bermuda or New York City. SEELEY G. MUDD ARCHIVES, PRINCETON UNIVERSITY

Warren G. Harding made love in a White House coat closet to Nan Britton, a young woman from his home town. LIBRARY OF CONGRESS

Florence Kling DeWolf Harding, Warren Harding's wife, was known as "The Duchess." LIBRARY OF CONGRESS

Carrie Phillips, Harding's first mistress and neighbor, was promised a regular monthly income as long as Harding was president. UPI/BETTMANN NEWS SERVICE

Nan Britton, Warren G. Harding's lover, wearing a fur coat, possibly paid for by Harding. UPI/BETTMANN NEWS SERVICE

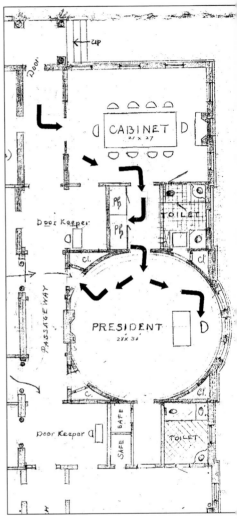

Floorplan of the Executive Office Building depicting the closet inside the president's office where Harding and Britton made love. Arrows show Nan's route into the closet through the cabinet room, her escape through the Oval Office, and Warren's escape route from the coat closet to his desk, where his wife, Florence, found him with a puzzled look on his face. NATIONAL ARCHIVES AND RECORDS ADMINISTRATION letters to Mrs. Peck were published. He wanted the colonel's advice about his rebuttal. Wilson's written statement declared:

> These letters are genuine, and I am now ashamed of them—not because the lady to whom they are addressed was not worthy of the most sincere admiration and affection, but because I did not have the moral right to offer her the ardent affection which they express.[12]

Colonel House told Wilson that he did not believe the letters would cause him serious harm and advised him not to yield to such blackmail. Woodrow had already decided not to surrender to blackmail, but he felt relieved when his judgment was validated. The colonel must have suspected (or known) that McAdoo's letter was fraudulent, since he was so unconcerned about the damage that might arise if the letters were published. It seems odd that the colonel would be so confident about this matter without having seen the letters, unless he already knew McAdoo's alleged letter was a fake. And Colonel House did meet with McAdoo before meeting with the president. Colonel House realized that Wilson was going to announce his engagement to Mrs. Galt no matter what advice he would give the president, so he gave his approval for a public announcement early the next month, even though only fourteen months had passed since Ellen Wilson's death.

On October 6, 1915, Woodrow penned the following engagement announcement and sent it to the newspapers:

> The engagement was announced today of Mrs. Norman Galt and President Woodrow Wilson.
>
> Mrs. Norman Galt is the widow of a well known business man of Washington who died some eight years ago. She has lived in Washington since her marriage in 1896. She was Miss Edith Bolling and was born in Wytheville, Virginia, where her girlhood was spent and where her father, the Hon. William H. Bolling, a man of remarkable character and charm, won distinction as one of the ablest, most interesting and most individual lawyers of a State famous for its lawyers. In the circle of cultivated and interesting people who have the privilege of knowing her Mrs. Galt has enjoyed an enviable distinction, not only because of her unusual beauty and natural charm, but also because of her very unusual character and gifts. She has always been sought out as a delightful friend, and her thoughtfulness and quick capacity for anything she chose to under-

take have made her friendship invaluable to those who were fortunate enough to win it.

It was Miss Margaret Wilson and her cousin Miss Bones who drew Mrs. Galt into the White House circle. They met her first in the early part of the present year, and were so much attracted by her that they sought her out more and more frequently and the friendship among them quickly ripened into an affectionate intimacy. It was through this association with his daughter and cousin that the President had the opportunity to meet Mrs. Galt, who spent a month at Cornish this summer as Miss Wilson's guest. It is, indeed, the most interesting circumstance connected with the engagement just announced that the President's daughters should have picked Mrs. Galt out for their special admiration and friendship before their father did.[13]

The editors of the *New York Times* were too embarrassed to publish the entire text of this gushy press release submitted by an infatuated president, so they printed the first paragraph and paraphrased the remainder of the text. The very next day, Woodrow and Edith went out in public for the first time. The president dined with Edith at her home for the next several weeks and was so ecstatic over his meetings with her and with his newfound freedom that he wanted to walk back to the White House. According to the Secret Service agents who would accompany him, Woodrow practically danced the entire way back home, all the while humming the words of the vaudeville show tune "Oh, you beautiful doll! You great big beautiful doll!"

Although the majority of people seemed to react favorably to news of the president's engagement, the Washington elite turned up their noses at his fiancée-commoner. After the announcement, ugly rumors began to circulate that perhaps Woodrow and Edith had been seeing each other before Ellen's death. Other stories suggested that he had neglected his wife's grave, failing to erect her headstone.

On October 9, 1915, a typographical error (or perhaps a Freudian slip) caused this embarrassing but comical mistake to be printed in an exclusive report about the president's courtship of Edith on the front page of the *Washington Post*: "The president spent much of the evening *entering* Mrs. Galt."[14] The reporter meant to say the president spent much of the evening *entertaining* Mrs. Galt. When the editors realized their mistake, they were horrified and scrambled to retrieve the errant story just as the newspapers were beginning to arrive at newsstands. They retrieved most of the papers, but not before a few copies were sold.

Woodrow and Edith were married on December 18, 1915. The small, private ceremony, in the bride's home in Washington, D.C., was attended by a group of close personal friends, family members, and members of the cabinet. Woodrow was fifty-eight, and Edith was fifteen years his junior. They honeymooned for two weeks at a resort in Hot Springs, Virginia.

There is some speculation as to whether Woodrow and Edith had become sexually intimate before they wed. At the White House the backstairs staff still occasionally tells the following joke about the love life of Woodrow Wilson: "What did Wilson's fiancée, Edith Bolling Galt, say when he proposed to her in the White House? Nothing. She was so shocked by his proposal that she fell out of the president's bed!"[15]

It is unlikely the couple made love at the White House before they wed. However, their letters are filled with references to sweet memories of times spent together in New England that seem to indicate they did consummate their relationship physically, during July 1915, five months before they were married. Woodrow was vacationing at his hideaway in Cornish, New Hampshire. Edith traveled to the vacation home two days before the president arrived, supposedly to visit his two daughters. However, after he arrived, Woodrow and Edith spent much time alone together for the next three weeks. He returned to Washington for a week in late July and then rejoined Edith for "another week of dalliance." During their final night together, before a planned monthlong separation designed to throw gossips and rumorsmongers off their trail, it appears she made love to Woodrow on the porch and again "on the big davenport in the living room."[16]

In Edith's letters to Woodrow, written in the weeks that followed their time together at Cornish, she described the home there as "my love nest." She also wrote the following words to him in two letters in the month following this vacation:

> I have come to look forward to this time (11 PM) with you every night
> . . . as the happiest part of the day . . . I hope you get to bed early and will

dream that I am with you and holding you safe in my arms while, with very tender fingers, I press down your tired lids and bid you sleep while I keep watch beside you.

A fond and very tender kiss my precious Woodrow, before we put out the light—and I feel your dear arms fold round me."[17]

During his courtship of Edith and even after their wedding, gossips charged that Woodrow did not respect the memory of his first wife, and even more ludicrous rumors arose suggesting that Woodrow and Edith had conspired to murder Ellen. Wilson's daughter tried to offset the bad publicity about some of his romantic love letters by publishing a book containing his letters to her mother.

During the war, rationing became a necessity. Edith set an example for the nation by reducing the consumption of gas, meat, and wheat at the White House and even had sheep brought to graze on the White House lawn to eliminate the need for an extra groundskeeper.

When Woodrow suffered a severe stroke in September 1919, Edith became his personal secretary. Since the ailing president was bedridden much of the time, Edith carefully screened all the correspondence and official papers that were sent to him and only allowed those matters that she considered truly important to be brought to his attention in an abbreviated form. She earned the nickname "Lady President" because of the important role she played in the last days of the Wilson administration. And it has been suggested that she became the first and only de facto woman president of the United States.

After leaving office in 1921, the Wilsons moved to S Street in Washington, D.C. Wilson finally had more time to read and write books. It was during this period that he wrote a five-volume *History of the American People*. Woodrow Wilson died in February 1924. He is buried in the National Cathedral of St. Peter and St. Paul in the nation's capital.

8

WARREN G. HARDING

Love in the White House
Coat Closet

☆

The president had just entered the coat closet with his young mistress, leaving Warren Ferguson, a Secret Service agent, to stand guard outside his office. He hadn't been in the closet more than five minutes when "the Duchess" arrived on the scene with arms flailing, shouting in a loud voice and demanding to see her husband at once. Ferguson quickly sandwiched himself between this lunatic woman and the office door. His special training hadn't prepared him to defend the president against this type of impassioned attack. Florence Harding, or the Duchess, as Warren liked to call her, had just discovered the location where her husband was busily engaged in sexual intimacies with Nan Britton, a much younger woman from his own hometown. Nan had already given birth to Warren Harding's illegitimate daughter, Elizabeth Ann.

Only those few people involved—Warren Harding, Nan, Florence, and Special Agent Ferguson—know exactly what happened that day. We only know about this event at all because Nan Britton, destitute after Warren's unexpected death and cut off from his surreptitious financial support, was compelled to write about her secret relationship with Warren Harding and their illegitimate daughter. The book told of their trysts

Warren G. Harding
Twenty-ninth President of the United States (1921–23)

Biographical Information

Born: November 2, 1865
Died: August 2, 1923
Wife: Florence ("Flossie") Kling DeWolfe (a.k.a. "the Duchess")
Children: None

Extramarital Affairs

Known and Suspected Sexual Partners:	Dates:	Locations:
Carrie (Fulton) Phillips	1905–20	Marion, Ohio
Nan Britton	1917–23	New York; Chicago; Washington, D.C.

Alleged Illegitimate Children: Elizabeth Ann Christian/Willets (Nan Britton's daughter)

---

in New York, Chicago, and Washington, D.C., and for the first time revealed their lovemaking in this most unusual place.

How did the president end up making love to a young woman in an unlit, five-foot-square coat closet in the White House? How did Nan Britton come to know Warren Harding, and how did Warren's wife find out about her husband's affair?

☆ ☆ ☆

Warren Harding was born on November 2, 1865, shortly after the Civil War ended, in Blooming Grove, Ohio, but grew up in neighboring Marion. His father, George Tyron Harding, was a country farmer turned doctor. His mother, Phoebe Dickerson Harding, became a schoolteacher and worked as a midwife to many of Marion's soon-to-be mothers.

Warren, the first of eight children, attended Ohio Central College in nearby Iberia and returned home to Marion in 1882 after graduating in July. At first, he taught school, then studied the law, but gave it up to sell insurance. Finally, he found his niche as an editor when his father bought a half interest in the *Star*, one of the local papers that had fallen on hard times.

Little is known about Warren's early romantic relationships. During his twenties Warren would occasionally visit the town's whorehouses in Marion's red-light district, located near the train station.[1] Perhaps this was where he first experimented sexually. As a U.S. senator, he would visit prostitutes in Washington from time to time.[2] Later, as president, he secured a special box at a burlesque theater in Washington where he could enjoy the shows without being observed. He certainly was attracted to beautiful young women and was considered attractive by the available young ladies in Marion. Tall and good-looking, at the age of twenty-five years he had already begun to gray at the temples and had a streak of gray running through his hair. His voice rang with a silvery resonance. When he walked down Marion's Center Street "he seemed the bull of the herd. Girls were drawn to his blatant maleness. He responded casually and directly," according to author Francis Russell.[3]

One of those girls was Florence "Flossie" Kling DeWolfe. Born into the richest family in Marion, she married her first husband, even though her father disapproved. A divorcée with a small child, she was said to be skinny and mean, possessing a plain-looking face, a manly stride, and a keen mind. Florence first met Warren when she was in his home giving one of his sisters a piano lesson. She was six years older than Harding. When Flossie made up her mind about something, she got her way, and she had decided that she wanted Warren. She pursued him relentlessly, until he finally agreed to marry her. One time, Warren saw her when he was arriving by train in Marion. He got off on the opposite side of the tracks and tried to sneak away. She shouted, "You needn't try to run away, Warren Harding. I see your big feet." They married in 1891, most assuredly not for love but for the opportunity she offered him to be part of the "in" crowd.

The *Star* grew and thrived under her control as circulation manager. Her managerial skills and business acumen freed Warren to become more involved in local politics. With her assistance he was elected state senator in 1896, U.S. senator in 1914, and U.S. president in 1920. After the presidential election she reportedly said to him, "Well, Warren Harding, I have got you the presidency. What are you going to do with it?"

Warren nicknamed her the Duchess because of her aloof and domineering manner. Warren was not satisfied romantically or sexually in this marriage, and he began to seek outlets for his affections. He may have dabbled occasionally with women in the red-light districts of Marion or in Washington D.C., but he only had two great loves in his life. These two women were Carrie Phillips and Nan Britton.

☆ ☆ ☆

Carrie (Fulton) Phillips was nine years younger than Warren. Tall and beautiful, with a round, pretty face and strawberry blond hair, she possessed a slender waist, full breasts, and a full, womanly figure. Carrie was sensual, exciting, and passionate. Like Warren, she, too, had married for opportunity and not love. Carrie wed Jim Phillips, a longtime Harding friend and part owner of the local Marion department store, in 1901 to escape the small town of Bucyrus, Ohio, where she taught school.

Carrie and Jim's two-year-old son, Jim Junior, died in 1904. Upon Warren's recommendation, Jim went away to calm his nerves after this tragedy to the same Battle Creek, Michigan, sanitarium that Warren had visited earlier, when he suffered his own nervous breakdown at age twenty-four. This left Carrie alone and grief-stricken. Florence was in Columbus being treated for a kidney ailment that she battled throughout her life.

Warren came to Carrie's home to console her. He found her alone in her bedroom. They began having an affair that night. It continued intermittently for the next fifteen years, until 1920. At first their affair was a well-kept secret. However, as in any small town, the gossip mill began to churn out rumors, fueled by speculation about the freshly laundered sheets that would appear on Carrie's clothesline after each of Warren's frequent daytime visits to her house "for tea." Warren discovered in Carrie "depths of sensuality he had not known before."[4] According to one of Harding's most respected biographers, Francis Russell, who read all of Warren's surviving love letters to Carrie, "She was the one great love of his life."

When they were apart, they began writing each other letters. Warren's letters often reached a length of forty pages or more. They were usually written in pencil on scratch paper. A few were written on stationery from the U.S. Senate. Many of the letters were enclosed in blue envelopes. His letters, very sentimental and at times erotic, described his longing for her hair, eyes, lips, cheekbones, earlobes, neck, shoulders, breasts, and thighs.[5] In 1911, Warren wrote her a letter which included the line "I love you garbed, but naked more." He underlined the word *naked* twice. Another of his letters to her, published in the *Washington Post* in 1976, contained the following passage: "There is one engulfing, enthralling rule of love, the song of your whole being which is a bit sweeter—Oh Warren! Oh Warren—when your body quivers with divine paroxysms and your soul hovers for flight with mine." Warren also wrote her a poem that began with the words "Carrie, take me panting to your heaving breast."[6]

Their spouses, Jim and Florence, must have suspected nothing, since they often saw each other socially. This foursome would take frequent drives together in the Hardings' Stevens-Duryea automobile.

They even vacationed together, and in February 1909 they took a monthlong cruise to Europe. Warren and Carrie would sneak out of their cabins at night and steal up to the deck for a quiet embrace in the dark shadows or a few minutes of comforting conversation. Carrie became torn during this trip, perhaps by guilt or the compromise of her integrity. She would feel her body drawn toward his but would suddenly push him away.

In 1911 they took an "economy" vacation to Bermuda. Anyone who has ever been to Bermuda knows that there is no such thing. Although it is a lovely little island and rich in history, it is somewhat pricey, since nearly everything but seafood must be imported. The locals consider it just another of the world's playgrounds for the rich and famous. The two couples boarded the *Bermudian* on March 21, 1911, and headed toward the island of pastel-colored limestone cottages. It would be their last joint vacation.

Although Warren was happy to maintain this arrangement, Carrie began to pressure him to divorce Florence and marry her. He refused, fearing Flossie's wrath and its effect on his political career. Carrie also ridiculed his political ambitions, which contributed to their breakup.

Angry at Warren because he refused to marry her, she packed her bags and took her daughter, Isabella, to Germany. She wrote to him and her husband telling them both she did not plan to return. She fell in love with the country and developed pro-German sentiments. Carrie did return, however, in 1914, when Germany was on the verge of war. Warren and Carrie resumed their affair, but it was not the same. Again, she pressured Warren to marry her. They had frequent conflicts and began to argue. Warren's continual refusal to wed Carrie and his anti-German stance during World War I created a wedge between them. She even threatened that if he did not support Germany in his Senate voting she would expose their affair publicly.

By 1914, Florence had become aware of their relationship. She made his life hell. At first, she made Warren accompany her to see a divorce lawyer. But he talked her out of the divorce while in the lawyer's office and was given a second chance. Although the revelation caused a brief gap in his affair with Carrie, it quickly resumed again with more intensity.[7]

Florence confronted Carrie when she would come by to talk with Warren in the evening while he was sitting on his front porch. On one occasion, Florence threw a feather duster at her to encourage her to leave. Next, Florence appeared with a wastepaper basket, which she also tossed at Carrie. Finally, she came out of the house brandishing a heavy wooden piano stool, and this time Carrie left, but not until she had blown Warren a kiss.

Although the affair began to become less intense, Warren and Carrie continued to write each other. Warren wrote Carrie the following poem, which he enclosed in a letter dated Christmas, 1915:

The Seventh Anniversary

I love you more than all the world
Possession wholly imploring
Mid passion I am oftime whirled
Oftimes admire—adoring
Oh God! If fate would only give
Us privilege to love and live!

Carrie's husband, Jim, did not learn of her affair until after it ended in 1920 and probably not until Carrie told him about it. Although she had promised to destroy all the letters Warren had sent her, she had saved them and was now threatening him with blackmail. And she had the proof. At one time, Harding had made her return the letters to him, but he later gave them back to her. Harding had already given her a Cadillac and offered her $5,000 a year "to avoid disgrace in the public eye, to escape ruin in the eyes of those who have trusted me in public life...."

During the presidential election campaign of 1920, the party bosses became worried that Warren's affair might become known and ruin their chances. The Republican National Committee sent Albert Lasker, an advertising executive and Harding's campaign manager in 1920, to offer the Carrie and Jim Phillips $20,000, a trip around the world, with an extended stay in the Orient, and $2,000 a month as long as they stayed out of the country until after the election and as long as Warren remained in public office.

Carrie and Jim Phillips lost their money during the Great Depression. Carrie became senile and was placed in a state home under the guardian-ship of Marion attorney Don Williamson. She died penniless in 1960.

In 1963, Williamson, the court-appointed attorney, found a locked box in a locked closet in Carrie's home. It contained 105 letters from Harding. Some were over forty pages in length. They proved beyond a reasonable doubt that Warren had engaged in a lengthy love affair with Carrie. They also helped to corroborate the story of Harding's other young lover, Nan Britton, who claimed he had also sent her similar let-ters during their love affair. All of Harding's letters to Carrie Phillips have been read by Francis Russell, who wrote the most comprehensive biog-raphy of Harding's life. The documents were delivered to the Ohio His-torical Society and are now in the possession of the Library of Congress. The letters were sealed by court order until July 29, 2014.

☆ ☆ ☆

Nan Britton was also born near Marion in 1896 and grew up in a house not far from Warren's. Her teacher in the school she attended was one of Warren's sisters, Abigail, or "Daisy," as she was known. Nan had an older sister named Elizabeth, after whom she eventually named her daughter, and two younger brothers, John and Howard, who was called

"Doc." Nan's father, a hardworking physician, died in 1913, when she was in junior high school. Her mother, a schoolteacher, had the burden of supporting the entire family from then on.

When Nan was fourteen years old, she saw Warren's picture on the Republican campaign posters around Marion and thought of him as her "ideal American." He was running for governor but lost. Nan said she knew she loved him at this young age—he was thirty years older than she—and began proclaiming her love to anyone who would listen. It brought her a good deal of ridicule and censure at times, and she eventually learned to curtail her confessions to the hometown folk.

Warren was amused by the ardent affections of this teenager. His wife was not at all amused. The members of the Twig Club, an important older ladies' gathering of all the socialites in Marion, thought Nan's behavior was absolutely scandalous. Florence called her friend, and Nan's next-door neighbor, and asked her to tell Nan's mother to constrain Nan's youthful enthusiasm for Mr. Harding. Florence, then age fifty-one or fifty-two, was probably jealous of this well-developed fourteen-year-old girl. She was described as having blond hair, a chubby but womanly figure, with rounded breasts, and a pouting, almost provocative face.

Nan worshiped Warren. One time, she said, "He was, to me, almost divine." She would have kissed the ground he walked on. In fact, she used to kiss his photograph and, later in life, the letters and gifts he would send her. On her first trip to the White House she lovingly caressed his chair in the empty cabinet room and sipped stale water out of the half-filled glass that sat at the head of the table. She had four identical pictures of him in frames of different types and sizes, cut from the ubiquitous campaign posters. One hung in her room directly above her bed. Nan said that she did this so she would see Warren's face first thing in the morning when she awoke and last thing at night before she fell asleep.

After school Nan would stand in the doorway of a building across the street from the *Marion Daily Star* newspaper office where Warren worked as editor. From her vantage point she could see the soles of his shoes when he propped them up on the windowsill, which seemed to give her a thrill. When Warren left his office, she would follow him home, or wherever he walked, being careful to remain about a block behind so that he would suspect nothing. Nan would call the Hardings' house on the telephone and ask to speak to Mrs. Harding but timed her calls when she knew Warren was at home and would likely answer.

Nan heard the rumors that Warren was very friendly with a "beautiful and extravagant" married woman in Marion who had a pampered daughter about Nan's age. Nan gave this woman a pseudonym in her book, Mrs. Henry Arnold, but surely she was referring to Carrie Phillips. Warren and Carrie's names had been connected by this small town's gossip, for everyone knew everyone else's business. It seems likely that Nan must have followed Warren quite often to the Phillips's house.

One day, when Nan was about fourteen, she was sent next door to bring home some milk. She got distracted by the flowers growing along the sidewalk and stopped to pick some of them. She had just created a makeshift bouquet when she looked up and saw Warren coming straight toward her. It was the closest she had ever been to him. She realized that it was too late to run and hide, so she just stood there stupefied as he passed. He gallantly stopped, tipped his hat, and said " How do you do?" Year's latter, Warren confessed that he had his "first desire to possess her" when he saw her that day.

Nan's only childhood visit to the Hardings' occurred when she and her sister, Elizabeth, rented a horse-drawn carriage for the afternoon and decided to stop by the Hardings' home. Nan was dumbfounded and couldn't think of anything to say. Her sister just prattled on. Nan remembers Mrs. Harding saying, "Now, Warren, you don't know anything about it," and, "Well, Warren, I know better," throughout the conversation.

Florence had developed the bad habit of putting Warren down in front of others and considered herself a know-it-all. Years later, Warren confided to Nan that Florence "puts me through Hell." All of these factors contributed to Warren's philandering. He often talked to Nan about his plans for the two of them if Florence were to die, which seemed a real possibility, since she was in poor health for long periods throughout their marriage.

Warren began secretly corresponding with Nan, writing her letters during the summer of 1914, when she was nearly eighteen. And she responded with letters of her own. This literary exchange seems to be the extent of their relationship at that time.[8]

After beginning a training program at the Ballard Secretarial Schools for Girls in New York City and moonlighting as a part-time secretary in the evenings to earn a little extra money, Nan decided that the time was right to look for a permanent position. In 1917 she typed Mr. Harding, then a U.S. senator, the following formal business letter, asking for his assistance in finding a secretarial position in Washington. Years before, he had said that he would try to help her in some way.

New York City
May 7, 1917

Hon. Warren G. Harding
United States Senate
Washington, D. C.
My Dear Mr. Harding:

I wonder if you will remember me; my father was Dr. Britton, of Marion Ohio.

I have been away from Marion for about two years, and up until last November, have been working. But it was work which promised no future.

Through the kindness of one of my father's Kenyon classmates, Mr. Grover Carter of this city, I have been enabled to take up a secretarial course, which course I shall finish in less than three weeks.

I have been reading of the imperative demand for stenographers and typists throughout the country, and the apparent scarcity, and it has occurred to me that you are in a position to help me along this line if there is an opening.

My experience is limited; I have done some work in the afternoon while going to school; the latter has been in connection with Madame Paderewska's Polish Refugee work. Now that I am about to look for an all-day position I do so want to get into something which will afford me prospects for long term advancement.

Any suggestions or help you might give me would be greatly appreciated, I assure you, and it would please me to hear from you.

Sincerely,
Nan Britton[9]

To her surprise she received his response three days later. Warren assured her that he did indeed remember her. He added: ". . . and I remember you most agreeably too." He told her that if he had a position available on his senatorial staff he would gladly give it to her. He asked her for a letter of recommendation and offered to "go personally to the war or navy department and urge [her] appointment." Warren also added that there was "every probability" of being in New York the following week." He indicated he would either attempt to call or look her up and would "take pleasure in doing it."

Although both letters seem innocent enough, it is likely Nan and Warren had more on their minds then finding Nan a job. Warren certainly did! Although he indicates in his letter that he might be in New York the following week, he latter admitted to Nan that the "sole motive" of his trip to New York was to see her. He obviously wanted to do more than act as a benevolent surrogate father or mentor.

The two quickly exchanged letters again. Nan informed him in more detail of her qualifications and told him how to contact her by phone. He commented on her writing ability and her intelligence and added, "I like your spirit and determination. It is like I always imagined you to be." Nan was soaring again. Warren G. Harding was thinking about her, imagining what she was like. It seemed like a dream that was too good to be true.

Before Nan could respond with another letter she was pleasantly surprised, in late May of 1917, by Warren's phone call at school. He made an appointment to meet her. She planned to wear her recently purchased "gray tailored suit and a dark blue sailor hat, the crown covered with gray veiling." However, it is unlikely she had time to change from her school outfit before arriving at the Manhattan Hotel, where he was staying. Warren was standing on the front steps of the hotel when she arrived at around 10:30 A.M. He probably flashed one of those warm, sincere Harding smiles she would remember so fondly in later years. He invited her to come inside to the reception room and talk of her need. They reminisced about her childhood affection for him, and she confessed frankly that she still had the same regard for him. This frank admission pleased Warren immensely. He suggested she come up to his room, the bridal chamber, where they might continue this discussion "without interruptions or annoyances." Nan wrote:

> . . . we had scarcely closed the door behind us when we shared our first
> kiss, it seemed sweetly appropriate. . . . I shall never forget how Mr. Hard-
> ing kept saying, after each kiss, "God! . . . God, Nan!" in high diminu-

endo, nor how he pleaded in tense voice, "Oh, dearie, tell me it isn't hateful to you to have me kiss you!" And as I kissed him back I thought that he surpassed even my gladdest dreams of him.[10]

According to Nan, they did not disturb the bed in the bridal chamber, and "there were no intimacies . . . beyond our very ardent kisses." They managed to find some time to talk about her need for a secretarial position. Although she wanted work in Washington, undoubtedly to be closer to Warren, he confessed that he would rather help her find a position in New York, where he would feel freer to come and spend time with her. Whether she fully grasped his proposition is not clear, but he was suggesting an illicit relationship; she would be little more than a kept woman. Before returning downstairs to lunch in the hotel's dining room, he "tucked $30 in her brand new silk stocking" to help with expenses for a trip she had planned to visit her sister in Chicago.

After lunch they decided to visit her landlady, Mrs. Phelps, and then took a taxi to the YWCA to talk about the quality of Nan's schoolwork. During the taxi ride Warren put his arm around Nan and dictated a letter to her, allegedly to see how fast she could take the information down. However, the content of his so-called letter indicates he had another objective in mind. He began the letter with " My Darling Nan." He told her he wanted and needed her and loved her more than the world. He wanted her to belong to him. "Could you?" he asked. He never finished dictating the letter, because Nan interrupted him with her kisses.

Later on in the day, after Warren found Nan a position with a major steel corporation in New York, he asked, "Now, do you believe that I love you?" Warren said, "I love you, dearie," to Nan many times and confided: "I'd like to make you my bride, Nan darling." He didn't seem to recall that he was already married, although they both knew that was the case.

One month later, in June 1917, when Nan was twenty, she received her first forty-page love letter from Warren. The letters were usually written in pencil on a scratch pad, sometimes on his stationery from the U.S. Senate, and enclosed in a blue envelope. Low on money, she wrote Warren about it, and he mailed her an American Express money order for forty-two dollars. In one of his earliest letters Warren expressed his great anticipation to be with her that "surpassed any longing he ever ex-

perienced in his life." He included a snapshot of himself which Nan cherished and used to kiss often. After she told him about this, Warren
wrote, saying, "Don't waste any more kisses on a likeness, Nan, when
the original yearns for your kisses." His letters varied in length from one
to sixty pages. He wrote them while sitting in the Senate chambers during the often dull proceedings and sent her letters weekly, which usually arrived by special delivery every Sunday morning. They decided to
destroy all their love letters to each other after reading them because of
the trouble they might eventually cause.

A week later, Warren invited Nan to Indianapolis, where he had a
speaking engagement. They checked into the Claypool Hotel. He registered her as his niece "Miss Harding." When Nan asked him what
Daisy, his sister and her former schoolteacher, would say if she saw them
together, he laughed and said, instead, that he would rather know what
his wife, Florence, would say.

U.S. senator Warren Harding and Nan planned to catch the midnight
train back to Chicago. He said he would obtain a berth for the two of
them to share if it was all right with her. In the taxi on the way to the
station he whispered repeatedly, "Dearie, 'r y' going t' sleep with me?"
However, at this time their relationship did not go beyond ardent kissing. During the train ride from Connersville, Indiana, to Chicago, Warren made "moving appeals" to Nan to become his 'totally. He told her
that if someone discovered they had shared the same sleeping quarters,
"we would invite as severe censure as though we had shared love's sweetest intimacy." Nan believed she was safe and would not become pregnant if she kept her clothes on. She tearfully asked Warren if he thought
she would have a child right away, even though he had done nothing
more than caress her in her nightgown.

Nan was very naive about love and sex. She did not even know the
simple facts of life, never having had a mother-daughter talk about sex.
She did not know how babies were brought into the world and wondered
aloud one time during one of their "kissing tours" why God had given
us navels. Warren had to explain all of this to her, answering her questions about sex. He also told her of his early sexual encounters, how he
had never been with a virgin before, and how it had been many years
since he had found his own marriage sexually satisfying.[11]

Back in Chicago they checked into another hotel. This time Warren registered them as man and wife. The clerk said to Warren, "If you can prove that she is your wife, I'll give you the room for nothing." Warren chuckled and told the clerk he didn't mind paying. Nan says their love-making that night was "restricted," which probably meant that they did not actually have intercourse. However, they must have been getting progressively closer.

Although Nan was determined to maintain her virginity, on July 30, 1917, Senator Harding and Nan registered again at a hotel on Broadway in New York by the name of Hardwick or Warwick (Nan couldn't remember which). She became "Mr. Harding's Bride" that day. The phone rang suddenly, startling them, and although Warren said the caller had the wrong number, two men knocked and let themselves into the hotel room. They immediately began questioning Nan, demanding her name. Warren was distressed but told her to tell the truth and said dejectedly, "They've got us!" Warren told them that Nan was twenty-two, but she corrected him and said she was only twenty. After Warren pleaded with them to let Nan go, they told him, "You'll have to tell that to the judge." After indicating they were sending for the police wagon, one of the men noticed the gold lettering in Warren's hat which read "W. G. Harding." The men suddenly became calm and respectful and left the room to let Warren and Nan finish dressing, but then returned to escort them out of the hotel by a side door to a waiting cab. Warren gave one of the men twenty dollars and, once safely in the taxi, confided to her, "Gee, Nan, I thought I wouldn't get out of that under one thousand dollars!"

On his next visit to New York, Warren asked the cabdriver if he knew of anyplace where he and Nan could go and not be disturbed. According to Nan, the driver took them to a shabby little hotel near Riverside Drive and Sixtieth Street, jumped out of the cab, leaving them inside, and did not return for fifteen minutes." Warren joked with the driver upon his return, saying he meant he wanted a "hotel." Nan and Warren visited this hotel six to seven times and were never raided once.

On another trip to New York, sometime in 1917 or 1918, Warren and Nan made love on a bench along a sheltered path in Central Park.

On August 17, 1918, Warren had a speaking engagement in Plattsburgh, New York. He sent Nan a letter suggesting she join him and enclosing ample money for her to make the trip. When she arrived at 8:00

A.M. he answered her knock at the hotel room door in his pajamas and said, "Gee, Nan, I'm s' glad t' see you!" They spent part of the day together in discussion, embraces, and lovemaking.

On Nan's first visit to see Warren in Washington, she stayed at the New Ebbit Hotel, registering as Elizabeth N. Christian, the name of Warren's secretary. He had promised to take her to the theater, but after showing her around town in a grand touring car, he dropped her off at the theater door with a ticket for the play *Good Morning, Judge!* He told her to "get back to the hotel and to bed" after the performance. She naively assumed they were going to the theater together and didn't realize until later in the evening that he needed to be more discreet in Washington than when they were in New York.

They "often talked about how wonderful it would be to have a child." Warren told Nan that he had wanted to adopt a child but his wife wouldn't hear of it. He said that Florence made his life hell and always spoke disparagingly about her to Nan. Florence was often sick, and he would tell Nan how he would marry her, live in the country, and buy a farm with "dogs, horses, chickens, and pigs" if his wife were to pass away. He told Nan she would make a darling wife and lovely bride! His letters always began with "Nan darling."

In early 1919, Nan came to Washington again. Warren was fifty-three; Nan, twenty-three. She visited his Senate office and stayed rather late. They made love in his office and later realized that their love child, Elizabeth Ann, was conceived that night. Not believing he would be lucky enough to have a child with Nan, Warren was careless and did not use any contraceptive that evening. And as Nan pointed out, "Of course the Senate Offices do not provide preventative facilities for use in such emergencies." By early February, Nan was certain she was pregnant. She wrote telling Warren the news. He wrote back telling her this "trouble was not so serious and could be handled." However, when he saw her again in late March or early April in Chicago at the New Willard Hotel, he was sweating and seemed nervous. He suggested an abortion, but Nan was determined to have his child. Warren began talking about how they would settle down on the farm he intended to buy for the two of them after he was "finished with politics." Then he became tense and troubled, grabbed both of Nan's arms, and said, "Look at me, dearie! You would be my wife, wouldn't you? If I only could . . . if we could only have our child together!" Nan nodded, assured him she would marry him, and said that at this moment "the very air seemed sacred."

Nan returned to New York in May 1919 and found a little apartment at the Hotel LaSalle Annex on East Sixtieth Street. During one of his visits, she told Warren she very much wanted a "wedding" ring. On a return trip he pulled a sapphire ring with little diamonds out of his pocket and put it on her finger. The two of them had a small ceremony during her fifth month of pregnancy and then he said that she "could not belong to him more utterly had we been joined together by fifty ministers."

One evening when Warren had prepared to spend the night at Nan's apartment and was already in her bed, a man they both knew from Marion knocked on the door. He had dined with Nan once before when he was in town and, after dinner, asked her not to tell his wife. Nan was greatly disturbed, since she felt they had done nothing wrong. This man now hoped to spend the night with her himself. But Nan, who had been preparing for her bath, sent him away without letting him through the door. When she returned to the bedroom, Warren was gone. She found the senator, and the future president of the United States, hiding in her wardrobe. They both laughed when Nan reminded him that his clothes were strewn all over her bedroom and that hiding would have done him little good, had it been another raid.

Nan left her apartment in New York and moved to Asbury Park, New Jersey, in July 1919, ostensibly "to summer" there, but in truth it was to have her baby. Together Warren and Nan devised a cover story. At first she stayed at the Hotel Monmouth, registering as Mrs. Edmund North Christian. She supposedly had married a Lieutenant Christian who was serving in the U.S. Army. She was living alone because the lieutenant's mother had disapproved of their marriage. Nan and Warren began referring to their unborn child as "the young lieutenant," thinking that the child would certainly be a boy. Three months later, on October 22, their daughter was born. When Nan was informed by the state's Department of Vital Statistics in Trenton that she would have to register the baby, she quickly named the child Elizabeth, after her sister, and chose Ann as a middle name; she thought it would sound better than Elizabeth Nan. Warren sent Nan $100–$150 monthly to pay for the baby's nurse.

During the presidential election campaign of 1920, Warren's candidacy was plagued with hints of scandal. Nan said that Mrs. Arnold (Carrie Phillips) and Warren's names were linked. Nan didn't know if the stories were true and never asked Warren about them. She didn't care what Warren had done before the two of them became "sweethearts," for she knew that she and Warren were faithful to each other during their six and one half years together. In fact, this was not the case. Warren's relationship with Carrie Phillips overlapped his relationship with Nan Britton by three or four years. He was seeing the two of them simultaneously. He sent each of them a five-pound box of Martha Washington chocolates as a Christmas present in 1917. Once, he mailed Carrie a letter written on stationery from the Witherill Hotel in Plattsburgh, dated August 17, 1918, which was the same weekend Nan remembered being at this hotel with Warren.[12]

Warren gave Nan a ticket to the convention that summer. She sat in the balcony as "unutterable emotion" swelled within her when the convention nominated Warren G. Harding as the Republican party's choice for the presidency of the United States. Nan recalled how, when she was just thirteen, she would write in the margin of her books, "Warren Harding—he's a darling! Warren Harding—President of the United States."[13] One biographer said that Nan's sister was also seated in the balcony, holding little Elizabeth Ann. After his nomination Warren became concerned that Nan might be "shadowed." Shortly after the convention, he visited Nan at her sister's house for two hours. She sat in his lap, and they kissed—almost like a loving father holding his little girl in his lap. This was one of their familiar romantic positions. When they were alone together, he often picked her up and carried her about the room. They talked and made plans for young Elizabeth Ann's care. Warren wanted Nan to give Elizabeth to her sister and brother-in-law. Although Nan suggested that they arrange for Warren to meet Elizabeth Ann, perhaps during one of her stroller rides in the park, he was reluctant to do so, thinking it unwise. Warren was probably wary of being seen together with his illegitimate daughter. Nan and Warren did not see each other again until after he was elected president.

For many months after she became a mother Nan was extremely tired. She left the child in her sister's care and went to Eagle Bay, a retreat in the Adirondacks, to regain her strength. The president's chief Secret Service agent, Jim Sloan, showed up with a note from Warren and $800.

Nan gave him the cover name Tim Slade in her book. Nan returned to Chicago and began working for Warren's election as a secretary for the Republican National Committee. On the day of the election Nan took a night train to Marion, hoping for a victory celebration, and was over-joyed after arriving the next morning when she was informed that War-ren would be the next president. She contacted Jim Sloan and asked to see Warren. He arranged a private meeting in one of the small houses they had rented for the campaign. Warren and Nan hugged, kissed, and probably made love in the darkened kitchen while the Secret Service man stood guard just outside the front door. Nan showed Warren sev-eral snapshots of the baby, and he gave her two or three $500 bills be-fore leaving.

After the inauguration, Nan made her first trip to the White House in June 1921. The president greeted her in the cabinet room and took her to his private office. He embraced her after pulling her into the cor-ner, away from the window. He complained, saying everyone seemed to have "eyes in the side of their heads." Warren had a remedy, though. In her book *The President's Daughter*, Nan wrote:

> Whereupon he introduced me to the one place where, he said, he thought we might share *kisses* in safety. This was a small closet in the ante-room, evidently a place for hats and coats, but entirely empty most of the times we used it, for we repaired there many times in the course of my visits to the White House, and in the darkness of a space not more than five feet square the President of the United States and his adoring sweetheart made love.[14]

In August 1921, Nan visited the White House again. Three-quarters of their time was spent in intimate embraces, and during the remaining time they discussed Elizabeth Ann's development and care.

In October, Warren Ferguson, a Secret Service man, met Nan at the train station in Washington when she came again to visit Warren. Jim Sloan was not available this time. Nan maintains that Ferguson met her at the train station only once, to escort her to the White House, although she could have been mistaken about this. After her meeting with the president, she said Ferguson gave her a private guided tour of the White House, even though there was a small risk she might bump into Mrs. Harding. It may have been on this occasion, or some other, that Ferguson was sent to bring Nan from the train station to the White House. The train arrived late. The president, frustrated and angry, shouted "Where have you been?" when they finally arrived. After he calmed down, Nan and Harding went directly to the coat closet, leaving Ferguson to stand guard outside the office door. Within five minutes, the Duchess showed up, arms flailing and with fire in her eyes. She ordered Ferguson to get out of her way, but he refused. When she realized that he would not be moved, she ran around to the front entrance to enter the closet through the anteroom office.

After Florence left, Ferguson banged loudly on the door to warn the president, slipped Nan out of the closet, and rushed her out the back door of the White House to his car. Florence was delayed coming around the other way just long enough for the president to slip out of the closet, jump behind his desk, and pretend to be working when the Duchess burst into the Oval Office from the other side. Ferguson felt that Mrs. Harding's own Secret Service man, Agent Barker, must have told her about the president's dallying in the coat closet. Several years earlier, Nan and Warren had wondered what Florence would say if she saw them together at the Claypool Hotel.

This was not the only close call at the White House. Years later, another first lady doubled back from a shopping trip and nearly caught the president frolicking naked in the White House swimming pool with several young, naked women. But not all presidents were so fortunate. Another president's wife allegedly caught him making love with a secretary on a couch in the Oval Office.

In January 1923, during Nan's last meeting with Warren in the White House, he confessed, "Nan, our matter worries me more than the combined worries of the whole administration. It is on my mind continually. Why dearie, sometimes in the night I think I shall lose my mind worrying over it." Nan, who was very naive, didn't understand why he was so worried and instead challenged him to give up everything, as some men had done, for love. He told her he wouldn't desert his party. There was nothing he could do. He said to her, "Nan, If you had been born earlier . . . Nan, darling, you must help me; our secret must not come out. Why, I would rather die than disappoint my party! . . . Oh, dearie, try!"[15]

Earlier he had referred to the White House as a prison and said he was in jail and couldn't get out. Now he seemed concerned about his chances for reelection, or perhaps he was simply worried about the consequences if their relationship ever became public knowledge. Nan was also worried, but not about the public exposure of their relationship. She was worried about Elizabeth Ann's future. According to Nan, Warren promised to provide for both of them as long as they both should live.

Harding died later that same year, the sixth president to die in office, while on a goodwill trip to Alaska. Nan was in France trying to forget all her troubles when she heard the news. Harding's death left Nan without a means of support and in great debt. Although she was sure Warren would have made some provision for Elizabeth Ann during his illness in the days shortly before his death, no money was ever found. Before his death, Harding sent Nan ample funds on which to live and support their daughter. He agreed to provide Nan's sister with $500 a month if she and her husband would adopt little Elizabeth Ann. Nan maintains that she was frugal and spent her money wisely, but she always seemed able to buy expensive clothes and other possessions. Warren chided her once on her spending habits after she appeared at one of their White House meetings in an expensive fur coat. In fact, Nan worked very little in the two years following her daughter's birth. Some of this time was spent recovering, since she seemed drained of her energy. Surely some of this lack of energy was from the stress of dealing with questions concerning Elizabeth Ann's care and guardianship.

In 1927, Nan Britton wrote *The President's Daughter*, which tells her story and the story of the love child she had with Warren Harding. In the foreword of the book she said the motivation for writing this book was to help obtain legal and social recognition and protection of all children born in the United States out of wedlock. Although this may have been a larger and more grandiose goal for the book, providing a means of financial support for herself and her daughter, Elizabeth Ann, was the immediate need and motivation. She also suggested changing the law to make it a criminal offense not to record the father's name at the birth of the child. Surely this change was proposed to ensure that so-called illegitimate children would have the same access to the financial resources of their fathers as those born in wedlock, an access that Nan no longer enjoyed.

9

FRANKLIN D. ROOSEVELT

Until Death Did They Part

☆

Since Franklin was still in bed recuperating from the double pneumonia he contracted during his voyage to Europe, Eleanor decided to unpack his bags and sort through his mail. She discovered several love letters addressed to Franklin written by her former secretary, Lucy Mercer. Suddenly, the bottom dropped out of her world. Eleanor's husband was seeing another woman—her own secretary. Her marriage had fallen apart, and she wasn't even aware of it until now. Eleanor cried, became angry, and then called Franklin's mother and asked her to come and be present when she confronted him with this irrefutable evidence.

Franklin did agree to end his affair with Lucy, but he quickly broke his promise, just as he had violated the marriage vows he had made to Eleanor thirteen years earlier. Franklin and Lucy continued to see each other secretly off and on for thirty years until his death in April 1945.

In a *Life* magazine poll published in August 1987, one-quarter of the voters said, "A long-term 'affair of the heart' was more acceptable in a President than casual infidelity." Although Franklin maintained a long-term love affair with Lucy Mercer and certainly was not casually unfaithful, it was not the sole extramarital affair in which he participated. He had an intimate relationship with Marguerite ("Missy") LeHand, his secretary of twenty years, and may have had an extramarital affair with

Franklin D. Roosevelt
Thirty-second President of the United States (1933–45)

Biographical Information

Born: January 30, 1882
Died: April 12, 1945
Wife: Anna Eleanor Roosevelt
Children: Five boys; one girl

Extramarital Affairs

Known and Suspected Sexual Partners:	Dates:	Locations:
Lucy Page Mercer Rutherfurd	1916–46	Washington, D.C.; Warm Springs, Ga.
Marguerite Alice ("Missy") LeHand	1921–40	Albany, N.Y.; Washington, D.C.
Dorothy Schiff	1938	Washington, D.C.
Princess Martha of Norway	1944–45	Washington, D.C.

Illegitimate Children: None

---

her, too. There is also some evidence that while in his mid-thirties he may have had numerous extramarital affairs while serving in Washington as the assistant secretary of the navy, until his battle with polio rendered him unable to walk. He may also have had one or two affairs in the late 1930s or earlier 1940s while serving as president of the United States.

☆ ☆ ☆

Franklin Delano Roosevelt was born in January 1882 in a palatial mansion in Hyde Park, an estate overlooking New York's Hudson River. He had private tutors until he was fourteen and then enrolled at the Groton School in Massachusetts. He attended Harvard University, served as the editor of the *Crimson* (the school's newspaper), and graduated in 1904. Afterward, he attended Colombia University Law School and was admitted to the bar in 1907 to practice law in New York City.

Franklin was tall, handsome, and charismatic. One newspaper account describes Franklin's appearance when he was in his early thirties this way:

> His face is long, firmly shaped and set with marks of confidence. There are faint wrinkles on a high straight forehead. Intensely blue eyes rest in light shadows. A firm, thin mouth breaks quietly to laugh, openly and freely. His voice is pitched well, goes forward without tripping. . . .[1]

Anna Eleanor Roosevelt was born in New York City on October 11, 1884. She was raised by her maternal grandmother from the time her parents had passed away when she was only eight years old. She was the niece of President Teddy Roosevelt, and Eleanor and Franklin were fifth cousins. Like her husband, she was raised in affluence and received her early education from private tutors. At age fifteen she was sent to London for three years to study at Allenswood, a private school for girls. She returned to New York in 1902, had her coming out party, and became a social worker working in the slums on New York City's Lower East Side.

Eleanor was not very attractive. She had large lips, protruding teeth, and a shrill voice. She did have a good figure, though, and an ample supply of blond hair. She was shy, serious, caring, and trusting.

In 1902 she met Franklin Roosevelt, then a young Harvard undergraduate student. He was smitten and proposed during a long walk after the Harvard-Yale football game on November 21, 1903. She accepted immediately, although they were not married until sixteen months later. According to several authors, Franklin and Eleanor never kissed before their wedding. Eleanor was certainly a product of her Victorian-era upbringing. She was a proper young woman, and it is likely this type of physical contact would have been inconsistent with her values.

Franklin and Eleanor were married on Saint Patrick's Day, 1905. He was twenty-three, and she was twenty. Teddy Roosevelt agreed to give away the fatherless young bride. The wedding took place at the home of her aunt in New York City. Since Franklin was still in law school, they only spent a week alone together in Springwood and later that summer sailed on the *Oceanic* for a three-month tour of Europe, which served as an extended honeymoon. Franklin began calling Eleanor "Babs," which was short for baby, during their honeymoon and continued to call her by this affectionate nickname for the rest of his life.

Overall, their marriage was not happy. There were a number of reasons, some of which may have contributed to Franklin's philandering. One was Franklin's mother. Another may have been Eleanor's own views toward the purpose of sexual relations between a husband and wife. Eleanor also tended to be critical.

Franklin's mother, Sara Delano Roosevelt, constantly interfered in their marriage. She ignored Eleanor's wishes and decorated the newlyweds' home according to her own tastes. She dominated their children and considered herself more their mother than was Eleanor. She gave the couple unsolicited advice about household matters whether they wanted it or not. Sara did not approve of their engagement, believing Franklin to be acting impulsively, so she arranged to take him on a Caribbean cruise in 1904, hoping to cool the relationship, but was unsuccessful.

Eleanor may have regarded sex as a marital obligation to be endured. Of course, she knew sex was required for the conception of her children but likely had little use for it otherwise. Years later, she had an awkward premarital conversation with her own daughter, Anna, and warned her that sex was "an ordeal to be borne." The Roosevelt's oldest son, Elliot, claimed that after the difficult birth of her last child and his brother, John, she declared that sexual relations with Franklin were a thing of the past. If this is true, then she must be held partly accountable for Franklin's philandering. This unilateral decree of celibacy, coupled with her unattractive physical appearance, may have pushed Franklin toward extramarital affairs. Although Eleanor was somewhat attractive as a young woman, she could hardly compete with the much younger, more attractive, and physically acquiescent young women to whom Franklin had easy access. Certainly by the end of 1918, if not sooner, they had ceased all conjugal activity.

Years after Franklin's death, Eleanor commented on their relationship and the role she played in his success:

FRANKLIN D. ROOSEVELT

> He might have been happier with a wife who was completely uncritical. That I was never able to be, and he had to find it in some other people. Nevertheless, I think I sometimes acted as a spur, even though the spurring was not always wanted or welcome.[2]

All of these factors, singularly and in combination, contributed to an unhappy marriage. Of course, Franklin's infidelity was the final blow.

Franklin's political career began in 1910. While in law school he carefully charted his course and planned to become president one day, following the example set by his distant cousin Teddy Roosevelt. First, he would be elected state senator; next, he would become the assistant secretary of the navy; then governor of New York and finally on to the presidency. He followed his plan exactly, and it worked.

He was elected Democratic state senator from New York, representing three election districts located along the Hudson River—a significant feat, since no Democrat had been elected to that position in fifty-four years. He was appointed assistant secretary of the navy by President Woodrow Wilson in April 1913.

Franklin was defeated when he ran for vice president as James M. Cox's running mate, losing to Warren Harding in 1920. He did not abandon his political aspirations, however.

In 1921, Franklin suffered a great personal misfortune. After a swim in the icy waters of the Bay of Fundy in Canada, he was diagnosed with polio. Although he was only thirty-nine, he never stood erect or walked again without some form of assistance. Frightened that he would die in a fire someday, Franklin practiced crawling in the unlikely event that he would be left alone in a burning building without anyone to help him escape. Although the havoc wreaked by the polio virus limited his mobility significantly, Franklin was still capable of sexual activity. Years later, after a physical examination, the three doctors who examined him reported, "No symptoms of *impotentia coeundi*." In other words, he remained potent.

He was elected governor of New York in 1928 and served two terms. With the help of the sage Democratic political boss James Farley and Roosevelt's popular financial-aid program which became known as the New Deal, he ran for president in 1932 and was elected by a landslide margin. He defeated incumbent president Herbert Hoover, capturing

472 of the 513 electoral votes. The only man to be elected president four times, he served for twelve years and thirty-nine days, longer than any other president.

Although he was loved by many Americans, who considered his character above reproach, Franklin was not above dubious political maneuvers. This included using rumors of sexual indiscretion as a weapon against his political opponents. During his reelection campaign in 1940, Franklin considered releasing news of Wendell Wilkie's suspected extramarital affair with a woman who was well known in New York literary circles. Franklin told his aides, "Spread it as a word-of-mouth thing, or by some people way, way down the line." He reasoned, if the other side wanted to play dirty politics, "we've got our own people" who could be used to do the same.

After giving these orders, Franklin reminded himself of another extramarital affair that occurred years earlier involving Jimmy Walker, then the mayor of New York City. Franklin said that Walker "was living openly with this gal all over New York, including the house across the street from me." According to FDR, Jimmy also "paid his wife ten thousand dollars to spend a weekend with him in Albany, New York, in order to maintain a proper public image." Before that weekend, Franklin claimed, Jimmy had never spent the whole weekend in Albany during his entire married life. "She was an extremely attractive little tart," he added. We know that Franklin gave these orders to campaign staffers because in 1982 secret recordings were discovered among his personal papers in the Roosevelt library. Franklin had made his own secret recordings in the White House Oval Office at this time, allegedly to protect himself "from being misquoted during the 1940 campaign." Although most Americans believe that Richard Nixon was the first president to make secret recordings in the Oval Office, this Democratic predecessor had done so thirty years earlier.

While it is likely that Roosevelt had long-term affairs with two women, he may have had brief illicit encounters with numerous other women. Livingston Davis, his old college chum and "jolly boy," insisted that "Franklin was an ardent ladies' man, a man of many affairs."[3] Davis would know if anyone did. He was undoubtedly one of Franklin's closest friends. Once, while in Havana, Davis suggested they attend one of the live sex shows that could be seen there for a price. After Franklin was stricken with polio, Davis wrote Franklin and encouraged him to look on the brighter side of this unfortunate situation. In his letter, Davis pointed out that during his convalescence Franklin would finally have time to write a book and suggested a number of subjects. One of the eight titles he suggested was "The Ladies of Washington: or Thirty Days and Evenings as a Bachelor."[4] Certainly this recommended book title may have represented a humorous exaggeration of Franklin's amorous behavior, but it may also have indicated that Franklin had been involved in many more than two extramarital affairs.

☆ ☆ ☆

Lucy Page Mercer served as Eleanor's social secretary from 1913 to 1914. Franklin met her at this time and undoubtedly was attracted to the twenty-two-year-old beauty. Duty and circumstances most likely prevented his manly desires from being fulfilled at this time. After all, some of his physical needs were still being fulfilled by Eleanor.

Lucy was five feet nine inches tall and had blue eyes and long light-brown hair which she wore on the top of her head in a classic Victorian style. Her skin was "exquisitely fine." Her voice was rich and velvety, and she had the most beautiful smile. Pretty and delightful, Lucy was described as geishalike, graceful, and seductive.

Franklin began an extramarital affair and a thirty-year relationship with Lucy Mercer during the summer of 1916. She was twenty-six; he was thirty-four. Franklin was living in the nation's capital while serving as assistant secretary of the navy. Eleanor was spending the summer with the children at Campobello in Canada to escape Washington's wretched heat and humidity. Lucy began accompanying Franklin to various social events that summer, and their love affair probably began at this time. She traveled with Franklin on an overnight weekend cruise up the Potomac River. They also spent the night in a Virginia Beach hotel after registering as husband and wife.

Eleanor must have suspected something was awry, for she wrote Franklin a letter during the summer of 1917 in which she speculated why he had decided to remain in Washington all summer rather than joining the children and her at Campobello. He wrote the following response:

July 16, 1917

Dearest Babs:

   I really can't stand that house all alone without you, and you were a goosy girl to think or even pretend to think that I don't want you here all the summer, because you know I do! . . . Kiss the chicks for me all round, and many many for you.

Your devoted
F[5]

The very next day he wrote her again:

July 17, 1917

Dearest Babs:

   It seems years since you left and I miss you horribly and hate the thought of the empty house . . . Love and kisses to you all.[6]

Eventually, Franklin did spend ten days in Campobello that summer. However, in 1917 he had even more difficulty freeing himself from his many duties to make the trip to this Canadian retreat to be with Eleanor or his family. However, he seemed to find time for leisurely trips during that same summer that always included Lucy Mercer.

   On Sunday, July 22, 1917, Franklin cruised down the Potomac River aboard the presidential yacht to Hampton Roads, Virginia, to inspect the naval fleet anchored there. He made this trip along with two other couples and with Lucy Mercer. He also invited Nigel Law, a bachelor and British military officer, to counter any appearance that he and Lucy had paired off like the two other married couples. Nigel was probably unaware that he was serving in an unofficial capacity as Franklin's "beard," that is, a single man brought along on an outing to supposedly escort a single woman and thereby obscure the fact that she is really traveling with a married man.

   In August, Franklin made another trip, this time by car to Harpers Ferry, West Virginia. He was accompanied by a single married couple and Lucy Mercer.

   On another occasion, Alice Roosevelt Longworth, Eleanor's distant cousin, phoned Franklin to inform him that she had seen him driving a car on an outing. She said, "I saw you twenty miles out in the country. You didn't see me. Your hands were on the wheel, but your eyes were on the perfectly lovely lady." As one author said, Franklin might have been thinking, "Better than the reverse being true." But instead of becoming defensive, he responded, "Isn't she perfectly lovely?"

Washington was abuzz with gossip. Yet somehow Eleanor remained blissfully ignorant of their blossoming relationship. Perhaps she did not want to know. Perhaps she was truly a trusting person and no one had brought these matters to her attention. She did not learn for certain of their love affair until September 1918, when she accidentally discovered several love letters written by Lucy to Franklin. When he was sick in bed with double pneumonia, after returning from a trip to Europe, Eleanor unpacked his belongings, sorted through Franklin's mail, and discovered the love letters that proved he was actively engaged in an affair with her former social secretary.

Eleanor was both tearful and angry. Years later, she described what followed her discovery when she told biographer Joseph P. Lash the following: "The bottom dropped out of my own particular world and I faced myself, my surroundings, my world, honestly for the first time. I really grew up that year."[7] We know she confronted Franklin and Lucy with their adulterous behavior. Franklin's mother, Sara, was present at the time. Sara threatened to cut Franklin off financially if he divorced Eleanor and told him she would "not give him another dollar." According to some accounts, Eleanor demanded that Franklin either end the relationship immediately or she would divorce him; according to others, she offered him a divorce, if he still wanted one after he carefully considered the impact it would have on their five children. Lucy claims that even though Eleanor may have offered him a divorce, it was never really an option, since "Eleanor was not willing to step aside."

In those days, ending a marriage was scandalous; the only grounds for divorce in New York State were adultery. This course of action would have been disastrous to Franklin's budding political career. Franklin and Lucy, a Roman Catholic who would not be free to marry a divorced man, anyway, reluctantly agreed to Eleanor's wishes in view of her threat. But they did not keep their promise. Franklin and Lucy continued to see each other secretly throughout his lifetime.

Eleanor agreed to continue as Franklin's helper but also made it clear that she would lead an independent life and look for emotional support and sustenance from others. Although Franklin and Eleanor maintained a close personal relationship for the rest of their lives, it was more of a limited partnership than a marriage. Perhaps resulting from a sense of guilt, Franklin supported Eleanor in every project she attempted. He would never allow anyone to criticize her.

When his train would make a side trip to Allamuchy, New Jersey, or Aiken, South Carolina, so he could visit Lucy, the press reporters chose selectively to exclude these excursions from their newspapers accounts.

In 1920, at age twenty-nine, Lucy married Winthrop Rutherfurd, a wealthy fifty-eight-year-old man with six children whose wife had died three years earlier. Although Lucy became absorbed in the logistics of meeting the needs of the instant family she inherited upon her marriage, she still found time to write Franklin letters and visit him occasionally. In March 1933, Franklin sent a presidential limo to bring Lucy to his first inauguration. In fact, he arranged for her to attend all four of his inaugurations and watch the proceedings from the privacy of a presidential limousine. He kept the knowledge of his special inaugural guest a secret from Eleanor. But she had her own secrets that day of which he was unaware.

Their relationship was much curtailed until 1940, when Franklin began phoning Lucy once or twice week and seeing her again. Lucy's husband had suffered a stroke and was very ill at the time. He was not in any shape to keep track of her movements. At first, Franklin would have the Secret Service drive him over to Georgetown, where he would slip into Lucy's car, or she into his, and they would drive through Rock Creek Park alone together and talk for a few hours. The Secret Service agents probably shadowed their movements to provide protection for the president. But Franklin was looking for companionship and not protection during these brief visits.

After her husband died in 1944, Lucy visited the White House often when Eleanor was away. That same year, while Eleanor was on a trip, her daughter, Anna, invited Lucy to dine at the White House with Franklin on several occasions. While there was nothing secretive about these dinners, Anna did keep knowledge of these visits with her father's former mistress from Eleanor. One time, Franklin Roosevelt Jr. made a surprise visit to his father's office and discovered Lucy massaging his withered legs.

Although Eleanor was not aware of it until years after Franklin's death, Lucy was with Franklin at his retreat in Warm Springs, Georgia, when he experienced his fatal stroke on April 12, 1945. He was working at his desk while Lucy sat opposite him, smiling warmly and laughing at his little jokes. He slumped forward in his chair, complained of a headache, and could not move. The servants quickly took him upstairs and called the doctor, who confirmed what they all feared, a massive stroke. Lucy was quickly shuttled away to prevent Eleanor from learning she was with Franklin shortly before he died. Lucy Mercer Rutherfurd died of leukemia in New York City three years later, in 1948.

The revelation of Franklin's extramarital affair with Lucy Mercer nearly destroyed his marriage of thirteen years. The news was kept secret, however, and not revealed to the public until 1946, after Franklin had died. When the news of the Mercer affair eventually came out, Eleanor's distant cousin, Alice Roosevelt Longworth, said, "Well, Franklin was entitled to a little fun. After all, he was married to Eleanor."

☆ ☆ ☆

In 1923, Marguerite Alice "Missy" LeHand had become Franklin's secretary. She worked for him for the next twenty years. She and Franklin had first met in 1920 during his failed vice-presidential campaign. Missy worked in the Democratic campaign headquarters in Washington. Although the extent of their personal relationship is not certain, author Shelley Ross wrote in *Fall From Grace*: ". . . FDR never hid his relationship with Missy from Eleanor, who accepted the young woman as her husband's mistress."

Missy was twenty-three years old. She was tall, had sad-looking but intense blue eyes, thin, willowy black hair, and was somewhat attractive. She was prim, capable, and at times amusing. Franklin was attracted to this type of woman.

Missy did far more than secretarial work. She traveled with Franklin wherever he went and took care of him. After he was stricken with polio in 1921, she was constantly by his side. She worked with him during his rehabilitation sessions, swam with him, and tried to cheer him up. On several occasions while Franklin cruised on his houseboat, the *Larooco*, she was seen sitting on his lap. Missy substituted as hostess when Eleanor was away.

After Franklin was elected governor of New York in 1928, Missy moved with the family into the governor's mansion. Her bedroom adjoined Franklin's, while Eleanor's was way down the hall. In was not uncommon for family members to find Missy in Franklin's bedroom clothed only in a nightgown.

After Franklin became president Missy lived in the White House. She had a three-room suite, consisting of her own bedroom, living room, and bath. But she would often be found in Franklin's bedroom at night, wearing only a nightgown. She was also often found sitting on Franklin's lap in the Oval Office.

Elliot Roosevelt, the president's son, believes that Missy was Franklin's mistress. Other family members, including Franklin's son, James Roosevelt, do not agree. Elliot claimed that the revelation of his father's affair with Missy LeHand did not surprise him. But he was surprised, he said, when he learned that Eleanor had knowledge of the affair at the time it occurred.

In 1940, Missy suffered a cerebral hemorrhage, was incapacitated, and had to be moved out of the White House; she died three years later. Franklin left half of his estate, valued at nearly $2 million, to Missy to pay for her medical bills.

☆ ☆ ☆

Two other women were rumored to have had affairs with Franklin. One was Princess Martha of Norway. She lived in the United States during World War II and had free run of the White House and Hyde Park. She and Franklin flirted openly, but there is little evidence that they did anything more.

The other woman was Dorothy Schiff, a former publisher of the *New York Post*. Dorothy claimed that she and Franklin had an intermittent love affair that included sex. Describing her relationship with Franklin, she said:

> He probably saw me as a sex object. This was a warm, sexy guy who was in an isolated position and was looking for a turn-on and companionship too. In a rather sweet way, he was fairly bold, and everything about his body—except his legs—was strong.[8]

It is difficult, if not impossible, to corroborate Dorothy's claims of a love affair with Franklin Roosevelt. There were no witnesses to confirm her account.

☆ ☆ ☆

Franklin may not have been alone in his adulterous behavior. There is some evidence suggesting Eleanor had her own extramarital affairs as well. With a woman.

In 1932, Eleanor met an Associated Press reporter named Lorena Hickok. Lorena had been assigned to cover the Democratic nominee's wife. Lorena was unattractive, overweight, sexless, and wore her hair in a bun. She looked a lot like J. Edgar Hoover, the former director of the Federal Bureau of Investigation (FBI). One of Lorena's female coworkers at the Associated Press said Lorena was a lesbian and claimed Lorena made a pass at her one night when they shared a hotel room during a news assignment. Rebuffed by the coworker, Lorena apologized for her indiscretion and admitted she usually kept her "tendency" in check but at times "went off the deep end" over certain women.[9]

Lorena eventually quit her job so she could spend all her time at Eleanor's side. She moved into the White House early in January 1941 but had been "visiting" Eleanor at the presidential residence for months at a time before officially changing her address. Lorena lived in the White House with Eleanor for the next four years. According to Lillian Rogers Parks, one of the back-stairs maids who worked at the White House during FDR's tenure, Lorena often slept on the daybed in Eleanor's room, even though she had her own room. Parks frequently witnessed Eleanor running back and forth between her room and Lorena's whenever Lorena chose to sleep in her own room. Franklin considered Lorena and some of Eleanor's other female friends "she-males" and once, referring to Lorena, was heard yelling, "I want that woman kept out of this house!"

Eleanor corresponded with Lorena for over thirty years, writing her between two thousand and three thousand letters. Lorena donated these letters to the Roosevelt Presidential Library at Hyde Park under the condition that they not be opened until ten years after her death, which occurred in 1968. A few of the letters contained passages that hinted at the degree of intimacy the two women shared. On March 7, 1933, Lorena's fortieth birthday, Eleanor wrote the following words in a letter to Hickok:

> Hick Darling, All day I've thought of you & another birthday I will be with you. . . . Oh! I want to put my arms around you. I ache to hold you close. Your ring is a great comfort. I look at it and think she does love me, or I wouldn't be wearing it.[10]

Eleanor wore this same sapphire-colored ring to Franklin's inauguration ceremony in March 1933. The night before the inauguration, Eleanor and Lorena spent the night together in the same room at the Mayflower Hotel in Washington.

In another letter Eleanor wrote:

> November 27, 1933
>
> Dear one:
> . . . and so you think they gossip about us, well they must at least think we stand separations rather well! I am always so much more optimistic than you are—I suppose because I care so little what "they" say.[11]

In another letter a few weeks later, Eleanor wrote:

> Dear:
> I've been trying today to bring back your face—to remember just how you look. Funny how even the dearest face will fade away in time. Most clearly I remember your eyes, with a kind reassuring smile in them, and the feeling of that soft spot just northeast of the corner of your mouth against my lips. I wonder what we'll do when we meet—what we'll say. Well, I'm rather proud of us, aren't you? I think we've done rather well. . . . Good night, dear one. I want to put my arms around you and kiss you at the corner of your mouth. And in a little more than a week now—I shall!"[12]

Although individually these letters could be explained away and may simply demonstrate innocent affection between two good female friends, taken together they suggest Eleanor and Lorena may have enjoyed a lesbian relationship.

Eleanor died in 1962. Before her death, she agreed that her body would be buried next to Franklin's in the rose garden at Hyde Park, as her husband had wished.

10

DWIGHT D. EISENHOWER

A Poignant Affair of the Heart

☆

Unlike most of the other presidents who strayed from their wives to in-volve themselves in numerous sexual liaisons, Dwight David Eisenhower (Ike) had only one known affair. It was with his Women's Auxiliary Corp staff driver, Kay Summersby, during World War II, when Ike was sta-tioned in Europe as the Supreme Allied Commander.

Ike was born in Denison, Texas, in October 1890. He was raised in Abilene, Kansas, on a dairy farm by a poor Mennonite couple who had five other sons. He wanted to further his education beyond high school, but since his family didn't have the means to finance his education, Ike applied to both the Naval Academy and West Point. He was hoping for a naval career but ended up at West Point, graduating in 1915.

Ike was a robust, strapping young man, and handsome. He had bright blue eyes, a ruddy complexion, and thinning, sandy-colored hair, He was famous for his broad, warm smile and the omnipresent "Eisenhower grin" that seemed to spread from ear to ear. During high school, girls came last in his list of priorities, which included other more important activities, like sports and academics. He was far more interested in im-pressing the boys and didn't want to show too much interest in girls for fear he would be considered a "sissy" by his fellow male classmates.

Ike met Mary ("Mamie") Geneva Doud in October 1915 while sta-

Dwight D. Eisenhower
Thirty-fourth President of the United States (1953–61)

Biographical Information

Born: October 14, 1890
Died: March 28, 1969
Wife: Mary ("Mamie") Geneva Doud
Children: Two boys

Extramarital Affairs

Known and Suspected Sexual Partners:	Dates:	Locations:
Kay Summersby	1943–44	London; North Africa; Germany

Illegitimate Children: None

---

tioned at Fort Sam Houston, near San Antonio, Texas. They liked each other instantly. Mamie was attractive, delicate, saucy, and vivacious. Ike asked her to accompany him on his rounds at the fort. He proposed on Valentine's Day in 1916. They married on July 1 of that same year. He was twenty-five; she was only nineteen.

Early on, Ike made it clear to Mamie that his country would always come first and she second. Their marriage was far from satisfying. She often refused to accompany him to remote posts. These long periods of separation couldn't have helped their relationship and must have increased the loneliness they both felt. The death of their first son, Doud Dwight, from scarlet fever at age three left them both traumatized and may have been another factor contributing to the emotional distance that developed between them. Ike admitted that "there was deep hurt on both sides, hurt so deep that they were never able to recapture their earlier relationship although it was not for want of trying." Ike once commented that something happened between Mamie and him that "killed something in me. Not all at once, but little by little. For years I never thought of making love, and when I did . . . when it had been on my mind for weeks, I failed."[1]

Before the war Ike's military career crept along at a snail's pace. Eventually his well-developed planning skills and poker-playing abilities brought him to the attention of generals George C. Marshall and Douglas MacArthur. During World War II, now as a two-star general, Ike was sent on a ten day fact-finding trip to Great Britain. It was there he met an attractive young Irishwoman named Kay Summersby.

Kathleen (Kay) Helen McCarthy-Morrogh Summersby grew up in Innis Beg, County Cork, Ireland. Kay was exuberant, flirtatious, and well educated. She had dark brown hair, sparkling blue eyes, a cute, slightly turned up nose, and a pert smile. She was a former model and aspiring movie actress when Ike first met her and twenty years his junior.

According to Kay, Ike eventually admitted he was attracted to her from the first moment he saw her. It was May 1942, and he had just arrived in London. Ike, fifty-one, was standing by a khaki-colored Packard with another general when Kay, age thirty-one, came running toward the car, trying to salute as she came to a sudden stop. She had been assigned to show Ike around war-torn London. She was not impressed with him, and because he had only two stars, she knew he couldn't be too important. Ike was startled to discover that his driver was a pretty, young, single woman. At the time, he was thinking how glamorous and beautiful she was.[2]

Before leaving the car at the Northholt Airport for his return flight to the States, Ike reached back in the car and gave Kay a box of chocolates, saying they were from General Clark and him. Ike also asked Kay if she would drive for him if he was ever back that way again. She told him, "I'd like that, sir," but never expected to see this likable American again.

When Ike arrived in the States, he unthinkingly described this young, attractive female driver to Mamie in an enthusiastic manner. She responded to him with expected coldness. Mamie didn't like the idea of Ike's being that far away from home with all the attractive young female WAACS, Red Cross volunteers, nurses, and drivers nearby. When she inquired about rumors in the press Ike wrote back: "Don't go bothering your pretty head about WAACS—etc, etc. You must realize that in such a confused life as we lead here all sorts of stories, gossip, lies and etc can get started without the slightest foundation in fact."[3]

In June Ike requested that Kay be assigned as his personal driver. The Brits complied, of course, and Ike and Kay continued a long, intimate personal relationship that lasted throughout the war. Kay was deeply touched because Ike not only remembered her; he thought so much of her that he had brought her a box of oranges and grapefruits from the States and had his aide scouring London looking for her.

One day when Ike had time for a little sightseeing, Kay took him to all of the typical tourist sights, including the Tower of London. She also drove by Bryanston Court, where Mrs. Simpson lived when she was being courted by the Prince of Wales. Ike commented that it was "a shame the King lost sight of his duty." Ike was of course referring to the duke of Windsor, who had chosen the love of a woman over duty to his country, for he had once been king but had to abdicate his throne to marry a nonroyal. Ike would face the same dilemma until the threat of utter ruin caused him to place duty to country ahead of personal happiness.

Ike stayed in several different London hotels, including the Claridge, which he detested. His ornate sitting room reminded him of a "goddamned fancy funeral parlor," and he said his bedroom was painted "whorehouse pink." It made him feel as if he were "living in sin." He moved on to other hotels, including the Dorchester, but felt like a prisoner whenever he stepped outside because his face had become so well known in London.

On numerous occasions, to unwind and relieve stress, Ike would ask Kay to bring the car around, and the two of them would go on long drives into the countryside. At times, he would ask Kay to pull the car over when he found a desirable spot so they could walk a bit. Sometimes they would stroll along at a leisurely pace and chat, but usually Ike launched out of the car at such a brisk pace that Kay would trot along after him nearly out of breath until he announced it was time to return to the car.

One of Ike's aides suggested that he rent a place outside London where he could get away for some fresh air and exercise. In August 1942 they found Telegraph Cottage. It looked like a Tudor-style dollhouse and included a living room with a big fireplace, dining room, kitchen with a big, old stove, five small bedrooms, and one bath. The property consisted of ten acres of woods and lawns and had flowering shrubs located throughout. It was very private. The house could not even be seen from the road. Its existence and location was TOP SECRET. It was here that Ike, Kay, and his close personal aides would get away for some much-needed rest and relaxation. Kay characterized the small, intimate group of friends as Ike's wartime family.

One day Ike asked Kay if she would like a dog. They found a perfect three-month-old black Scottie pup. He peed in the center of the general's rug the first time he appeared for Ike's inspection, then marched around as if he were proud of himself. However, since Kay loved the dog, Ike selected him. Officially the dog belonged to Ike, but Kay understood that he was buying the dog for her. Ike named the pup Telek and said, "It's a combination of Telegraph Cottage and Kay. Two parts of my life that make me very happy."

Kay considered waging war and making love both creative processes. She said that the fervor of commitment she and Ike shared to win the war plus their affair produced the same high-tension euphoria. She felt as if she and Ike were living in a transparent, invisible tunnel that bound them together in a special way.

Ike spent at least thirty minutes each day reading Mamie's letters from home and writing her numerous ones in return, many of which were published in 1978 by his son, John S. D. Eisenhower, at Mamie's request in the book *Letters to Mamie*. Ike reassured Mamie constantly that he was not interested in any other woman but her. He wrote:

I've liked some—been intrigued by others—but haven't been in love with anyone else and don't want any other wife.[4]

I'm old—my days of romance may be all behind me—but I swear I think I miss you more and love you more than I ever did.[5]

Ike neglected to mention in his letters home to Mamie that Kay was driving him around again and accompanying him on long horseback rides two or three times weekly. Since his whereabouts were reported daily by the press, Mamie was aware of this developing relationship. Kay also appeared in numerous photographs standing next to or just behind Ike. Certainly these images troubled Mamie. After Mamie learned from *Life* magazine that Kay had accompanied Ike to Algiers, she wrote to him inquiring about his "London driver." Ike assured her that Kay had come there to marry Col. Richard R. Arnold and was very much in love with him. In reality, Ike invited Kay to join him when it was time for him to leave for Algiers because he wanted her near him. Ike left first. Kay came later on a ship, the *Strathallen*, which was torpedoed just off the coast. When Ike heard the news about the sinking of Kay's ship, he was sick with worry and for the first time admitted to himself just how deeply he cared for Kay. But he did not tell her so at the time. He was not sure he ever would. Kay's lifeboat was rescued by another ship that was sent out from the Algerian coast after the threat of another submarine attack had passed.

Kay was known as Ike's "shadow," since she went nearly everywhere with him. Rumors soon began to swirl about their relationship, although they were unfounded at first. Kay was already engaged to marry Colonel Arnold when she and Ike first met.

Kay had once driven Ike to the front outside of Algiers. When they returned to Algiers, one of Ike's aides, named Tex, took Kay aside and informed her that there was a lot of gossip about her and the boss. He was too embarrassed to tell her about the exact nature of the gossip until she pried out of him that there was talk that she and Ike slept together when they went on trips. She burst out laughing and said, "We did, Tex. We did!"

Kay explained that on her most recent trip to the front it was very late and Ike was off inspecting the troops. She was exhausted and asked if there was anyplace she could lie down and get some sleep before the general returned and they would need to make the return trip to Algiers. She was directed to an old tent that had several cots for sleeping. When Ike returned, it was too late to begin the journey back to Algiers, and he found his driver sleeping in the tent. The troops thought they should wake her and move her elsewhere so that Ike could sleep alone. Ike growled, "Jesus Christ, don't do that. Let her sleep." He threw his sleeping bag on one of the cots and was out cold, snoring in minutes. So in a way they did sleep together. At least in the same tent. Kay reminded Tex that she was engaged to marry Colonel Arnold and thought the gossip both ridiculous and very funny.

Arnold was later killed in an accident when inspecting a minefield in

Oran in North Africa. Ike was the one who told Kay the sad news. They were in the living room at his villa in Algiers. Ike was silent and had acted withdrawn during the entire ride home. Finally, he said, "Kay, I am just going to give this to you straight. Dick has been killed." He explained the circumstances to Kay and then added, "I am very, very sorry, Kay."

After pacing up and down the hall for a while, Kay returned to the living room and said to Ike, "It's all right, I'm all right," and then burst into tears. Ike put his arm around her shoulder, led her over to the couch, and held her while she bawled. Patting her, he said, "There, there." From time to time he would tell her to blow her nose. Ike had ordered a box of a dozen handkerchiefs and had placed them on the table to afford her a fresh one each time she filled one with her tears. He spoon-fed her a cup of hot tea and then suggested she take a few days off and spend it at a cottage called Sailor's Delight, where she could be alone. He also suggested that she go horseback riding while she was there.

"Activity helps. I have learned that myself," he told her. He was likely referring to his own ordeal when faced with the death of his first son but may also have been alluding to the difficulties he experienced in his marriage to Mamie. Kay took Ike's advice.

When she returned to work, Ike kept her busy driving him around and answering his correspondence. She even drove the king of England around on his visit to Algiers. Ike had arranged the assignment to keep her mind off her loss.

One day Ike surprised Kay when he informed her that he was having some new uniforms made for himself and had told the tailor to make her several uniforms, too. She protested because of the expense and said, "You do so many nice things for me. How can I ever thank you?" Then Ike made his first overture of love when he answered the question she had just raised. In her book *Past Forgetting: My Love Affair With Dwight D. Eisenhower*, Kay described his response this way:

> "You can't possibly know how much I would like to do for you," he said. There was a strange quality to his voice. He was looking at me, his teeth clenched. That kind of look from which you cannot tell if a person is going to laugh or cry. Startled, I sat there at his desk looking at him. Neither of us said a word. Then Ike took off those reading glasses of his and stretched out his hand. "Kay, you are someone very special to me." I felt

tears rising in my eyes. He was someone very special to me, too. I had never realized how special before. But he was. Very.

He laid his hand over mine. And he smiled. This was not the famous Eisenhower grin. This was a tender, almost tremulous smile, even a bit rueful. And full of love. I could not return it. I felt shaken, timid, almost as if I were undressing in front of him very slowly. In my face, in my eyes, there was nothing but absolute naked adoration. I could not hide it.

We just sat there and looked at each other. I felt overpoweringly shy. We were both silent, serious, eyes searching eyes. It was a communion, a pledging, an avowal of love.

. . . So this is love, I thought.

. . . Love had grown so naturally that it was part of our lives, something precious that I had taken for granted without ever putting a name to it.

Yes, I loved this middle-aged man with his thinning hair, his eye-glasses, his drawn, tired face. I wanted to hold him in my arms, to cuddle him, delight him. I wanted to lie on some grassy lawn and see those broad shoulders above me, feel the intensity of those eyes on mine, feel that hard body against mine, I loved this man.[6]

After leaving his office and overcoming the shock of the experience, Kay was soon soaring with happiness and contentment. She began to recount the excuses they made for touching each other over the previous months. She remembered how they would sit after work on the sofa in the evening and find themselves holding hands without either of them really noticing it. Neither Ike nor Kay spoke as she drove him back to the cottage for lunch that afternoon. After lunch they returned to the car to drive back to headquarters, and Ike apologized for his actions, saying, "I'm sorry about this morning, Kay. That shouldn't have happened. I spoke out of turn. Please forget it." Kay struggled to drive and hold back the tears at the same time. Ike became frustrated and began to cuss, using his favorite word, Goddamnit, repeatedly. He told her it was impossible and he was a damn fool for suggesting it. He ordered her to stop crying. At first, she refused to speak to him; then, when she did speak, she wouldn't admit to crying; she blamed the tears on the Algerian dust.

Later that afternoon, he called her into his office and informed her without even looking at her that the tailor would be by in the morning to take her measurements for the new uniforms he was having made for her. She responded coolly with "Oh, I think not. What I've got will serve perfectly well. Thank you, but I think I should say no." This made Ike so mad that he turned bright red, stood up, walked around his desk, called Kay a "goddamned stubborn Irish mule," and then added, "You're going to get measured for those uniforms. . . . That's an order." They both stood there glaring at each other, daring the other to make the next move. Finally, Ike barked, "Goddamnit, can't you tell I'm crazy about you?" Kay described what happened next this way:

> It was like an explosion. We were suddenly in each other's arms. His kisses absolutely unraveled me. Hungry, strong, demanding. And I responded every bit as passionately. He stopped, took my face between his hands. "Goddamnit," he said, "I love you."
>
> We were breathing as if we had run up a dozen flights of stairs. God must have been watching over us, because no one came bursting into the office. It was lovers' luck, but we both came to our senses, remembering how Tex had walked in earlier that day. Ike had lipstick smudges on his face. I started scrubbing at them frantically with my handkerchief, worrying—What if someone comes in?
>
> Ike put his hands on my shoulders. "We have to be very careful," he said. "I don't want you to be hurt. I don't want people to gossip about you. God, I wish things were different."
>
> "I think things are wonderful." I whispered. I knew what he was talking about. I understood the problem. And I did not believe for a moment that love conquers all. But still everything *was* wonderful. I did not expect anything to be easy. But I was not one to deny love. I could see no reason to deny it. This is part of the business of living in this special dimension, in our case the tunnel of war, where all your feelings, all your energies are absorbed by one great purpose. Your world is different from that of other people, divorced from the world outside the tunnel. What was important here and now was that there was love—pulsating, irrepressible love.[7]

Ike, the first to admit his love earlier that morning, repeated the avowal that same afternoon before initiating this first physical and sexual prelude to lovemaking.

Ike and Kay resumed their normal routines. They had to be careful now. However, they were always on a quest for privacy. They continued their horseback riding, during which they could speak privately without arousing suspicion, but were rarely ever left completely alone. During one ride Ike admitted that it was hard for him to talk about his feelings. He told Kay that talking about love made him feel uncomfortable and that he had always kept his feelings in check and rarely even thought about them.

In the evenings they would sit on the high-back sofa and steal a few kisses when no one else was in the room. Ike told Kay that he was so good at concealing his feelings that he was no good at determining what he actually felt but only at what he was supposed to feel. One evening he told her he was "very out of practice in love." She did not think much about his statement at the time because he was such a thoughtful, considerate, and loving man. Ike was undoubtedly referring to the sexual and physical side of love. Perhaps he saw the day drawing nearer and wanted to gently prepare Kay for what he feared would happen. On another evening he told Kay he had received some new records and wanted her to tell him what she thought of them. They were all popular, contemporary songs, but the last was an old favorite of hers that she had once confided to him was the most romantic song she had ever heard. It was the waltz "I'll See You Again" by Noël Coward. After listening to the song, Ike said he didn't like it because it was too sad, since it focused on goodbyes and missing each other. Although they argued over just how romantic the song was, Kay considered it so tender that Ike remembered the name of the song for several months and had searched out a copy for her.

In the fall of 1943, on a flight aboard a C-54 transport to the Cairo Conference, Ike and Kay spent a few minutes necking in the shadows of the plane after the lights were dimmed and the other members of the party were asleep and snoring. Later, after the conference one evening, they embraced and held each other tight for a few minutes behind closed doors. Ike had been asked to take a couple of days off, so he, Kay, and the rest of the party toured the pyramids and the tombs of the pharaohs in the Valley of the Kings. They also visited Jerusalem and Bethlehem in the Holy Land. They returned to Algiers after the conference and touring had ended.

Ike was called home to the United States for twelve days. Kay began thinking about Ike's being at home with Mamie and found herself becoming very jealous. Kay decided that Ike loved her and that was all that mattered. If they had met under different circumstances, she might have asked him to make up his mind and choose between the two of them, but this was wartime, and no tomorrow was guaranteed. Kay chose to follow her heart and live for the moment.

When he returned to England, Kay picked up Ike at the train station, for he had flown into Scotland because of the fog and taken the train to London. They stopped at headquarters at 20 Grosvenor Lane for a few minutes, and then Kay drove the general and his aides to his new house off Berkeley Square. Everyone was exhausted and quickly went to bed, but Ike claimed he was too wound up to sleep. He asked Kay to join him for a nightcap. She consented, knowing that no one would disturb them in the living room that night. Ike held her in his arms on the sofa as they chatted and caught up on events of the previous few days. They had several drinks, and then Kay described what happened next in her book *Past Forgetting*:

> . . . we found ourselves in each other's arms in an unrestrained embrace. Our ties came off. Our jackets came off. Buttons were unbuttoned. It was as if we were frantic. And we were.
>
> But this was not what I had expected. Wearily, we slowly calmed down. He snuggled his face into the hollow between my neck and shoulder and said, "Oh God, Kay. I'm sorry. I'm not going to be any good for you." I didn't know what to say except "You're good enough for me. What you need is some sleep." It was a bit embarrassing struggling back into the clothes that had been flung on the floor. Finally we were dressed. Ike looked troubled. "I don't want to let you go," he said. "But you can't stay here. God, I'm sorry. I can't even drive you home."
>
> "Don't worry," I told him "I'll be fine. It's just around the corner." We kissed good night. As he let me out the door, I saluted. "Good night, General. I'll be here in the morning.' " One never knew who might be lurking in the fog ready to catch an indiscreet word.
>
> . . . My last thought as I dropped off to sleep was to the effect that things are never the way you think they'll be.[8]

Ike was impotent. The next day he apologized for his failure to perform the previous night and reminded Kay that he had told her sometime ago that he was "out of practice in love." Kay thought it was due to his physical exhaustion and age. Ike was relieved to know that she was not terribly disappointed in him. Kay said she knew that someday they were going to consummate their relationship. "Maybe," Ike said, indicating not his lack of desire but his lack of confidence in his ability to perform sexually.

Ike decided to move headquarters to Bushey Park so that he could spend his evenings at Telegraph College again. Kay said that Ike and she were never totally alone at Telegraph Cottage, but it was a place where they could relax and just enjoy each other's company. They did have a favorite secluded bench where they could sit and hold hands and she could place her head on Ike's shoulder.

One evening he confided to Kay that he had hell to pay from the very beginning of his trip home to Mamie because he kept calling her "Kay" and she would become furious. Ike recounted the trouble he had experienced in his marriage, how there was such deep hurt on both sides, that he had not thought about making love for a long time and when he did, he failed his wife. And now he had disappointed Kay. Kay held Ike's head to her breast and, as he cried, told him it would be all right. She promised him that someday things would be different and said she was not a stubborn Irishwoman for nothing.

One evening after Kay brought Telek home from his six-month quarantine at the kennel, Ike and Kay noticed how much the reunion was like having a child come home from boarding school for the first time. He asked Kay whether she would like to have a child, and she told him she would love to have *his* baby. They concluded that it was impossible, but after some reflection Ike thought that it might be possible somehow. He told her he would like it if they had a child together but was also worried that he would be too old.

Months later, after V-E Day, Ike and Kay again found themselves on the secluded park bench at Telegraph Cottage one afternoon. Ike asked if she remembered their conversation about having a baby the day she brought Telek home from the kennel, then admitted that he wanted to do something about it if he could. He promised to "try my damnedest." Kay was not at all sure what he meant. He may have been talking about another attempt at lovemaking, or perhaps he was considering divorce. This would have been about the time he purportedly sent the famous letter to General Marshall describing his intentions to divorce Mamie and marry Kay.

To celebrate the end of the war, they went to London to see a show.

Kay sat next to Ike in his theater box. After the theater they went to dinner at Ciro's and spent most of the evening chatting and dancing together.

On October 15, 1945, the day after Ike's birthday, Ike and Kay were spending the afternoon in Frankfurt alone together after returning from one of their frequent horseback rides. Ike had arranged for Kay to fly to Washington and apply to become a U.S. citizen. This way she could work for him at the Pentagon. They spent the afternoon making plans for the future while sitting on the sofa in Ike's house, all the while holding hands and kissing. This would be at least their second unsuccessful attempt at lovemaking. Kay recorded what happened next in her book *Past Forgetting* and remembered it this way:

> Never in all the time I had known him had I had to hold Ike back. He had always been very circumspect, but this afternoon he was an eager lover. The door was closed and I knew that nobody from the household would be walking in. This was quite a formal household in Germany, not like the villa in Algiers or the cottage. People did not burst into rooms here. A closed door would never be opened.
>
> The fire was warm. The sofa was soft. We held each other close, closer. Excitedly. I remember thinking, the way one thinks odd thoughts at significant moments, Wouldn't it be wonderful if this were the day we conceived a baby—our very first time. Ike was tender, careful, loving. But it didn't work.
>
> "Wait," I said. "You're too excited. It will be all right."
>
> "No," he said flatly. "It won't. It's too late. I can't." He was bitter. We dressed slowly. Kissing occasionally. Smiling a bit sadly.
>
> ". . . It's not that important," I told him earnestly. "It's not the least bit important. It just takes time. That's all. And I'm very stubborn. You've said so yourself."
>
> "I know you are," he said. "But I'm not sure that you are right." There was no point in arguing with him, I thought. Only time would show him that he was wrong. We dropped the subject.
>
> Two weeks later I left for Washington in Ike's Flying Fortress.[9]

When Kay returned to Frankfurt, she was surprised to discover that Ike had been summoned to Washington to take over the Pentagon. President Truman had sent General Marshall on a special mission to China, and Ike was needed as Marshall's replacement. Ike said he would return in a few weeks, but he never came back. Kay learned that Ike was too ill with pneumonia to return to Frankfurt, and his staff was told to prepare to leave for Washington within ten days. Then, shortly before they were scheduled to go, a telex from the Pentagon indicated that she had been dropped from the list of those selected to report to Washington. At first, she thought there had been some mistake, but soon the realization of what was happening set in. Kay was purposefully being left behind. She cried until midnight. Eventually, after a couple of uneventful assignments, Kay put in for a discharge and moved to New York, where she wrote her first book, *Eisenhower Was My Boss.*

After learning that Ike would be moving to New York to become president of Columbia University, she spent a lot of time becoming familiar with the campus until she ran into Ike one day. She realized she still loved him and certainly knew their paths would cross if she spent enough time at the university. He was surprised to see her and acted irritated and distraught. He said, "Kay, it's impossible. There's nothing I can do." She told him, "I understand," as she stood there, trying to smile, tears welling up in her eyes. Their relationship was truly over.

Kay went to England during the summer to visit her mother. They read in the papers that General Eisenhower and his wife were visiting London. Kay's mother convinced her to send the Eisenhowers an invitation to come to tea. Kay did not receive a reply, but a few days later a young major was sent to take her out for a drink and deliver a message from Ike. The major said, "Kay, it's impossible. The General is really on a tight leash. He is not his own master."[10] Kay was thankful that Ike cared enough about her to send a special envoy. From the time Ike successfully led the Allies to victory over Germany he was a prime presidential candidate. Both political parties tried to recruit him. Undoubtedly, his Republican party handlers wanted to end Ike's relationship with Kay as quickly and quietly as possible.

As early as 1952 rumors began to circulate that Ike had written a letter to General Marshall indicating his plans to divorce Mamie and marry Kay. Harry Truman's White House aide, Maj. Gen. Harry Vaughan, confirmed that such rumors began at about this time. Shortly before the Republican National Convention, when Sen. Robert Taft and Eisenhower were both positioning themselves to win the nomination, the Taft camp heard about the letters between Eisenhower and Marshall and tried to get their hands on them; they were unsuccessful.

Ike eventually won the Republican nomination and was elected president in 1952 and again in 1956. According to Traphes Bryant, the White House dog keeper, the rumors among the back-stairs staff at the White House were that after World War II ended, Ike wanted to divorce Mamie and marry his pretty Irish chauffeur, Kay Summersby. They also understood that Mamie had asked Gen. George C. Marshall to station Ike's son, John, with his father to cool down the steamy relationship and save the Eisenhowers' marriage. However, it appears that John's presence did little to calm the relationship.

In about the 1971–72 time frame, Kay received a call one day from news producer David Susskind. Susskind wanted Kay to appear on his program and talk about "the letter." Kay did not have the foggiest idea what letter he was referring to. When he explained about the letter Ike had puportedly penned to General Marshall declaring his intention to divorce Mamie and marry her, Kay thought he was pulling her leg and was using this ruse to flush out an interview.

Their love affair remained secret for nearly thirty years, until 1973, when Merle Miller, in *Plain Speaking: An Oral Biography of Harry S. Truman*, revealed that Truman claimed to have seen and destroyed the letter Ike sent to General Marshall asking that he be relieved of his duties, since he planned to return to the United States, divorce Mamie, and marry Kay Summersby. In *Plain Speaking*, Truman also claimed to have seen the blistering reply Marshall wrote to Ike in which Marshall said:

> . . . if Eisenhower even came close to doing such a thing, he'd not only bust him out of the Army, he'd see to it that never for the rest of his life would he be able to draw a peaceful breath. He said it wouldn't matter if he was in the Army or wasn't. Or even what country he was in.[11]

Harry Truman, a real straight shooter, didn't think these personal letters should be used for dirty politics. Although he did not support Eisenhower for president, neither did he think that this type of activity was fair, so he had the letters removed from Ike's file in the Pentagon and destroyed. Years later, Kay speculated that the letters were not actually destroyed but sent to Marshall with a note from Truman saying that the letters belonged in Marshall's personal files. If she was right, perhaps one day the letters will surface among Marshall's many official and personal papers.

In 1976, *Past Forgetting: My Love Affair With Dwight D. Eisenhower* by Kay Summersby Morgan was published shortly after her death. A portion of the title of the book came from Kay's favorite song "I'll See You Again," which includes the line "But what has been, / Is *past forgetting*." This book is truly the retelling of the romantic love affair that Kay had thirty years earlier. Kay conceded that she did not know for certain whether Ike wrote the now-famous letter to General Marshall indicating his plans to divorce Mamie and marry her, since Ike never mentioned it to her, but she also admitted that she believed that Ike did send it. Her faith was inspired by Harry Truman's truthfulness and integrity. She did not believe that Truman would have fabricated the story. Kay also said that it was this same belief that Ike had written the letter that gave her the strength and courage needed to write her tell-all book.

Ike died of a heart attack on March 28, 1969. Kay Summersby died in 1975, the year before *Past Forgetting* was published. Mamie died on November 11, 1979, after a severe stroke the previous September.

Most historians believe that Ike and Kay never fully consummated their physical relationship because of his impotence. Kay Summersby's book would seem to support that belief. She wrote the book with the help of a ghostwriter named Barbara Wyden, who had written another bestseller. But Wyden was the second ghostwriter assigned to this book project. The first was Sigrid Hedin. She claimed in the *New York Post* during June 1977 that "there was a lot in the final version of *Past Forgetting* that is not quite correct." Sigrid claims to have the real manuscript and said it indicated that Ike was not completely impotent but had to be taught the ways of love by Kay. If true, the Eisenhower-Summersby love affair may have been consummated, after all.

11

JOHN F. KENNEDY

The Secret Service Called Him Lancer

. . . Let the word go forth from this time and place, to friend and foe alike, that the torch has been passed to a new generation of Americans—born in this century, tempered by war, disciplined by a hard and bitter peace, proud of our ancient heritage—and unwilling to witness or permit the slow undoing of those human rights to which this nation has always been committed, and to which we are committed today at home and around the world. . . . Ask not what your country can do for you: Ask . . ."[1]

"Where are the broads?"[2]

These words were uttered by John Fitzgerald ("Jack") Kennedy on January 20, 1961. The first group of inspiring words we remember well. They were delivered during his inaugural on that cold, snowy day in January when a handsome, robust, and coatless man in his early forties was sworn in as America's thirty-fifth President.

The last four words were spoken later that same day during a late-night party at columnist Joe Alsop's Georgetown house. In fact, they were the first words out of Jack's mouth when he arrived at the party. John Kennedy was the author of this crude, heartfelt question but not the au-

John F. Kennedy
Thirty-fifth President of the United States (1961–63)

Biographical Information

Born: May 29, 1917
Died: November 22, 1963
Wife: Jacqueline Lee Bouvier
Children: Two boys; two girls

Extramarital Affairs
Known and Suspected

Sexual Partners:	Dates:	Locations:
Beauty Queens		
Inga "Inga Binga" Arvad Fejos	1941–44	Washington, D.C.; Charlestown, S.C.
Strippers		
Tempest Storm	1955	Washington, D.C.
Blaze Starr	1960	New Orleans
Call Girls		
Suzy Chang	1960–61	New York City
Marie Novotny	1960–61	New York City
Various prostitutes		
Acquaintances		
Joan Lundberg	1959–60	Santa Monica, Calif.
Pamela Turnure	1956–63	Washington, D.C.
White House Staff		
Priscilla Weir and Jill Cowan (a.k.a. Fiddle and Faddle)	1960–63	Palm Beach, Fla.; Nassau, Bahamas; Yosemite, Calif.
Secretaries and aides	1960–63	Washington, D.C.

Socialites

Florence Prichett Smith	1957–60	Cuba; Palm Beach, Fla.
Judy Campbell Exner	1960–62	Chicago; Las Vegas; Los Angeles; Miami Beach; New York City; Palm Beach, Fla. Palm Springs, Calif.; Washington, D.C.
Mary Pinchot Meyer	1962–63	White House

Actresses

Gene Tierney	1946–47	Los Angeles
Jayne Mansfield	1960–63	Hollywood
Angie Dickinson	1961–62	Palm Springs, Calif.
Marilyn Monroe	1954–62	New York; California; Washington, D.C., Air Force One

Others

Airline stewardesses	1950s, 1960s	Washington, D.C. Santa Monica, Calif.
Campaign workers	1950s, 1960s	Massachusetts; Washington, D.C.
Willing women sent by Jack's male friends	1950s, 1960s	Washington, D.C.

Alleged Illegitimate Child: Ronald McCoy (Inga Arvad's son) thor of those inspiring words he spoke during his inaugural speech. They were written by Ted Sorensen, Jack's gifted speechwriter. But even Sorensen did not create the most famous phrase from this speech without some help. Those words originally appeared in an earlier speech by President Warren G. Harding, who said, "Think more of what you can do for your Government than of what your Government can do for you."

That inaugural night Jack had his choice of the young party girls and movie starlets at Alsop's party. One European ambassador offered his niece to the new president. Six attractive young starlets, supplied by actor Peter Lawford, Jack's brother-in-law, volunteered to sleep with the new president of the United States. Peter lined them up, and after inspection Jack selected one or two to take to bed. One account says he selected two and took them into a spare bedroom at the same time for a *ménage-à-trois*–type sexual encounter.[3]

George Smathers, Jack's close friend in the Senate, said that having two girls at once was one of Jack's "favorite pastimes." Jack once told several reporters, "I'm never through with a girl until I've had her three ways." It is not entirely clear what Jack meant by this statement. He may have been referring either to a *ménage-à-trois* sexual encounter or to the three most common forms of intercourse—oral, anal, and vaginal sex.

Earlier that same evening, while attending the second of five inaugural balls at the Statler-Hilton Hotel with Vice President and Mrs. Johnson and his wife, Jacqueline ("Jackie") Bouvier Kennedy, Jack excused himself, slipped away, and quickly went upstairs to a private party given by Frank Sinatra. Actresses Angie Dickinson, Janet Leigh, and Kim Novak were at Sinatra's party. Earlier in the day, Angie and Kim had also attended a private dinner party given for Jack by his loyal friends and campaign workers, George and Janet Wheeler. So as not to arouse any suspicion, Angie was accompanied by her official escort, or beard, Red Fay. Fay was the undersecretary of the navy. Jack had requested that Fay escort Angie to these various events. Jack returned to the presidential box a half hour later with a copy of the *Washington Post* tucked under his arm to give the impression that he had left the ball to purchase a newspaper. Jackie asked, "Anything interesting going on in the world tonight?" He looked embarrassed but managed to smile. Jackie said nothing further but gave him a cold, angry look.

The media knew about Kennedy's philandering but looked the other way. One former Associated Press reporter said, "There used to be a gentlemen's agreement about reporting such things."[4] The same sentiment was echoed by another observer, who said, "There was a sort of gentlemen's agreement in Washington that you don't talk about my private life and I don't talk about yours. . . ." Even Ben Bradlee, former chief of the Washington, D.C., bureau of *Newsweek* magazine and later an editor of the *Washington Post*, acted surprised years later when news of Kennedy's womanizing began to appear in press reports. However, Bradlee did admit: "John Kennedy was a hungry man, ravenous sometimes for the nourishment he found in the life he led and the people he loved. . . . This was both literally and figuratively true."[5] Jack knew that his philandering was off-limits to the press. He once said, "They can't touch me while I'm alive, and after I'm dead who cares?"

To understand Jack's sexual behavior on the evening of the inaugural and put it in context, we must go back in time to Jack's early developmental years, to the beginning of his political career, and then resume the story after his inauguration.

☆ ☆ ☆

Jack Kennedy was only twelve years old when his father and family patriarch, Joseph Kennedy, brought his mistress, screen star Gloria Swanson, into their Hyannis Port home to have dinner with his wife, Rose, and their children. Rose pretended not to know what was going on. This insensitive and brazen act must have hurt Rose deeply and affected Jack, if not then, later, when he became old enough to understand. Joe Kennedy did not attempt to hide his womanizing; according to Jack, he advised "all the boys to get laid as often as possible." Dr. John E. Schowalter, the Albert Solnit Professor of Child Psychiatry at the Yale Child Study Center in New Haven, Connecticut, said, "A father's sexual ethics can exert a powerful influence on his son's attitude toward women."[6] Jack learned at a young age that women were little more than sex objects.

☆ ☆ ☆

Accompanied by his best friend Lemoyne "Lem" Billings, Jack lost his virginity in a brothel in Harlem at age seventeen. Jack suggested they lose it together to the same woman to strengthen the bond of friendship that existed between them even further. They traveled to Harlem and hired a prostitute. Jack went to her first, and Lem stood guard outside the door. Some accounts say that Lem lost his nerve and did not participate. Other accounts say Billings—always willing to follow Jack's lead—did afterward. Later, the thought of contracting a venereal disease caused them both to panic, so they went to a hospital and got medicine and salves. They even phoned a doctor, waking him in the middle of the night for his assistance in administering the medicine.

☆ ☆ ☆

Jack attended Princeton in 1935 but eventually transferred to Harvard in the fall of 1936 and graduated cum laude in June 1940. He continued to chase girls while in college. He once wrote his friend Lem Billings about a movie extra he pursued while on vacation in Hollywood. Jack called her "the best looking thing I have ever seen," then signed the letter with a postscript: "The Extra's delight, or how I got my tail in Hollywood." While at Harvard he wrote Lem again, saying, "I can now get tail as often and as free as I want . . . which is a step in the right direction." Jack even nicknamed his penis "JJ" and wrote, "JJ has never been in better shape or doing better service."

On another vacation to Mexico he wrote about his sexual escapades in a letter to Lem entitled "Travels in a Mexican Whore-house With Your Roomie." He claimed he had sex with a prostitute for sixty-five cents and joked about getting ". . . the biggest juiciest load of the claps." He signed the letter: "Your gonnereick roomie."

During college he seriously dated Olive Cawley, Frances A. Cannon, Charlottee McDonnell, and Harriet "Flip" Price and may have considered marriage to all four women. Eventually, these relationships fizzled. After college Jack attended the Stanford Business school briefly and toured South America.

He joined the navy in September 1941 and served until April 1945. At first, he was assigned to the Office of Naval Intelligence (ONI) in Washington and worked at encoding and decoding secret messages. His father, Joseph Kennedy, used his influence with the secretary of the navy to have Jack transferred to another duty assignment in

Charlestown, South Carolina. Jack had been sleeping with a married woman named Inga Arvad Fejos. It was a serious love affair, but Inga was suspected by the FBI of being a German spy. Their relationship seemed to a take serious turn, and Jack contemplated marriage, even though he knew it was impossible and would ruin any hopes he had of a postnavy career in politics. Jack was the skipper of a PT-109 until it was rammed by a Japanese destroyer and cut in two. He reinjured his weak back and was released from military service several months later.

Jack was six feet one inch tall, handsome, and youthful. He had blue-gray eyes and bristly reddish-brown hair. He was very personable, energetic, mischievous, and charismatic. Jack could be fiercely competitive, but he also had a good sense of humor and was a good listener. He had all the qualities needed by a successful politician. Although he hated campaigning, Jack understood that it was a necessary evil. He had the ability to weave ideas and words together in a way that captured the imagination and left his listeners inspired and impressed. One time Jack said, "A politician is a dream merchant. . . . But he must back up the dream." Like every politician, Jack understood the difference between myth and reality. But he may have consciously decided to settle for shadow instead of substance, believing anything more to be impossible. Jack carefully crafted many myths, using the press as a tool. For example, he used the press to create the illusion that he and Jackie were a happy couple when that was not the case.

Jack was elected to the House of Representatives from Massachusetts for the first time in 1946 and then reelected twice. He was elected to the U.S. Senate in 1952, defeating incumbent Henry Cabot Lodge by seventy thousand votes. Thanks to a 1953 article in the *Saturday Evening Post*, Jack became known as the "Senate's Gay Young Bachelor." He wrote *Profiles in Courage* while recuperating from back problems, and the book earned him the Pulitzer Prize. Published in 1956, it chronicled the unpopular but principled stands taken by several well-known U.S. politicians throughout our nation's history. The book helped him gain even greater national recognition.

Jack sought the vice-presidential nomination in 1956, but he was unsuccessful, losing his bid to Tennessee senator Estes Kefauver. He was reelected to the Senate in 1958. After this political victory he began to position himself for a run for the presidency two years later.

Jack met Jackie Bouvier at a dinner party given by a mutual friend and newsman, Charles Bartlett, in May 1951. Jackie was a social columnist and photographer for the *Times Herald*. She was sent to the Hill from time to time to take some politician's photo. And she interviewed Jack in her column. She visited Senator Kennedy's office from time to time, bringing him a hot lunch in a picnic basket. Jackie enlisted the aid of William "Fishbait" Miller, the congressional doorkeeper, to help trap Jack for herself.

Demure and proud, Jackie had dark brown hair and brown eyes. She carried herself in a cool, reserved, and distinguished manner at all times.

One of their earliest sexual encounters occurred in Arlington, Virginia, in the backseat of Jack's convertible. It was interrupted by a policeman's flashlight soon after Jack had removed Jackie's bra. Recognizing the senator, the embarrassed policeman apologized and left them alone to finish their lovemaking. At this time, Jackie was engaged to be married to John Husted, but she quickly broke off the engagement, shedding him for Jack. Although a mutual friend told Jackie that Jack was a playboy congressman and a womanizer and that "no good would come" from their relationship, she chose not to listen to the advice, believing she could conquer and reform him.[7]

Jack and Jackie were married on September 12, 1953, at Saint Mary's Church in Newport, Rhode Island. He was thirty-six; she was twenty-four. Jackie was born on July 28, 1929. Like Kennedy, she had grown up in an environment of wealth and privilege. Her parents had divorced in 1940 when she was only eleven years old. She attended Vassar College and the Sorbonne in Paris but graduated from George Washington University in 1951. Her father, John V. "Black Jack" Bouvier III, was a stockbroker. He was also an alcoholic and a known philanderer. He was drunk during Jackie's wedding and failed to show up to walk her down the aisle. Her mother's second husband, Hugh Auchincloss, escorted her instead.

Close friends noticed that the tension in their marriage could be traced back to their honeymoon, when Jack flirted with every attractive woman who came his way. Soon after the honeymoon ended, Jack returned to his life of traveling and politics. Jack and fellow senator George Smathers kept an apartment at the Carroll Arms in Washington, D.C., for rendezvous with women. Jack liked to have sex with a couple of young secretaries at the same time. Smathers said, "He liked groups."

By September or October 1954, Jack had a friend arrange a "house party" for him at a cottage in Maine when Jackie was away in Europe. Jack's friend devised a clever scheme that would prevent anyone from being able to attribute any scandalous behavior to Jack. There were seven revelers in all—three men and four women. They decided to conduct all the social activities in odd-numbered groups so it would appear that Jack did not have a date. To throw the reporters off track, Jack's friend even arranged for him to take a distinguished-looking elderly lady to church on Sunday morning after a night of hard partying.

Whereas Jack maintained a nonchalant attitude toward philandering during his political campaigns, his aides became frantic over any new revelation that would come to their attention. When he was once shown a photograph of himself and a well-endowed brunet lying naked together on a beach, he smiled and said, "Yes, I remember her. She was great!" When aides worried that Nixon might use the photograph against him, Jack seemed unconcerned and simply said, "He won't use it." However, during the presidential campaign of 1960, Jack worried privately about whether news of his philandering would be revealed. In one of his personal notes, in his own handwriting, he wrote, "I suppose they are going to hit me with something before we are finished."

And he had a lot to worry about. Jack knew there had been an endless number of past sexual liaisons throughout his political career, any of which could be suddenly revealed with devastating consequences. In another personal note he wrote, "I got into the blond." He probably didn't even know her name. She was just one of hundreds of potential time bombs. In still another note Jack finally lamented, "My poon days are over."[8]

If this information had appeared during the election, it would certainly have been disastrous for Kennedy. He won the general election by only 118,000 votes out of the 68.3 million ballots cast, an average of two to three votes per precinct nationwide. According to a *Life* magazine poll that appeared in its August 1984 issue, "A third of Americans say that if they had known of his [Kennedy's] affairs, they would not have voted for him." It is likely that Richard Nixon would have been elected president in 1960 if these sexual indiscretions had been revealed during the campaign. The outlook for his reelection in 1964 would also have been grim if his sexual indiscretions were publicly known.

Despite his sexual indiscretions, Jack and Jackie shared a certain intimacy. Jack gave strict orders that they not be disturbed in the afternoons, when they spent time alone in the private family quarters while their two children napped. Jackie even confided to one of her girlfriends how many times a week she and Jack had sex.

Jack had numerous sexual encounters with many woman. Some were well-known movie stars and burlesque queens. Others were high-class call girls and common prostitutes. His sexual partners also included White House staffers, secretaries, stewardesses, socialites, campaign workers, and acquaintances of his trusted male friends. Hundreds of others will probably never come to light.

☆ ☆ ☆

During his brief tour of duty for the navy in Washington, Jack's sister, Kathleen, introduced him to a former Miss Denmark named Inga Arvad. Jack referred to her affectionately as "Inga Binga." She had blond hair and blue eyes. Inga was gorgeous, sophisticated, and well groomed. She was also experienced in the boudoir and enjoyed sex. Inga may have been the closest any woman ever came to being the one great love of Jack's life. Jack and Inga discussed marriage, but it never came to pass. He was twenty-four when they met, and she was twenty-eight. They shared an apartment in Washington, even though Inga was married at the time.

Inga claimed that the only thing Jack ever wore around her apartment was a towel. She said that although Jack was compassionate, he could also be insensitive and insistent when it came to sex. If he wanted it, he would demand it then. If they had to leave for a party in fifteen minutes, he would look at his watch and say, "We've got ten minutes, let's go."

Before coming to the United States, Inga had previously acted in German films, worked as a correspondent, and had interviewed Adolf Hitler and other Nazi leaders personally. Hitler was so taken with her that he persuaded her to visit whenever she was in Berlin. Since she was suspected of being a spy, the FBI had bugged Inga's apartment and made secret recordings of her sexual encounters with Jack. Because of these relationships the U.S. Navy tried to force Jack to end his relationship with her and transferred him to a post in Charlestown, South Carolina, but he continued to see her secretly for some time. The FBI continued its wiretaps in Charlestown, and its director, J. Edgar Hoover, was delighted to find that the wiretaps confirmed that Jack and Inga had "engaged in sexual intercourse on a number of occasions."

Even before Jack was elected president, Hoover began keeping extensive files on Jack's extramarital sexual activity. He added a lot of information to this file after Kennedy became president in order to retain his appointed position as director. Hoover considered Kennedy a pervert. Jack once referred to Hoover as a "queer son of a bitch." Although advisers wanted Jack to fire Hoover soon after taking office, Jack was reluctant, knowing Hoover had the secret recordings of his lovemaking sessions with Inga Arvad and possibly other information about his philandering. In fact, after Jack became president, Hoover had discovered, and he let Bobby Kennedy know it, that Jack had impregnated his former fiancée, Mrs. Alice Darr Purdom, in 1951 and then sent Bobby to her in 1961 with an offer of $500,000 in hush money to keep the affair out of the press. Alice had filed divorce proceedings against her husband, who countersued, naming Jack as a correspondent. After Bobby's visit, she dropped her divorce proceedings in the United States and got a "quickie" Mexican divorce instead.

On Friday, February 6, 1942, Inga checked into room 132 of the Fort Sumter Hotel in Charlestown, registering under the alias Barbara White. Jack arrived at 5:35 P.M. in his black two-door Buick convertible. Except for a dinner break, he did not leave until the next morning. They spent all day Saturday and much of Sunday in the room. This type of detailed information about their affair was recorded in classified FBI reports.

Inga visited Charlestown again during the weekend of February 21–23. Jack met her plane at the airport and whisked her off to the Francis Marion Hotel, where they spent the next three days making love. This time Inga registered under the alias Barbara Smith.

Lem Billings tipped Jack off in a letter that he learned from Joe Kennedy that Inga's apartment was bugged and her phone was tapped by the FBI. Reacting quickly, Jack received special permission to fly to Washington on February 28, where, after spending the night with Inga again, he broke off their relationship. They continued to talk by phone, and Jack saw her occasionally, but their affair had ended.

Inga told Jack she was worried she might become pregnant and accused him of "taking every pleasure of youth but none of the responsibility." Inga did eventually become pregnant, but it was not clear who fathered the child. Jack allegedly fathered Inga's son, Ronald McCoy. Ronald said his mother once told him that Jack Kennedy was really his father.

☆ ☆ ☆

Jack also had sex with two famous burlesque queens, Tempest Storm and Blaze Starr. Jack met stripper Tempest Storm in 1955. She performed at the Casino Royale Theatre in Washington. He would see her whenever she was in town. She was six feet tall, very well endowed, and performed as well in bed as she did on the stage. Tempest said that Jack was "almost insatiable in bed."[9]

Jack spent twenty minutes making love to stripper Blaze Starr in a closet in a New Orleans hotel in 1960 while her fiancée, Gov. Earl Long, was at a campaign party next door. Blaze maintained that Jack told her about the time President Warren G. Harding had made love to his mistress, Nan Britton, in the White House coat closet while she and Jack were having sex. This was not the first time Jack had made love in a closet and was probably not the last. In the early 1950s, when Jack was still a freshman senator from Massachusetts, he irritated the distinguished guests at a white-tie charity benefit in the Vanderbilts' old mansion in Newport, Rhode Island. The frustrated guests were told that the coat closet was closed temporarily and waited impatiently outside in a long line until after Jack emerged from the coat room with his date.

☆ ☆ ☆

During June 1963, Jack's secret sexual behavior was nearly revealed to the public. Don Frasca and James Horan wrote in the *New York Journal-American* that one of the "biggest names in American politics," who currently held "a very high" elected office, had previously had sexual encounters during 1960–61 in New York City with a beautiful model and actress from London named Suzy Chang. It addition, the two authors privately claimed that they also had proof that this officeholder had group sex with a nineteen-year-old London call girl named Marie Novotny and two other prostitutes. During a joint FBI–Scotland Yard investigation, Novotny admitted meeting Jack when she was only nineteen in December 1960 at a party hosted by entertainer Vic Damone in a New York hotel. Peter Lawford introduced Maria to Jack, and they found an empty bedroom and used it to have sex. Novotny also admitted in an interview that Peter Lawford asked her to arrange "something a bit more interesting for the president." They met in an apartment on West Fifty-fifth Street in Manhattan to play the age-old game of doctor. Lawford procured Maria's services, along with two prostitutes, who dressed up as nurses to provide sexual services to their patient, Jack Kennedy. Kennedy's name was left out of the article. Jack's brother Bobby, then the U.S. attorney general, threatened the journal with an antitrust suit if it printed any more stories. None were published.[10]

☆ ☆ ☆

Joan Lundberg, a divorced mother of two children, met Jack shortly after he narrowly missed the opportunity to become the vice president on the Democratic party ticket in 1956. She was in a bar in Santa Monica visiting friends when she noticed Kennedy. Jack was there with his sister Pat and her husband, Peter Lawford. Joan engaged Jack in a discussion about the record she was going to play on the jukebox near his table. Jack's sexual antennae were up as usual, and after leaving, he placed a call to the bar, asked to speak to her, and invited her to a party that was already under way at the Lawfords' home. After she arrived, Jack chose to spend the evening with her and commented that she resembled his sister Pat. Joan said the physical resemblance helped them maintain a discreet three-year affair, since people assumed they were related when they traveled alone together.

Jack provided the financial support necessary to make Joan a kept woman, even offering to pay $400 for an abortion when it became necessary. They used the Lawfords' house for their liaisons until people became suspicious and began to talk. Joan was eventually banned from the Lawfords' home.

Joan said of Jack, "He loved threesomes—himself and two girls. He was also a voyeur, (i.e., someone who gains gratification from seeing sex organs and watching sex acts). Perhaps Joan meant that Jack liked looking at a girl's naked body. But she may also have meant that he enjoyed watching two girls having homosexual relations either before or after he had sex with them.

Joan said Jack confided that he worried about whether Jackie was conducting any illicit affairs of her own. At one particular party at the White House, Jackie drank too much champagne, kicked off her shoes, and danced and flirted with every man in attendance. She enjoyed making Jack jealous and evoking this natural male response. Jackie knew that Jack worried whether she was doing the same thing he was.

Until recently there was little evidence that Jackie had any affairs of her own. One rumor suggested that she had an affair with a Secret Service agent charged with her protection. This appears to have been just so much gossip. One Secret Service agent admitted to Jackie that he was quite taken with her. But instead of having an affair, Jackie had him transferred to another assignment immediately. But in March 1995, Jack Kennedy's secretary, Evelyn Lincoln, was interviewed by award-winning director Charles Furneaux for a British documentary about Jack and Jackie Kennedy. Furneaux was surprised when Lincoln said that Jackie coped with JFK's philandering by taking lovers of her own. According to Lincoln, Jackie had a fling with a "dashing Italian count" and "was one month into a torrid affair with Aristotle Onassis" in November 1963, when her husband was assassinated in Dallas.[11]

Joan said she spent the night with Jack in his Georgetown town house when Jackie was away. They most likely made love in the same bed Jack and Jackie used when Jackie was home. Their four-year affair ended the night Jack received the democratic nomination for the presidency. They parted after exchanging amicable goodbyes.

☆ ☆ ☆

Pamela Turnure met Jack when he was a U.S. senator, and they became intimate. He was forty, and she was only twenty. Pam was described by one photographer as "bright, attractive, well-groomed, well-spoken." She was gentle, tasteful, and dignified. Pam had brown hair, blue-green eyes, and a pale complexion. Others said she resembled Jackie and even looked and sounded like her. Eventually, Pam began to mimic Jackie's style of dress and even her voice. Pam became Jack's receptionist, and he often had many late-night meetings at her apartment in Georgetown.

Pam's landlords, the Katers, became incensed over Pam and Jack's late-night behavior in the apartment they were renting to her, so they began to set up secret tape recorders to obtain some evidence of the senator's behavior. One night the Katers heard a noise at 1:00 A.M., looked outside, and saw Jack tossing pebbles at Pam's window. He was shouting, "If you don't come down, I'll climb up your balcony." They even waited outside one night and snapped a few photos of Jack leaving Pam's apartment at 1:00 A.M. When Mrs. Kater confronted Jack with the photo, he simply brushed it aside. Even though the landlords sent copies of the tape recordings and the photographs to the FBI and the media, little was done. As a result, the Katers began showing up at Jack's political rallies with crude handmade signs charging him with adultery. They visited Cardinal Cushing in Boston. Mrs. Kater even picketed the White House after Jack was elected president. She carried a sign that read: Do You Want an Adulterer in the White House?

After Jack became president, Pam was given a staff job as Jackie's press secretary, even though she had no experience in this field. Her office was located in the White House so that she was nearby and always available to satisfy Jack's physical needs. Witnesses saw her take the elevator up to the family's private family quarters minutes after Jack would disappear from some White House function. It seems certain that Jackie knew of their relationship but thought it better to have Pam nearby, where she could keep a closer watch on the two of them. Jackie once asked a friend if she knew that Jack "was having an affair with Pamela Turnure." George Smathers surmised that Jackie allowed Pam to be nearby and provide Jack with sex so frequently that he would get bored with it. Jackie may have been right! Jack onced phoned a friend and said, "There are two naked girls in the room, but I'm sitting here reading the *Wall Street Journal.* Does that mean I'm getting old?"

☆ ☆ ☆

Jack used at least two of the secretaries in the White House secretarial pool for recreational sex. They were Priscilla Weir and Jill Cowan. Both were described as attractive, bright, charming, and in their early twenties. Priscilla was a blonde and Jill a brunet. They applied for White House jobs together, wearing identical dresses.

The Secret Service gave them the code names Fiddle and Faddle when they referred to them over the radio communication channels for an added measure of security. Jackie referred to them disdainfully as the "White House dogs." One time, when Jackie was giving an Italian journalist a private tour of the White House, she opened the door to Jill and Priscilla's office and said, "Those two are my husband's lovers."

On another occasion, Peter Lawford brought some "poppers" to the White House. This drug, known clinically as amyl nitrate, was supposed to heighten sexual pleasure. Although Jack wanted to try some, Peter convinced him that it would be dangerous and unwise to experiment with the drug. So Jack gave some to either Priscilla or Jill and watched curiously as she began to hyperventilate.

The Secret Service also had code words to refer to Jack, Jackie, and their children. Jack was Lancer. Jackie was Lace. The two children, Caroline and John junior, were referred to as Lyric and Lark, respectively. It is not clear how Jack's code name was chosen. It could have been randomly selected, but this is not usually the case. It is unlikely Lancer is short for Lancelot, the knight in King Arthur's court, from the movie and play *Camelot*. Although this story was one of Jack's favorites and his administration became known as the "Thousand Days of Camelot," this royal image was not created until after Jack's death. The code name might have been derived from Jack's frequent sexual activity. It is not clear whether the Secret Service agent who gave Jack this code name knew about his philandering ways when he assigned it, but it is likely he knew, since the Secret Service had been guarding Kennedy from the moment he became the president-elect in November 1960. Nevertheless, Lancer was an appropriate code name for a person who regularly engaged in promiscuous sexual activity.

Although Jill and Priscilla did not have any noteworthy secretarial skills and were not assigned any routine duties, they traveled frequently with Jack to places like Nassau, Palm Beach, and Yosemite National Park. They were usually housed near Jack. He would call them to his private quarters very late in the evening for "work." They usually returned physically worn out. Since Jack was fond of *ménage-à-trois* liaisons, it seems reasonable to assume that they participated in this type of sexual activity. According to George Reedy, Lyndon Johnson's press secretary, Fiddle and Faddle had three-way sex with Kennedy and also swam nude with him in the White House swimming pool.[12]

☆ ☆ ☆

Florence Prichett Smith, the fashion editor of the *New York Journal-American*, was the wife of E. T. Smith, the U.S. ambassador to Cuba during the Eisenhower presidency. During 1957 and 1958, Jack slipped out of the country and visited Florence in Cuba on several different occasions. She was five-seven, had brown hair and eyes, and was "terribly good-looking." Florence was also intelligent, fun, and had a great personality. He also saw her in Miami and Palm Beach when she was visiting the United States. On one of her trips to Palm Beach, after Jack had been elected president, the FBI, the Secret Service, and the local chief of police finally found Jack a few hours after he had given them the slip. Jack and Florence were in her swimming pool, and according to the chief of police, "They weren't doing the Australian crawl."

☆ ☆ ☆

Jack met Judith "Judy" Eileen Katherine Immoor Campbell during his campaign for the presidency in February 1960. Judy was a young, sensuous, and vivacious woman with raven-black hair and clear blue eyes. Some have remarked that she resembled Elizabeth Taylor or even Jackie Kennedy. Frank Sinatra, the famous entertainer, introduced Judy to Jack on February 7, 1960, when Jack visited the Sands Hotel in Las Vegas on a campaign layover to see Sinatra's show. It was 10:00 P.M. when they met, and Judy thought, "He looked so handsome in his pinstriped suit. Those strong white teeth and smiling Irish eyes."[13] Judy began to learn that evening that Jack was the "world's greatest listener," for he appeared totally focused and absorbed in what she was saying. He even leaned forward in his chair so as not to miss even a single word. They had a three-hour lunch the next day on Sinatra's patio, where they got acquainted.

Judy arrived for lunch at 12:30 P.M. wearing a burgundy knit suit, a black-leather belt and shoes, and a matching handbag.

Judy also attended a reception later that evening in Jack's honor and then had an intimate dinner with him while watching a show in the Copa Room. Jack would pat or squeeze Judy's hand whenever he reached over for his drink. Judy admitted she was wearing her heart on her sleeve that evening but sensed that the feeling was mutual. Jack said he wanted to see a lot of her if she was willing. She responded with "I'm willing. Don't worry about that."

After the show, they were separated, and Jack was whisked off to another party. When he realized that Judy had not come along, he called her hotel around midnight and pleaded with her to join him in the Copa Room again for the late show. She agreed. This time they exchanged telephone numbers during the show. Within a week Jack sent Judy a dozen red roses and began calling her nearly every day. He told her how much he missed her, how glad he was they had met, and how he wanted to arrange another meeting with her.

Their next meeting, and first sexual encounter, took place one month later in room 1651 of the Plaza Hotel in New York on March 7, 1960, on the eve of the New Hampshire primary election. It had been a month since she last saw Jack, and Judy was nervous. She heard a light knock at the door, and after opening it, Jack entered her room, appearing out of breath. Jack hugged her, told her it was good to see her, and told her she looked sensational. Judy had a bottle of Jack Daniel's on ice and led Jack over to two chairs, where they could sit, have a drink, and chat. She couldn't keep her eyes off her bed. It seemed to grow to a gigantic size in proportion to the room. Judy was ambivalent about taking their relationship to the next level. She wanted to but knew it would bring new difficulties, and she was afraid of being hurt. Still, she realized what was transpiring, and she let it happen. Judy thought, "That damn bed was getting bigger by the minute."

Finally, Jack initiated the next move. He got Judy to her feet and began kissing her. She said, "He was very amorous and just very loving." In her mind she was resisting what was happening but let it continue nonetheless. Jack led her over to the bed, gently pushing her onto her back, and became even more amorous, kissing her more passionately. Suddenly, Judy pushed him away and said, "No, Jack!" Astounded, he tried to talk her into continuing and told her, "I have so looked forward to being close to you." After sensing that further discussion was futile, Jack walked over to get his jacket. He had his hand on the doorknob before Judy called him back. He told her he didn't mean to appear impatient but he had been so looking forward to this moment for an entire month. He confessed that he could have walked into the room and carried her immediately to the bed to make love and they could have laid in each other's arms and talked intimately in the way only two lovers can talk after they have just finished having sex.

They began kissing. Judy went into the bathroom to undress. She found Jack already in bed. Smiling, he reached out for her. Jack was very gentle and loving and appeared to be very considerate and concerned about Judy's feelings that night. After making love, they held each other and talked. Later, they continued drinking Jack Daniel's while sitting in bed until Jack had to leave. Jack didn't seem concerned about the election and never mentioned the primary once that evening. The next morning, Judy received a dozen roses and a card that read: "Thinking of you," signed only with the initial J. She was delighted by his thoughtful gesture and excited after learning he had won the New Hampshire primary. He called the following day and suggested another meeting in the next few days in Washington. Judy agreed.

At first, Judy found Jack very sensitive. However, over time, she became dissatisfied with his performance in bed. She felt as if Jack were interested in being serviced sexually and claimed that his favorite lovemaking position was on his back. Although she acknowledged that this preference may have been due partially to his weak back, she eventually sensed an attitude in Jack that indicated that she was there primarily to meet his physical needs.

On April 5, 1960, Judy dined with Jack in his Georgetown home at 3307 N Street, NW, at 7:30 P.M., while his pregnant wife was in Florida. She arrived wearing a black knit suit and a new black diamond mink coat. Jack raised his eyebrows when he saw her, and he said, "You look fantastic." After dinner, Jack gave Judy a tour of the rest of the house, and they ended up in the master bedroom, which had twin beds with pale green sheets. They began to kiss passionately while sitting on one of the beds. Judy took this as the signal and went into the bathroom to undress. She found Jack already in bed when she returned, and they made love. Judy felt somewhat uncomfortable making love in the same bed that Jack shared with Jackie. But she admitted that her need to be with Jack was stronger than her conscience.

Afterward, he held very tight her in his arms, and they talked for several hours. He told Judy that if he did not win the presidential nomination, they would go off to a beach on a deserted island somewhere for a whole month. Judy asked if he meant somewhere where it was warm enough for them to "make love in the sunlight and moonlight." Jack responded with "Yes, and never wear clothes." He asked to meet her again a week later in Miami, and she told him she would do so.

On April 12, Jack met Judy in her room at the Fontainebleau. He only stayed an hour, and they did not make love. Jack indicated that if he did not win the presidential nomination, he was going to make some major changes in his life. He implied that he and Jackie would divorce: he claimed "their marriage was unhappy, and things hadn't worked out between them. Judy got the impression that if he did not win, Jackie would be leaving him and that any divorce was a mutual decision between them." He made no promises to Judy and didn't imply he was leaving Jackie for her, but he certainly did indicate that he would be more available to spend time with her. Before leaving that evening, Jack handed Judy an envelope with strict instructions that she not open it until after he left. It contained two $1,000 bills. He wanted to do something nice for her and instructed her to use the money to pay for the new mink coat she had just bought. It was the one time Judy accepted a gift of cash from Jack.

On May 31, Jack visited Judy, who was recovering from surgery at her parents' home in Los Angeles. He drove across town in the merciless heat just to be with her for a few minutes and deliver a dozen red roses along with a warm smile. For this simple act of kindness, at that moment Judy felt she loved him more than at any other time in their relationship.

After the first evening session of the 1960 Democratic National Convention, held in Los Angeles on July 11, Jack spent some time with Judy alone in Peter Lawford's hotel suite (room 724) in the Beverly Hilton Hotel. It was during this meeting that Jack tried to talk Judy into a ménage-à-trois sexual encounter with a tall, thin secretarial type in her late twenties. After the party ended, Jack asked Judy to accompany him to the bedroom. She was surprised when she discovered another woman there waiting for them. The woman went into the bathroom and closed the door, and Jack talked to Judy about the three of them going to bed together.

She could not believe what she was hearing. He tried to kiss Judy, but she wouldn't let him. He told her not to be afraid, that there was nothing wrong with a threesome and that it was widely practiced. Although Judy became very upset and protested, Jack repeatedly said, "I know you. I know you'll enjoy it." Judy told Jack off and began to cry. She remained firm in her rebuff of his offer, however, and Jack later apologized for his actions. Judy decided to leave and was very upset, of course, but before doing so, Jack tried to persuade her to promise to call him after she got home to let him know if she was all right. Judy only said that she would think about calling after she got home. She heard the phone ring several times after she arrived home, but knowing it was Jack, she refused to answer.

The next morning, the phone began ringing again, and when she answered, it was Jack. He asked her to try to forget about the previous night and "think kind thoughts." He asked her to attend the convention and told her that there would be four tickets waiting for her, but her mother went instead. Judy did wish him good luck at the convention before hanging up the phone.

Judy moved into an apartment in the Navarro in New York. Jack called on August 3 and asked if he could drop by. They had made up by then, and Judy decided to forgive him. She joked about the deserted island Jack had promised to take her to and make love around the clock if he lost the primary elections. She said that he must have been there without her, because he had a great tan. He laughed and chided her about hitting below the belt, but soon they were hugging and kissing again and made love that evening. Jack returned the next day for more lovemaking, and again on August 11 and 16, 1960.

On August 19, Jack arranged for Judy to meet him at his home in Georgetown for the second time. She slept with him in his and Jackie's bed and joked afterward about his trip the next day to Independence, Missouri, to see former president Harry Truman, who was considering endorsing Jack's campaign for the presidency.

The day after his election victory Jack invited Judy to attend his inauguration in January 1961. She refused, telling him, "I just wouldn't feel comfortable with your wife and family being there." Later, she changed her mind and said she would come. Jack's secretary, Evelyn Lincoln, told Judy that she would get her the best available seats. But she changed her mind again and watched Jack on television instead. She did save her personal invitation and tickets to the inauguration as mementos of the historic occasion.

Judy claims that she made frequent phone calls to Jack and visited the White House more than twenty times for intimate meetings with him during the summer of 1961. Judy made at least seventy calls to Kennedy in the White House between 1961 and early 1962. The last known call between Jack and Judy, recorded in the White House phone logs, came only hours after J. Edgar Hoover met with Jack in the White House on March 22, 1962. It is believed that Hoover warned Kennedy to end his relationship with Judy and informed him that she was also seeing Chicago mobster boss Sam "Momo" Giancana. Hoover was briefed about Campbell before leaving the FBI for his meeting with the president. But Judy contends that she continued contact with Kennedy as late as June 1962. Several of their meetings in the White House resulted in lovemaking in the family's private quarters.

When Jack discovered that Judy and Sam Giancana were friends, he asked if she could arrange a meeting between the two of them, since Jack thought Sam might be able to help with the campaign. Giancana sent one of his lieutenants, Paul "Skinny" D'Amato, to West Virginia to help Jack defeat Hubert Humphrey in the primary. D'Amato was supplied with $50,000 cash to hand out among the leaders of the West Virginia democratic political machine if they would turn the vote out for Jack. D'Amato also had the authority to forgive the gambling debts many of these pols had run up in the Mafia-backed casinos in New Jersey.

On April 12, 1961, Judy was happy to discover that Jack was going to be in Chicago. She was staying in suite 839-40 at the Ambassador East Hotel. Jack made arrangements for a brief twenty-minute visit. Even though they had not seen each other in some time, Judy said that it was as if they had never been apart and sensed that Jack missed her as much as she had missed him. They kissed and agreed that she would come to the White House in early May.

On May 4, Judy checked into room 424 at the Mayflower Hotel in Washington. Evelyn Lincoln called to say that Jack could not see her until 4:30 P.M. the following day. Judy arrived by cab at the West Gate and was escorted into the Cabinet Room and left alone to wait for the president. Judy was very nervous until Jack walked into the room. He told her he was feeling good now that she was finally here and said, "What a way to end the day. You look ravishing. . . . I had forgotten how beautiful you really are." She was wearing her magenta Dior suit. They talked for thirty to forty minutes, then embraced before she left. Judy agreed to return the next day at 1:15 P.M.

On Saturday, May 6, 1961, Judy had lunch with Jack and his assistant Dave Powers in the White House. Jack had sent a car to pick Judy up at the Mayflower, and she was greeted shortly after arriving at the West Gate by Dave Powers. Jack placed his arm around her and escorted her down the hallway to the swimming pool. "How about a swim before lunch?" he asked. Judy refused on the grounds that she hadn't gotten all dolled up to go swimming. Jack was probably envisioning a nude swim in the pool with Judy and perhaps some lovemaking in one of the deck chairs before lunch.

Judy probably never suspected what he had in mind. Jack would often swim in the nude with girls he invited to the White House—a practice he had learned from his father, who was also very fond of skinny-dipping with naked young women. Since Judy refused his offer, Jack asked if she would mind if he took a swim alone before lunch. She said it would be fine. Dave Powers took Judy upstairs to the private family quarters to fix her a drink. As she passed through the living room, she recognized much of the furniture, having seen it twice before in the Kennedys' town house in Georgetown. Jack arrived soon after, and they had drinks before moving into the dining room for lunch.

After lunch, Jack led Judy through the master bedroom, where she noticed the same twin beds from his town house in Georgetown, then into another bedroom with a large double bed, where they kissed and embraced. Jack put the music from *Camelot* on the stereo. He said, "What a way to spend a Saturday afternoon." As usual, Judy went into the bathroom to ready herself for their lovemaking and returned to find Jack already undressed, lying in bed in his favorite position, on his back. She said he was having trouble with his back; it was the first time during their lovemaking that he stayed on his back the whole time. Somehow this position made her feel as if she were there just to service him. However, after they finished making love, Jack was very considerate. They laid in bed for a long time afterward, talking and caressing.

On August 8, 1961, Jack invited Judy to the White House again. She arrived wearing an "apple green Chanel-style silk suit." Apparently, Jack was concerned that word of his proposal to have a *ménage à trois* with Judy and another woman had leaked out. He said it had gotten back to him that Judy had mentioned it to a friend. Jack openly discussed the matter with Judy in front of his aide Dave Powers, which embarrassed and angered Judy greatly. She said, "Jack, you know damn well I would never repeat that story to anyone." But Judy was not telling the whole truth. She had told her doctor and one or two of her acquaintances. Of course, she was not about to tell Jack this.

Two weeks later, on August 24, after Judy's anger subsided, she returned to the White House again for another round of lovemaking in that same big double bed. This time Jack had a little surprise waiting for her afterward. He presented Judy with a flower-shaped gold brooch filled with diamonds and rubies. She said he only gave her the gift because he was still feeling guilty about the proposed *ménage à trois*. He responded with "Let this remind you that if my intentions go astray from time to time, my heart is still in the right place." This was only the second and last gift Judy ever accepted from Jack.

Sometime on or before August 31, Jack visited Judy at her suite in the Plaza Hotel, number 1529-31. It was very large, and after she gave Jack a tour, they ended up in bed together again. But soon it was time for Jack to go.

In November 1961, Jack visited Judy at her apartment on North Flores in Los Angeles. She gave him a tour, and they ended up in the bedroom and within minutes were frolicking on her king-sized bed. She said that there was nothing wrong with Jack's back that evening. He made her promise to see him again in Palm Beach.

A month later, in December, Judy visited Jack in Florida at his one-story, pastel-colored house, surrounded by a five-foot wall. It had a large swimming pool and a sprawling lawn. After strolling along the beach and eating a seafood salad for lunch, they made love in the bedroom with the windows wide open and the sun beaming down on their naked bodies. Judy didn't know that when he was staying at this house alone, Jack would regularly cruise down Worth Avenue in Palm Beach and point out attractive women to his aides, who would recruit them for an afternoon or evening of lovemaking, usually at the home of a neighbor or friend.

Judy made further visits to the White House during the summer and again in the fall. In fact, she was a fairly frequent visitor at the White House until the summer of 1962. Although they made love there, Judy never stayed overnight. Jack said, "If only I could keep you right here, and have you waiting for me when I came back. Then in the morning we could make love before breakfast, and after lunch, of course."[14]

During the spring of 1962, Judy claims, they began to argue on the phone; she resented the fact that he wanted her to run to him every time he called. Their telephone contact waned and by the summer their relationship had ended. There was no big argument or explosion, just a gradual drifting away from each other. Judy couldn't have known, but by this time Jack was already seeing Mary Pinchot Meyer on a regular basis. Both Judy and Mary had similar qualities. They were artists, and both were strong, independent, and spirited women who enjoyed Jack Kennedy sexually.

Judy was staying at the Beverly Crest Hotel in November when she learned that Jack had been killed by a gunman in Dallas on November 22, 1963. She was in shock and had difficulty coping with her loss. She would go for days without eating and drink herself to sleep.

Jack and Judy's affair did not become public knowledge until December 1975, twelve years later. Earlier that year, in September, Judy had been called to testify in secret session before the Senate Select Committee on Intelligence Operations by its chairman, Sen. Frank Church. The committee wanted to learn if Judy knew anything about the CIA's (Central Intelligence Agency) plot to assassinate Cuba's dictator, Fidel Castro. She told them she had a close personal relationship with Kennedy but knew nothing of the CIA's activities. Her testimony was immediately sealed and will not be available to the public until the year 2025. Convinced she knew nothing about the plot, the committee referred to her in its November report only as a "close friend" of Jack Kennedy's. However, the *Washington Post* soon revealed that Kennedy's close friend was a woman and his mistress. Washington was abuzz with gossip. Judy called a press conference and on December 17, 1975, appeared in San Diego behind numerous microphones and cameras wearing big black sunglasses to read the following prepared statement:

> I can at this time emphatically state that my personal relationship with Jack Kennedy was of a close, personal nature and did not involve conspiratorial shenanigans of any kind. My relationship with Sam Giancana and my friendship with Johnny Roselli were of a personal nature and in no way related to or affected my relationship with Jack Kennedy. Nor did I discuss either of them with the other.[15]

But Judy was not telling the whole truth. In 1988, after learning she was slowly dying of cancer, Judy and biographer Kitty Kelley collaborated on a feature article for *People* magazine (for which they split the $100,000 payment). In this article Judy admitted lying to the Senate committee in 1975 and in her book, published in 1977 and written with the help of Ovid Demaris, entitled *My Story*. She feared that if she had told the truth, she would be killed. Her fears were justified, for Sam Giancana was murdered in his home while under police protection in June 1975, just two days before he was scheduled to testify before the Senate committee about his role in the CIA plot to murder Castro. He had been shot seven times in the head. Johnny Roselli, who did testify before the committee about Giancana's role in the CIA plot, was murdered about a year later, shortly before he was scheduled to testify before the committee a second time. His body was found floating in an oil drum secured by heavy chains in the ocean near Miami.

In *My Story*, Judy summed up her thoughts about mobsters and politicians with the following words:

> No one really knows why Sam was murdered, or Jack, for that matter, and now Johnny. Life in the underworld of crime and the netherworld of politics is cheap. From what I have observed, it is impossible to tell good men from the bad.[16]

☆ ☆ ☆

Mary Pinchot Meyer was a socialite and sister-in-law of Benjamin Bradlee. She met Jack when he was a student at Choate. She continued seeing him while she attended Vassar and he studied at Harvard. One acquaintance described Mary as "intelligent, charming and beautiful, with blond hair and pert features." An author described Mary as an "attractive, medium-blonde, half-serious girl with a mysterious hidden quality. Talented, cheerful, sexy, a super girl." Another set of authors described Mary this way: "Mary Pinchot reminded men of a cat walking on the roof in the moonlight. She was a writer, a painter, and a liberated woman, long before those pursuits became fashionable."[17]

After divorcing her husband of fourteen years in 1959, she began a new bohemian lifestyle. With the help of a family inheritance, she established a modest art studio in a garage in Georgetown, where she spent time working on paintings that were displayed in a trendy Washington, D.C., art gallery. Once, while vacationing in Italy, Mary saw a handsome Italian on his yacht. She swam out to meet him, shedding her bikini before climbing aboard.

Mary was usually present at the private dinner parties Ben and Toni Bradlee gave for Jack and Jackie. Ben Bradlee claimed that he did not know that Jack and Mary were having an affair. Mary did tell her best friend, Ann Truitt, about the affair. Ann's husband, Jim, then a vice president of the *Washington Post*, made this affair known many years after Mary's murder in 1976 in an interview with the *National Enquirer*.

Jack bedded Mary for the first time in January 1962 in the White House. They were seeing each other on a regular basis by the spring of 1962. There affair continued up until November 1963, when Jack was assassinated in Dallas.

Mary was also one of Jackie's friends. They saw each other until the time Jack was elected president. Mary never visited Jackie in the White House, but she did visit Jack there secretly. She also had sex with Jack in the White House in 1962, at which time she introduced him to drugs.

The president of the United States hid inside a White House closet and smoked marijuana with his mistress a week before a White House conference on drugs. During one of her visits, Mary took Jack into the closet and pulled out a little box with six marijuana cigarettes. They smoked one of the joints together. And Jack joked about the upcoming conference. After Jack and Mary shared a few more joints, they joked about Jack's being incapacitated if the time came for him to push "the button" in the event of a nuclear attack by the Russians. "Suppose the Russians drop a bomb," he said. Peter Lawford had already introduced

Jack to cocaine and hashish. Mary also reportedly introduced Jack to LSD as well. According to author C. David Heymann, Jack and Mary apparently took a "mild trip" while making love. For Jack, this activity may have been more of an experiment than curiosity about a new form of drug. Perhaps he thought it would heighten his sexual pleasure.

Mary was murdered in October 1964 while jogging along the towpath of the old Chesapeake and Ohio Canal which runs parallel with the Potomac River. She was shot once in the head and chest. This is the same spot where she used to walk with her friend, Jackie Kennedy, several years earlier. One eyewitness claimed that he saw a black man, standing over Mary's body and dressed in a windbreaker, dark slacks, and a dark cap, place a dark object in the pocket of his jacket. Another witness identified a laborer named Raymond Crump as the man he had seen struggling with Mary shortly before her murder. But since no murder weapon was ever found and there was no apparent motive, Crump was acquitted.

Mary kept a diary which included many details of her affair with Jack, but it disappeared after her murder. Some have surmised that the murderer was looking for Mary's diary. Ben Bradlee, Mary's brother-in-law, claimed that his wife found the diary and that he turned it over to his friend James Angleton, then chief of counterintelligence at the CIA. Angleton maintains that he destroyed the diary, not to protect the late president but to protect Mary's privacy, since she was survived by two young sons.

☆ ☆ ☆

In 1946, while on a six-week vacation that included a stop in Los Angeles, Jack met actress Gene Tierney. Jack was bent on "knocking a name" while he was in Hollywood. Gene was wearing a lavender dress while filming on the set of *Dragonwyck* and turned to find herself "staring into the most perfect blue eyes I had ever seen on a man." She was married at the time to Oleg Cassini, the famous fashion designer, but their marriage was breaking up. Jack and Gene began an affair that lasted for a year.

Describing Jack's way with women, she said, "Gifts and flowers were not his style. He gave you his time, his interest. He knew the strength of the phrase What do you think?" She also said, "He had the kind of bantering, unforced Irish charm that women so often find fatal." Gene was so infatuated with Jack that she even refused the advances of Tyrone Power.

Gene once said, "I was deeply in love with John [Kennedy], and I would have married him in a minute if he had been able to ask me. But Rose made it clear that no good Irish Catholic would marry a divorced woman."

☆ ☆ ☆

After Jayne Mansfield's untimely and accidental death, her publicist, Raymond Strait, wrote *Jayne Mansfield and the American Fifties* and *Here They Are: Jayne Mansfield*. In these books he claimed that Jayne confessed to an intermittent, multiyear love affair with Jack Kennedy. He said that Jayne liked to talk about Jack when she had been drinking. Strait produced no evidence other than his own recollections of these events.

According to Strait, Peter Lawford, Jack Kennedy's brother-in-law, was a close personal friend of Jayne Mansfield's. Lawford acted as a panderer on Kennedy's behalf when Jack was a still a senator from Massachusetts. And the Kennedy-Mansfield affair began at this time.

According to Strait, on two occasions when he knew President Kennedy was in the vicinity, Jayne received mysterious calls from a Mr. J. (a.k.a. Jack Kennedy). One call came when Kennedy was vacationing in Palm Springs; the other, when he was visiting Peter Lawford at his beach house in Santa Monica.

The first time, the caller said, "Please tell Miss Mansfield that Mister J. called. The meeting is scheduled for two this afternoon." Strait did not recognize the caller at first, even though his voice and Massachusetts accent sounded familiar. Later, after returning from her mystery date with Mr. J., Jayne dropped by Strait's apartment for a cup of coffee and a cigarette and accidentally left a book of matches behind. The cover of the book was imprinted with the presidential seal. Only then did Strait recognize the caller's voice and realize it had been Jack Kennedy.

The second call from Mr. J. came a year later, when Jayne was pregnant and ready to deliver her fourth child. Strait told Mr. J. that he was unable to contact Jayne but would keep trying. Mr. J. agreed to call back.

When Strait got through to Jayne, she rushed over to Ray's apartment to await Mr. J.'s follow-up call. He wanted her to come down to Palm Springs. Jayne was very excited and ready to go. When Strait confronted her with the combined evidence of the match cover she left behind and the Massachusetts accent of the mystery caller, Mr. J., she admitted she was involved in an affair with the president of the United States.

On another occasion when Jayne had been drinking, she bragged about the time Senator Kennedy invited her to a party. It was during the Democratic National Convention in 1960. Jayne drove over to Jack's West Hollywood apartment, only to discover that she was going to be the party. No one else had been invited. She was eight months pregnant. They had sex, even though her belly was the size of a balloon, and Jack was wearing some kind of corset because of a back injury he attributed to the war. Jayne liked and respected Jack and remembered he was "very considerate of my condition."

Jack once told Jayne that her voice reminded him of Jackie's. Years later, Jayne found the comparison insulting and depressing. Jayne said, "I don't sound like her. She doesn't sound like anything."

Strait also claimed that Fred Otash, Hollywood's premier gumshoe, had bugged a room that Jack and Jayne used in order to obtain some dirt on this senator who would be president. Otash was allegedly working for Kennedy enemy and president of the Teamsters Union, Jimmy Hoffa. Otash and Strait collaborated on the writing of two books, and Strait said that he had listened to Otash's secret audiotape recordings of the private meetings between Jack and Jayne.

After hearing about Marilyn Monroe's death, Jayne became afraid for her own life and said, "I may be next." Monroe, of course, was another of Jack's sexual conquests. Some sources say she was threatening to call a press conference and go public about her affairs with both Jack and Bobby Kennedy just days before she was discovered dead in her house.

☆ ☆ ☆

Another of Jack's starlet friends was Angie Dickinson. It is not clear when their relationship began. According to one witness, Jack and Angie spent several days alone at a cottage in Palm Springs before he was inaugurated.[18]

Angie attended a $100-a-plate fund-raising diner for Jack hosted by fellow actor Frank Sinatra during the Democratic National Convention in 1960. Angie was also on hand during the inaugural celebrations in 1961 with her beard, Red Fay, the undersecretary of the navy. She and Jack probably spent the most time together in 1962. Jack was also seeing several other woman, including fellow actresses Jayne Mansfield and Marilyn Monroe and socialites Mary Pinchot Meyer and Judy Campbell.

Angie has never directly confirmed or denied whether her relationship with Jack was of an intimate sexual nature. She once said, "I have nothing to hide about my relationship with the Kennedys. People keep throwing up the rumor, trying to make something more of it than it was." But she has also hinted coyly at the extent of the relationship by making several suggestive remarks with double entendres like "He's the only presidential candidate who has ever turned me on" and "He was wonderful. . . . It would be bad manners to say more."[19]

One celebrity magazine claimed in the late 1980s that Angie still kept a autographed picture of Jack on her dresser with an inscription that read: "Angie. To the only woman I've ever loved."

In 1993 she told columnist James Brady of *Parade* Magazine that she did not want to see Oliver Stone's controversial movie *JFK*. It seems likely that it would have been too painful for her, especially if she had had an intimate relationship with Jack Kennedy.

☆ ☆ ☆

Marilyn Monroe was introduced to Jack Kennedy in 1954 at a party at the home of agent Charles Feldeman. Actor Peter Lawford had arranged for the Kennedys to receive an invitation, since he knew Marilyn would be there and was trying to arrange for Jack to meet Marilyn. She had to talk her new husband of six months, baseball legend Joe DiMaggio, into going, for he hated Hollywood parties. Jack couldn't take his eyes off Marilyn, which made her feel both uncomfortable and flattered at the same time. Both Joe and Jackie saw what was going on. Joe tried to force Marilyn to leave every few minutes, stating he had had enough. Before Joe shuffled her out of the party, Marilyn managed to slip her phone number to Jack. Jack called her the next day, but Joe answered the phone. When he asked who was calling, Kennedy responded with

"A friend," and Joe hung up. After Marilyn divorced Joe in early 1955, she began seeing Jack when she visited New York City, whenever he was in town.

A few months later, Jack entered the hospital to have back surgery during which he nearly died. Friends who came to visit found that Jack had a color poster of Marilyn hung upside down on his wall. She was pictured in shorts standing with her shapely legs spread far apart.

Although Marilyn married playwright Arthur Miller, she continued to tryst with Jack for the remainder of the decade. Whenever she fought with Miller she could escape from their home in Connecticut to her apartment on Fifty-seventh Street. When Jack was in New York, she would meet him at his private bachelor pad in the Carlyle Hotel. This penthouse had huge plate-glass windows and a spectacular view of the city below.

Jack saw Marilyn at Peter Lawford's house in 1957 and spent several days with her in 1959 in Palm Springs. The Lawfords' beach house was the scene of much debauchery. When Jack came to visit Peter Lawford and his wife, Patricia, was away, Peter would throw wild parties at his beach house, some of which became legendary. One of Peter's neighbors described the scene as a "goddamn whorehouse," and others referred to the parties as orgies. On one occasion, someone was running around during the party nude. Peter always made sure there was an ample supply of party girls, starlets, models, and prostitutes. At times, Jack would take one or two girls back to his Beverly Hills Hotel after the party ended.

Lady Lawford, Peter's mother, also claimed that Jack kept two airline stewardesses at Peter Lawford's beach house when he was a U.S. senator and met movie starlets and Marilyn Monroe there as well. He would see them when he traveled to the West Coast. She said that although she liked Jack best of all the Kennedys, she never would have voted for him since his mind was always down between his legs. She also wrote in her book *Bitch*, "I find it difficult to place my complete trust in a president of the United States who always had his mind on his cock!"

During the second night of the Democratic National Convention in 1960, Jack was surprised and embarrassed to find that Marilyn wore no underwear when he reached his hand up under her dress during a dinner party in the Puccini restaurant. They probably had sex earlier that evening before dinner because Marilyn told Peter Lawford that Jack's performance had been "very democratic" and "very penetrating." On July 15, 1960, late in the same evening that Jack gave an inspiring acceptance speech at the convention, Marilyn attended a nude swimming party with Jack in the Lawfords' pool. Jack even delayed his return from Los Angeles to Boston by one day to spend it with Marilyn.

They had another sexual encounter during a 1961 Christmas party at the Lawfords' home. Jack and Marilyn slipped away to one of the upstairs bedrooms. They took a bubble bath together during which Marilyn poured sparkling cold champagne over Jack's shoulders. One author said that on one occasion Peter Lawford snapped several photographs of Marilyn performing fellatio on Jack while he lounged in a large marble tub. This may have been the location where the photographs were taken.[20] Afterward, Jack made love to Marilyn for an hour in the bed that was once owned by film mogul Louis B. Mayer.

Their next meeting came early in 1962, when they spent the night together at the Beverly Hilton, feasting on lobster thermidor that was delivered by room service. They also slept together once in a penthouse room at the same hotel and made love on the beach in Santa Monica.

During an official visit to Bing Crosby's estate in Palm Springs on March 24, 1962, Jack sent *Air Force One* on a side trip to Los Angeles to pick up Peter Lawford, who was accompanied by Marilyn, disguised as his secretary. This was done to prevent the Secret Service and other political aides from knowing her true identity. Marilyn wore an inexpensive gray suit from Sears, Roebuck, a cheap brunet wig, and sunglasses. Lawford made her carry a steno pad and even take dictation to make the disguise seem all the more real.

After a formal dinner with the Crosbys, Jack changed into his favorite clothes: a pair of khaki trousers, a sweater, and loafers with no socks. He threw a private party for a select group of democratic pols in the secluded guest house where he was staying. Marilyn was there, too, dressed in pajamas and a silk robe. She acted as Jack's unofficial hostess. She had been drinking heavily. One of the politicos at the party, Philip Watson, said, "It was obvious they were intimate." It was also obvious that Marilyn intended to stay the night. From their bed that evening, Marilyn placed a call to her friend and masseur Ralph Roberts. Marilyn told Roberts she was giving "her friend" a massage and that they had had a disagreement about the location of certain muscles. Marilyn wanted Roberts to back up her position. She also had Roberts explain to Jack the muscles she had developed through regular exercise for the famous "Marilyn walk." Kennedy asked her masseur for some personal advice about how massage might help his almost constant back pain. After the phone conversation ended, Marilyn jokingly told Jack that Ralph could give him a better massage than she could. Jack quipped: "That wouldn't really be the same, would it?" Marilyn laughed and confided later to Roberts, "But I think I made his back feel better."

In *Show Business Laid Bare*, published in 1974, Earl Wilson said: "Marilyn Monroe's sexual pyrotechnics excited the President of the United States." Jack liked to pat and squeeze Marilyn when he cuddled with her. According to author Peter Harry Brown, Marilyn's studio maid, Hazel Washington, said, "She slept with him [Kennedy] off and on—whenever there was a scrap of time."

Marilyn later confided to both Ralph Roberts and writer Bob Slatzer that Jack was "both brutal and perfunctory in bed." She "insisted he made love like an adolescent."[21] "He was in and out in a few seconds," she said. Overall, Marilyn was disappointed by Jack's performance in bed, which she said was "less than inspired." She also confessed that many times nothing happened at all because of Jack's weakened back. Other women who slept with Jack confirmed that he was "a lousy lay," a "bam-bam, thank you ma'am" who considered sex "a dessert" and "good, clean fun."

Marilyn later confided to Ralph that she hoped that one day Jack and Jackie would divorce so she could become the first lady. She once wondered out loud why Jack was married to that statue and said, "Boy is she ever stiff," referring to Jackie. Marilyn guessed that Jack probably did not put his hand up Jackie's dress, as he did hers. She confided to Roberts that she could tell Jack was not in love with Jackie. On another occasion, in 1962, Marilyn asked a girlfriend, "Can't you just see me as first lady?" Marilyn even called Jackie once at the White House and asked her to divorce Jack so she could marry him. According to Peter Lawford, Marilyn also fantasized about having Jack's children.

In April 1962, at Jack's request, Marilyn attended a private $10,000-a-plate fund-raiser given by socialite Fifi Fell for the rich and privileged in a penthouse on Park Avenue in Manhattan. When she arrived, fashionably late, of course, Peter Lawford was frantic, since he was charged with making sure she made it to the party. Jack was furious. Dinner had been held up until after 10:00 P.M., waiting for her arrival. However, after she arrived, it was as if time stood still. The idle chatter of the New York socialites stopped. All eyes were fixed on her. Her every move was watched. Marilyn's publicist said that he realized Marilyn had fallen in love with Jack after overhearing a little of their intimate conversation. The presidential limousine took her back to her apartment on Fifty-seventh Street after the fund-raiser ended around four in the morning, but Marilyn quickly changed clothes and then took a cab back to Jack's rooftop, garden-style apartment at the Carlyle Hotel.

Jack gave Marilyn the private phone number of the Oval Office. She made scores of phone calls, first from the privacy of her bedroom and later, as she became more open about their relationship, from her dressing room on the lot at Fox Studios. This number rolled over to Jack's private family quarters on the second floor of the White House after hours. According to Patricia Kennedy Lawford, Jack's sister, Jackie often answered the phone when Marilyn called. Jackie allowed the two of them to have phone conversations in her presence and was aware of their relationship.

Although they were somewhat discreet about their affair during the previous decade, by the 1960s their relationship had become so obvious that Jack's advisers warned him of the consequences if there was ever a full public disclosure. One of them, Peter Summers, saw Jack and Marilyn emerge from the same shower together. A Secret Service agent claimed that Jack and Marilyn had sex in the loft above his brother Bobby's office at the Department of Justice. There was a big double bed in the loft, which is located between the fifth and sixth floors, that was used by the attorney general when he needed to stay at his office overnight during periods of crisis. A private elevator leading directly to this little-known bedroom from the basement of the Justice Department building made it possible for Jack and Marilyn to slip into the loft unnoticed for a few hours of passionate lovemaking.[22]

Marilyn agreed to perform at the star-studded party at Madison Square Garden honoring Jack's forty-fifth birthday in May 1962. Several members of the cabinet protested. The director of the birthday gala was also concerned that Marilyn was not the right kind of girl for this type of affair. When Jackie found this out, knowing of Jack's affair with Marilyn and not about to be embarrassed and upstaged by this sensuous blond actress, she gave Jack an ultimatum and made him choose between the two of them. When he chose Marilyn, Jackie decided not to attend and instead spent the weekend in Virginia.

One of Marilyn's Fox Studios screenwriters, Nunnally Johnson, said, "Many of us felt her appearance at Madison Square Garden would be like Marilyn making love to the President publicly after doing it privately all these months." And Johnson was right. This was exactly the message that Marilyn intended to send. She sang a sensuous rendition of "Happy Birthday, Mr. President" and a special version of "Thanks for the Memories." She wore a $5,000 see-through gown, designed by Jean-Louis, made from two hundred pieces of silk, with rhinestones placed in strategic locations. The gown, which weighed about an ounce, created the illusion that Marilyn was nude. "Skin and beads" was the way one politico described Marilyn's dress. It was so tight that she had to be sewn into it. Marilyn combined sexual gestures, like tracing the outline of her body and cupping her breast with her hand, with breathy voice tones as she cooed her way through the performance. One observer said it was as if Marilyn were trying to give the impression during her performance that she was going to be the president's birthday present.

Jack turned to writer Gene Schoor, sitting in his box, and said, "Jesus Christ, look at that dress." While staring at her every movement, Jack added, "What an ass, Gene. *What* an ass," as Marilyn's hips gyrated through her performance. After she finished her performance and the grand finale of the show that night, Jack came to the microphone and said, "I can now retire from politics after having had 'Happy Birthday' sung to me in such a sweet, wholesome way."

Although she was exhausted and suffering from a high fever, Marilyn insisted that she attend the public party at Arthur Krim's apartment and Jack's private party later that evening at the Carlyle Hotel. Jack and Marilyn left Krim's party at about one in the morning, accompanied by a few others, and took a private elevator to the basement. Then they navigated a series of tunnels under the streets of New York until they reached the Carlyle Hotel. They met alone in his suite and slept together probably for the last time that night. Marilyn did not return to her own apartment until 4:00 A.M.

After the birthday gala, Jack had little use for Marilyn. He had had an affair with the most popular and desirable movie star of the day. She had just topped it off with a show-stopping performance that was as close as one could come to making love in public to the president, or "the Prez," as she called him.

Jack soon stopped taking Marilyn's phone calls. She became angry, realizing he had used her and was now no longer interested in continuing their relationship. Marilyn became irrational and threatened to call a press conference and go public about their affair. Jack sent brother Bobby, the U.S. attorney general, to calm her down, and eventually he, too, became involved in an affair with Marilyn. She then started to fantasize about Bobby in the same way she had about Jack. He may have even led her to believe that he was going to divorce Ethel to marry her.

Marilyn died on August 4, 1962. The cause of death was officially reported as a suicide due to an overdose of sleeping pills. Much controversy has surrounded her death, and some authors have suggested she was murdered to prevent her from revealing her affairs with the Kennedy brothers.

Although Marilyn's affair with Bobby was in full bloom at the time of her death and her affair with Jack had ended, she was trying to arrange another date with Jack in Washington, D.C., after attending a new Irving Berlin musical called *Mr. President*. But Marilyn never made the opening of the play. Jack and Jackie attended, however, and he continued with his womanizing. He danced with many of the women there and was even seen kissing one on the ear.

☆ ☆ ☆

Jack's womanizing continued throughout his tenure as a congressman and U.S. senator. While a freshman congressman, he threw frequent parties in his Georgetown apartment, which he shared with his sister Eunice. After she moved out, girls went through his bed like shoppers through a revolving door. There were so many that he did not even bother to learn their first names.

During his first congressional campaign, one of his aides walked into campaign headquarters and surprised Jack and one of the secretaries provided by the publicity agency hired by Jack's father. The aide described what he saw:

... I found him humping this girl on one of the desks in his office. I said, "Sorry," and left! Later, the girl told my wife she had missed her period, then learned she was expecting. I told Jack.

"Oh shit!" was all he said! He didn't care a damn about the girl—it was just the inconvenience that bothered him! In that sense he was a pretty selfish guy.[23]

According to an FBI report, Jack maintained a "personal playpen" in room 812 of the Mayflower Hotel in Washington from 1955 through 1959. Kennedy frequently threw parties there. One FBI informant maintains that he attended a party in Jack's apartment when Jack and Sen. Estes Kefauver both had sex with their dates in full view of the other guests, then switched girls and did it again.

Senator Kennedy liked to pat women on the behind when riding in the elevators on Capitol Hill. When making love in his office, congressman and later senator Kennedy was known to prefer the hard floor with just the office rug under him rather than the office couch. Perhaps the floor gave his weak back more support. We know from several of his sexual partners that the position was his favorite.

Fellow senator George Smathers said Jack had "the most active libido of any man I've ever known." He also said, "Just in terms of the time he spent with a woman, he was a lousy lover. He went in more for quantity than quality." Smathers also said, "No one was off-limits to Jack—not your wife, your mother, your sister." Once, after Jack and Smathers took two girls up to their private apartment, Smathers received word that he was wanted back at the Senate. Halfway there, he realized something was awry when he remembered that the Senate was no longer in session. He quickly returned to find Jack chasing both of their dates around the apartment. On anther occasion, after Jack was rebuffed when attempting to seduce historian Dr. Margaret Louise Coit, she asked, "Do you do this to all the women you meet?" Jack looked surprised and responded humorously, "My, god, no—I don't have the strength." When Kennedy and a congressional buddy (probably Smathers) were in another city, they used to get one hotel room, two girls, and trade them.

In August 1956, after losing the nomination for vice president to Sen. Estes Kefauver at the democratic convention in Chicago, Jack took a Mediterranean cruise aboard the *Washington Star*. He was accompanied by George Smathers and a sexy blonde known to friends as "Pooh," or simply "P." She was a rich, stunning, and uninhibited socialite. There were several other young women aboard the boat, including a French movie starlet. Jackie, who was seven months pregnant, suffered an abdominal hemorrhage and was rushed to Newport Hospital. An emergency cesarean section was performed, but it was too late to save the baby, who died before birth. The press was told that Jack could not be reached until several days later, when the boat came to shore in Genoa. In reality, he learned of Jackie's tragic condition while still aboard ship but was unwilling to cut short his vacation and return to Jackie until Smathers set him straight and convinced him it would ruin his political career if he did not return home soon.

One columnist said that Jack did not womanize during an election campaign, but this is simply not true. During the presidential campaign Jack's advance men had an additional duty—finding girls for Jack to sleep with during each leg of his trip. The day before the first-ever televised presidential debate in 1960 against Republican candidate Richard Nixon, Jack asked one of his men, "Any girls lined up for tomorrow?" The next day, the call girl was waiting in a hotel room at the Palmer House. Jack arrived to have sex with her just ninety minutes before airtime. He was introduced to the girl, who had already been paid for the services she would provide, spent fifteen minutes in her hotel room, and afterward emerged with a big grin on his face. After doing well against Nixon during the first debate, Jack insisted that a girl be lined up for him before each of the remaining broadcasts.

During the Democratic National Convention in 1960, the Kennedy camp was sending anything the delegates wanted up to their hotel rooms, including booze and women. While Hollywood stars, including Frank Sinatra and the rest of his Rat Pack, cruised the convention floor looking for votes, Jack was busy with women. Jack's stayed officially at the Biltmore Hotel, but he also kept a private suite at a nearby apartment house. After reporters discovered his private playpen, he tried to evade them by sneaking out a window and climbing down a fire escape but was caught while climbing over the fence at the rear of the building. He shouted that he was off to "meet my father." No reporter believed him. Later, it was discovered that he had spent the night with the wife of a former diplomat. If all accounts are accurate, Jack had sex with Marilyn Monroe, Jayne Mansfield, Judy Campbell, a former ambassador's wife, and several other party girls and prostitutes during this five-day convention.

☆ ☆ ☆

Jack's philandering continued throughout the presidential campaign and on into the White House. The back-stairs traffic at the White House was heavy during the summertime when Jackie and the kids were vacationing in Cape Cod. Attractive women were seen being escorted upstairs to the private family quarters. They would enter the southwest service entrance of the White House to prevent being noticed. Jack's trusted male friends would send willing young women to the White House sometimes with a note introducing them to Jack. One time, after receiving a gorgeous brunet for some lovemaking who was purportedly a *Playboy* centerfold model, Jack sent a note back to the columnist, who had sent her with one, that said, "I got your message—both of them." On another occasion, during the summer of 1963, Jack reportedly reinjured his back while engaging in one of these sexual encounters.

One afternoon when Jack was in bed with a young woman, he heard a knock at the door of the Lincoln bedroom. Angry at being disturbed, he flung open the door, revealing to two foreign-aid advisers a young woman in bed. They must have been standing there with their mouths and eyes wide open. Jack did not even bother to close the door. He walked over to a chair, sat down, read the classified cables, made his decision, gave the advisers direction, returned the cables, shut the door, and went on with his lovemaking.

The family's living quarters were on the second floor of the White House. Jack's bedroom was nearest the elevator so that he could go quickly to his office in the West Wing. The room had white walls, a huge four-poster bed made of dark mahogany wood, and dark colonial blue-and-white furnishings and accessories. Under Jack's bed were the speakers from the stereo system, placed in a large closet that separated his

bedroom from Jackie's. At the foot of his bed Jack kept a table that contained all of his newspapers and magazines.

Jackie's bedroom was located next to Jack's. The color scheme of the
room consisted of pale shades of blue and green. Most of her bedroom
furniture was brought over from their Georgetown town house. Jackie
had an upholstered bench at the foot of her bed. It held her typical reading materials, which included: *Art à la Mode; Elle; Femme Chic; Figaro
Litéraire; L'Officiale; Paris-Match; Realités;* and *Spectator.*[24]

Jack liked to listen to soft, romantic music when he was in bed. One
time when the speakers were accidentally switched to loud, White House
staff heard the sound of German military music coming from the balcony.
He must have been in a different mood that day.

According to Traphes Bryant, the White House dog keeper, Jack
would pass the word to his staff that the private family quarters on the
second floor of the White House were off-limits when Jackie was gone
and he wanted to be alone with his female companions. Once, Bryant
was riding the elevator to the third floor, and it stopped on its own at
the second floor. When the door opened, Bryant witnessed a naked
blond office girl running through the hall with breasts swinging as she
went. He quickly punched the basement button, fleeing from the scene.

In the Peter Davis television documentary about John F. Kennedy entitled *Jack,* which aired in November 1993, one woman, identified only
as Susannah M., maintains that she had a four-year relationship with
Kennedy that included visits to the White House for sex. She would be
escorted up to the family quarters and after arriving would note, "There
didn't seem to be a lot of people around. In fact, there wasn't anybody
around." She remembered their sexual encounters fondly.

It's doubtful, however, that there was anything romantic about most
of Jack's back-stairs sexual encounters. Kennedy treated woman as sex
objects. One observer who knew Jack said he only had one use for
women, and that was horizontal.

As president, Jack was on a tight schedule. He did not have much time
to spend with each of these woman. One woman said, "He was as com-
pulsive as Mussolini. 'Up against the wall, Signora, if you have five minutes,' that sort of thing." Jack used these brief sexual encounters for
diversion from stress or to prevent headaches. During a conference in

Nassau in either 1961 or 1962, Jack casually confessed to Prime Minister Harold Macmillan and Foreign Minister R. A. B. Butler that he would suffer from severe headaches if he went too long without a woman. He also confided to a female friend, Nancy Dickerson, "I can't get to sleep unless I've had a lay."

The Secret Service was given instructions by Jack to pass woman along to him. Although these casual liaisons with relatively unknown woman worried them, there was little they could do. They did put Jack's regular female visitors through background investigations. It would be interesting to see what the Secret Service noted as the reason for granting them access to the president. Lem Billings said it never occurred to Jack that one of these unknown party girls could have posed a danger to him.

When asked once what the president of the United States would like to have for his birthday, Jack named a certain television actress. Peter Lawford and Dave Powers helped to make Jack's birthday wish come true.

During the Cuban Missile Crisis, Jackie returned home from her house at Glen Ora, Virginia, to be near her husband in his hour of need. However, in spite of this national crisis, Jack's mind was still on womanizing. After giving the Russians the ultimatum to remove their missiles from Cuba or else, Jack noticed an attractive new secretary who was filling in during this tense evening. He whispered to Robert McNamara, "Bob, I want her name and number. We may avert war here tonight."

During June 1963, Jack visited Germany to give a speech in West Berlin and to see the Berlin Wall. During the day he made speeches promising U.S. protection against the Russians. At night he was chasing women. One was a German secretary that worked at the American embassy in Berlin named Ursula.

☆ ☆ ☆

There can be little doubt that Jackie knew about the President's philandering. Peter Lawford claims she told him she knew about Jack's affairs and that she had once caught him in the act. It was on a cruise aboard the presidential yacht *Honey Fitz* during Jack's forty-sixth birthday celebration. George Smathers confirmed that Jackie once said that

Franklin D. Roosevelt had an affair with his wife's personal secretary, Lucy Mercer. FRANKLIN D. ROOSEVELT LIBRARY

Eleanor Roosevelt refused to sleep with FDR after discovering his affair with Lucy. FRANKLIN D. ROOSEVELT LIBRARY

Lucy Mercer was with Franklin when he died. FRANKLIN D. ROOSEVELT LIBRARY

Missy LeHand was often seen sitting on Franklin's lap at the White House and aboard his yacht. FRANKLIN D. ROOSEVELT LIBRARY

Dwight D. Eisenhower, the Supreme Allied Commander, had an affair with his wartime driver, Kay Summersby. DWIGHT D. EISENHOWER LIBRARY

Mamie D. Eisenhower's wartime letters intimated she suspected Ike's extramarital relationship. DWIGHT D. EISENHOWER LIBRARY

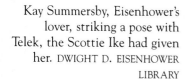

Kay Summersby, Eisenhower's lover, striking a pose with Telek, the Scottie Ike had given her. DWIGHT D. EISENHOWER LIBRARY

John F. Kennedy, the playboy president who sought pleasure and power, had the most active extramarital sex life of any president. LIBRARY OF CONGRESS

Jacqueline Bouvier Kennedy, one of the most beautiful first ladies, even pointed out two of the president's lovers when giving a private tour of the White House to a friend. JOHN F. KENNEDY LIBRARY

Pamela Turnure was given a job as Jackie Kennedy's press secretary and an office in the White House to be near JFK. JOHN F. KENNEDY LIBRARY

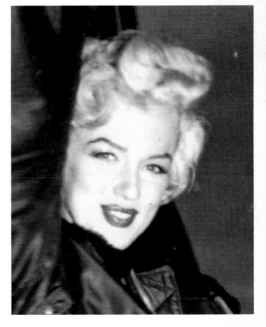

Marilyn Monroe, the reigning sex symbol of the 1950s and early 1960s, had an affair with JFK. NATIONAL ARCHIVES AND RECORDS ADMINISTRATION

Inga Arvad, JFK's lover during the war years. Arvad's son may have been fathered by JFK. UPI/BETTMANN NEWS SERVICE

Jayne Mansfield claimed she had sex with JFK when she was several months pregnant. Jack wore a corset while they were having sex to strengthen his weak back. AP/WIDE WORLD PHOTOS

The apartment house where JFK lounged in a bath towel between lovemaking episodes with Arvad. The FBI taped the sounds of JFK and Inga making love. AUTHOR'S PHOTOGRAPH

Judith Campbell Exner, JFK's mistress for over two years, wrote a book entitled *My Story* describing her trysts with Kennedy. AP/WIDE WORLD PHOTOS

The Georgetown townhouse where JFK lived with Jackie and also made love to Judy Campbell and Joan Lundberg. AUTHOR'S PHOTOGRAPH

Mary Pinchot Meyer, last mistress of the president, smoked marijuana with JFK in a White House coat closet days before a White House conference on drugs. She later died under mysterious circumstances. UPI/BETTMANN NEWS SERVICE

According to a Secret Service man, Lady Bird caught Lyndon Baines Johnson having sex in the Oval Office with a secretary. LYNDON BAINES JOHNSON LIBRARY AND MUSEUM

Claudia Alta Taylor "Lady Bird" Johnson, a virtuous woman who loved LBJ despite his many flaws. LYNDON BAINES JOHNSON LIBRARY AND MUSEUM

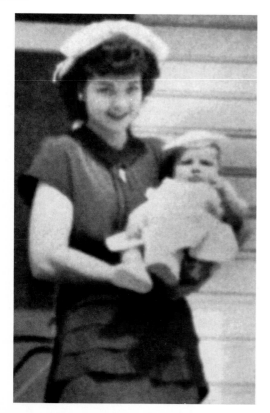

Madeleine Brown, the president's mistress, alleges that Lyndon Johnson fathered her child, Steven Brown. BROWN FAMILY

Alice Glass was the president's mistress while
married to newspaper mogul Charles Marsh.
LYNDON BAINES JOHNSON LIBRARY AND
MUSEUM, CASSON STUDIOS

The Mayflower Hotel, location of the secret rendezvous
between LBJ and Alice Glass and between JFK and Judy
Campbell. AUTHOR'S PHOTOGRAPH

Bill Clinton was the first sitting president to be sued for sexual misconduct. THE WHITE HOUSE

Hillary Rodham Clinton, disgusted with Bill's philandering, threatened to have an extramarital affair of her own. THE WHITE HOUSE

Gennifer Flowers, at a radio show in New York in May 1994, talking about her affair with Bill Clinton. Clinton claimed she was just a "friendly accquaintance." AP/WIDE WORLD PHOTOS

Paula Corbin Jones, who sued President Clinton, speaking with reporters in February 1994 about her allegations of sexual misconduct against the president when he was governor of Arkansas. AP/WIDE WORLD PHOTOS she had caught Jack making love to the wife of David Niven, a famous movie star. While on a birthday cruise for Jackie, who was then five months pregnant, Jack convinced Niven's wife to slip into a cabin with him for a quick sexual encounter lasting only a few minutes. Smathers did not say how Jackie responded to this discovery.

She may have felt it was better to have woman service him nearby in the White House than for him to sneak off for some illicit rendezvous. She once said to a friend, "I don't think that there are any men who are faithful to their wives. Men are such a combination of good and bad." This is not to say that she was happy about this arrangement, though. She once found a pair of panties tucked inside her pillowcase and brought them to Jack, dangling then delicately between her thumb and forefinger. She said in a chilly tone, "Would you please shop around and see who these belong to? They're not my size."

On another occasion, after leaving for a trip to Atoka, Virginia, Jackie doubled back to the White House. Perhaps she suspected something or had been tipped off by her Secret Service agent.

One of the naked girls, a beautiful, tall blonde, had stopped in the gymnasium to disrobe before continuing on to the presidential swimming pool. She found Jack sitting naked in a lounge chair, nursing a daiquiri, when she arrived. After swimming nude for a few minutes, one of the aides announced that Jackie was on her way back to the White House and was headed toward the pool. Jack had been joined by brother Bobby, other male friends, and several naked girls.

One time, when asked why he wasn't worried that Jackie would return from an outing earlier than planned and catch him with a woman, Jack boasted, "Jackie can't get within two hundred yards of this place without my knowing about it." But now he was scrambling! According to one witness, "naked bodies were scurrying every which way." The ushers quickly cleared away all of the highball glasses, and Jackie returned to the pool to find Jack swimming alone. She left after finding nothing amiss. After receiving word that Jackie's car had left a second time, the skinny-dipping party resumed. White House workers would sometimes come up to the glass doors leading into the pool area to gawk at the nude swimming parties. Jack eventually had the doors frosted to prevent onlookers from seeing what was happening in the pool.

According to Traphes Bryant, the White House staff was used to cover up evidence that Jack had just entertained a female guest in the private family quarters. After Jack had finished, the staff was sent to scour the room where the liaison had taken place, looking for bobby pins, blond hairs, and any other telltale signs that Jack had been with a woman. One of the upstairs maids complained, "Why do we always have to be searching for blond hairs and blond bobby pins? Why can't he get himself a steady brunet?"

Joseph Kennedy reportedly offered Jackie $1 million not to divorce Jack but to stay with him throughout the presidential campaign and as long as he remained in the White House. According to the rumor mill at the White House, Jack's father made this offer after Jackie learned that their baby-sitter had accused Jack of getting her pregnant. This act of philandering exceeded the limits of Jackie's toleration, and she supposedly threatened Jack with divorce. The baby-sitter was only fifteen years old at the time.

In *A Woman Named Jackie* by C. David Heymann, the author reported that Jack impregnated the baby-sitter of a famous newsman's children. The baby-sitter had accompanied the newsman to Camp David when he was doing a feature story on Jack. During this trip the newsman discovered that his baby-sitter was involved in a steamy tryst with Jack. He did not know that Jack had previously financed an abortion for her in Puerto Rico after impregnating her. He also learned that Jack and others lounged around and swam naked in the Camp David pool. Needless to say, he reported none of this information in his news article.

Lady Lawford, a feisty and outspoken Englishwoman and Peter Lawford's mother, says in her book *Bitch* that Joe Kennedy's million-dollar offer came after Jackie became upset and threatened to divorce Jack when she accidentally found a photograph of Jack coming out of a Beverly Hills call house. According to Lady Lawford, Jackie's response to Joe's monetary offer was "Make it tax-free and it's a deal."

Thomas C. Reeves, in his book *A Question of Character,* implies that Joe Kennedy made the million-dollar offer to Jackie when she learned why Jack had at first refused to return to her bedside shortly after she lost her second child. Jack had been unwinding and womanizing aboard a yacht during his Mediterranean-cruise vacation after his vice-presidential defeat in 1956.

JOHN F. KENNEDY

☆ ☆ ☆

In his book *The Kennedys: Dynasty and Disaster 1848–1983*, John H. Davis wrote: "Kennedy . . . was a classic sexual adventurer, a libertine who thoroughly enjoyed the hunt, the chase and the conquest, who took women where he found them and discarded them as quickly as he took them."[25]

Jack once confided to a friend, "I'm not interested—once I get a woman, I'm not interested in carrying on, for the most part. I like the conquest. That's the challenge. I like the contest between male and female—that's what I like. It's the chase I like—not the kill!"

To explain Jack's relentless sexual activity we need to return to his childhood. Neither Jack's father nor his mother was physically affectionate. Jack once told a friend that during his childhood his mother was never around when he needed her and never held or hugged him. Close friends said that although on the surface Jack appeared to be friendly and concerned about others, he really "had a total lack of ability to relate emotionally to anyone." Another lifelong friend said that Jack was aloof and had an "inability to love or express feelings."

A woman who knew the Kennedy family once asked Jack "why he was acting like his father, why he was avoiding real relationships, why he was taking a chance on getting caught in a scandal at the same time that he was trying to make his career take off." After thinking it over for long time, a look came over his face like a little boy about to cry. He finally shrugged and said, "I don't know, really. I guess I can't help it."

Jack may have also been recklessly promiscuous due in part to his health and bad back. Realizing that you only live once, he seemed to be cramming in the wild living because he was not sure how long his back would hold out or even how long he would live. Jack had Addison's disease. His treatment included frequent injections of Novocain, daily doses of cortisone tablets, and desoxycorticosterone acetate pellets implanted in his thigh every three months. This combination of medication tended to stimulate his sex drive and may in part have accounted for his overactive libido. During the 1960 Democratic National Convention, the Lyndon Johnson campaign had released word that Jack had the mysterious Addison's disease and, despite his young age, might not live long enough to serve even a single term in office. Jack once said about his struggle with Addison's disease, "They keep giving me all of these chemical because I have this disease. It'll finish me off by the time I'm forty-five."

☆ ☆ ☆

In spite of his many failings, Jack did have quite a sense of humor, especially when it came to the topic of sex. One time Ted Sorensen joked, "This administration [Kennedy's] is going to do for sex what the last one [Eisenhower's] did for golf. Jack responded with "You mean nineteen holes in one day?"

When Jack asked his doctor for a shot of painkiller for his back shortly before his forty-sixth birthday party, the doctor warned him it would "remove all feeling below the waist." Jack responded with "We can't have that, can we, Jacqueline?"

Jack Kennedy had the most active extramarital sex life of any sitting president and probably had more sexual partners than any other man who became president.

12

LYNDON B. JOHNSON
The Unrestrained Texan

☆

Today, with the advent of interlocking worldwide computer communication networks like the Internet, parents must worry about the type of sexually explicit information and images that may end up on their children's computer desktop. Lyndon Johnson did not need to master the personal computer, but he did need to be concerned about a different kind of sex on the desktop.

We don't know the exact details of Lyndon Johnson's lovemaking activities with his "harem" of secretaries in the Oval Office, but secretaries, aides, Secret Service agents, and others who knew Johnson personally claimed that this type of activity took place there. In *Lone Star Rising: Lyndon Johnson and His Times, 1908–1960*, author Robert Dallek wrote that one unnamed secretary said she had sex with Johnson atop a desk in the White House. The secretary didn't specify whether the desk was in the Oval Office or not. And in *Inside the White House* another author, Ronald Kessler, said that a Secret Service agent claimed that Lady Bird caught Lyndon having sex with a secretary on a couch in the Oval Office.

To learn more about what we do know of Lyndon Johnson's sexual escapades and to thoroughly understand the type of man and husband he was, we must return to his early beginnings and trace them forward

Lyndon Johnson
Thirty-sixth President of the United States (1963–69)

Biographical Information

Born: August 27, 1908
Died: January 22, 1973
Wife: Claudia Alta Taylor (a.k.a. "Lady Bird")
Children: Two girls

Extramarital Affairs

Known and Suspected Sexual Partners:	Dates:	Locations:
Alice Glass	1938–65	Washington, D.C.; Houston; Longlea, Calif.
Madeleine Brown	1948–69	Austin, Dallas, Houston, San Antonio

Alleged Illegitimate Child: Steven Brown

toward the present, stopping from time to time to examine sexual behavior that would eventually contribute to his sexual conduct as president of the United States.

☆ ☆ ☆

Johnson was born near Stonewall, Texas, just after the turn of the century. His father, Sam Ealy Johnson Jr., was a local politician. After Lyndon graduated from high school he took a job as a highway laborer, as his family lacked the financial resources to send him to college. He also worked as a car washer, elevator operator, and handyman. He eventually saved enough money to enroll in Southwest Teachers College and after graduation taught debate and public speaking at high schools in Pearsall, Texas, and Houston from 1930 to 1931.

Lyndon B. Johnson

At age twenty Lyndon was six feet three inches tall but weighed only 135 pounds. He had a full head of dark, wavy hair and was considered very good-looking by some of the women he knew. He was described by those who knew him as charming, energetic, and sentimental. But Lyndon was also chameleon-like, crude, and self-absorbed. In truth, Lyndon was a mixture of all these qualities.

In 1928 he met Carol Davis, the daughter of a wealthy banker living in a small town near Johnson City, Texas. They began dating. It was obvious that Lyndon was interested in her money and had made it known that he was looking to marry a rich girl. Carol was the first woman Lyndon seriously considered marrying. He was the first man who had showed her any serious attention. Lyndon described her this way:

> . . . very beautiful, tall and blonde with dark blue eyes. Her skin was pale and very soft. She was clever and everyone admired her. I fell in love with her the first moment we met. She seemed so much more alive than all the other girls I knew, interested in politics and loved the out-of-doors.[1]

However, when Carol took him home to meet her parents, it was obvious that they had already formed a negative opinion of him even before he arrived. Lyndon received a very chilly reception. Carol's father offended Lyndon by saying that everyone knew that his grandfather, Sam Ealy Johnson, was "nothing but an old cattle rustler." Davis went on to dash their marriage plans and told his daughter:

> I won't let you, I won't have my daughter marrying into that no-account Johnson family. I've known that bunch all my life, one generation after another of shiftless dirt farmers and grubby politicians. Always sticking together and leeching onto one another so the minute one starts to make it, the others drag him down. None of them will ever amount to a damn.[2]

According to Lyndon, even though Carol was willing to ignore her father's wishes and marry Lyndon, he realized it would not work out, refused to marry her, and did not see her again for years. Other accounts indicate that it was Carol who grew cool to the idea of marriage when she realized they had little in common. Since Lyndon's greatest love was politics, something she had little interest in, and since he was not concerned about the things that interested her, she decided against the marriage.

From 1931 to 1934, Lyndon served as secretary to Richard M. Kleberg, one of the Democratic representatives from Texas. Lyndon's public-speaking skills served him well, for he was elected as speaker of the "Little Congress," an organization of congressional secretaries.

While living in Houston, Lyndon dated Claudia Alta Taylor, the daughter of a rich rancher and merchant, Thomas Jefferson Taylor. Claudia had been nicknamed Lady Bird as an infant by her nursemaid, and the name stuck. Lady Bird was described as sensitive, supportive, and shrewd.

She was born on December 22, 1912. Her mother died when she was only five. She was raised by her father and her mother's sister, aunt Effie Pattillo. Lady Bird graduated with honors near the top of her class at the University of Texas and received a B.A. degree in education in 1933 and a second bachelor's degree in journalism in 1934.

She met Lyndon at the home of a mutual friend in 1934. Lyndon invited her to eat breakfast with him the next morning and proposed to her later that same day. She refused to marry him at first, but Lyndon was persistent. He called or wrote her nearly every day for weeks. She finally agreed to marry him just seven weeks later, after Lyndon delivered a now-or-never ultimatum and after much encouragement from her father. When she brought Lyndon home to meet her father, he was warmly received, unlike the rejection he had experienced at the home of Carol Davis. After meeting Lyndon for the first time, Lady Bird's father said, "Well, daughter, you've brought home a lot of boys, but this time you brought home a man!"[3]

When Lady Bird finally said yes, Lyndon phoned his friend, Dan Quill, and had him make all the wedding arrangements while he and Lady Bird drove 450 miles across Texas from Texarkana to San Antonio to get married. Quill filled out the marriage license himself, got a clerk to sign it, rushed down to the local Sears, Roebuck store, bought a dozen cheap wedding rings for $2.50 a piece, since he did not know Lady Bird's size, rounded up a local Episcopal minister to perform the ceremony before Lady Bird changed her mind, and finally served as Lyndon's best man. Lyndon and Lady Bird were married on November 17, 1934, at Saint Mark's Episcopal Church in San Antonio, only two months after they had first met. Lyndon was twenty-six; Lady Bird, twenty-one. They honeymooned in Mexico after spending their wedding night at San Antonio's Plaza Hotel.

Lyndon served as the director of the National Youth Administration (NYA) in Texas from 1935 to 1937, which helped provide part-time positions for college students and training and public-works jobs for needy high school students who were not going on to college. As director of the NYA, Lyndon's name become known across the state and helped him earn votes when he embarked on his first political campaign at the end of his two-year term.

In 1937, Lyndon borrowed enough money from his father-in-law to finance his first congressional campaign and ran for the U.S. House of Representatives' seat for the Tenth District. He won a special run-off election after apparent voting fraud put him over the top. He served in the House of Representatives until 1949.

Lyndon joined the naval reserve in January 1940 and saw active duty in the U.S. Navy from December 1941 until July 1942. His aircraft was attacked during an intelligence-gathering mission over New Guinea, but he survived and was awarded a Silver Star by order of Gen. Douglas MacArthur.

He was elected to the U.S. Senate in 1948. Lady Bird gradually gained the confidence and experience she needed to become a skilled politician's wife. Although she would come whenever Lyndon called, she was not deeply involved in any of his elections until his senatorial campaign of 1948. He served as the Senate majority leader from 1956 until 1961, when he became vice president. Lady Bird also joined his vice-presidential campaign in 1960 and traveled over thirty-five thousand miles in a little over two months gleaning votes for her beloved husband.

After John Kennedy was assassinated in Dallas during November, 1963, Lyndon was sworn in as the thirty-sixth President of the United States, with Lady Bird standing on his right side and Jackie Kennedy on his left. They were aboard *Air Force One* with the body of the slain former president.

Lady Bird was also very involved in his election campaign of 1964, when Johnson was elected to serve a full four-year term. He elected not to run for a second term in 1968.

☆ ☆ ☆

Lyndon Johnson was a womanizer and proud of it. He had a continual need for sexual conquests and persisted in seeking them out even in his fifties. Lyndon once confided to a young associate that "he didn't see anything wrong with people having sex outside of marriage." Although the associate was shocked and responded with "Well, wouldn't that bother you in your own family?" Lyndon answered the probing question with "Well, not really." However, the young associate sensed that Johnson's answer was not entirely honest.

Lyndon bragged constantly about his sexual conquests, his sexual appetites, and the size of his sex organs. According to Johnson's presidential press secretary, George Reedy, Lyndon made little attempt to conceal his philandering. Although his womanizing was well known to those around him, during this era the press kept his sexual exploits secret from the American public, considering them a private family matter. In his book *The Years of Lyndon Johnson: The Path to Power*, Johnson biographer Robert Caro described Johnson's need to brag about his sexual conquests this way:

> Displaying that same coarseness that, at college, had led him to exhibit his penis and call it "Jumbo," he would show no reticence whatever about the most intimate details of extramarital relationships. His description of his amours were not only exhibitionistic but boastful; particularly with cronies, he would seem almost to need to make other men acknowledge his sexual prowess. There was, seemingly, no aspect of an afternoon in bed—not even the most intimate details of a partner's anatomy that he did not consider grist for his vivid storytelling ability.[4]

He was not at all modest and would often parade around in his bedroom completely naked. One time, he asked that his favorite dog, Yuki, be brought to him, walked out of his bedroom wearing only the top of his pajamas, and ordered the White House dog keeper to hold the dog until he put on his pajama bottoms.[5]

Lyndon considered himself a ladies' man but was jealous of John F. Kennedy's reputation as a womanizer. According to William "Fishbait" Miller, the congressional doorkeeper, Lyndon became angry at then senator Kennedy during the 1960 Democratic National Convention in Los

Angeles because he was jealous that Jack was off fooling around with girls in some hotel room while he had to work hard to gain votes for him. Lyndon said, "[Jack] probably got himself a half-dozen starlets" while "I'm working my ass off and he's playing tiddlewinks." On another occasion when Kennedy's success with women was mentioned, Lyndon became furious, pounded his fist on a desk, and shouted, "I had more women by accident than Kennedy had on purpose."[6] However, unlike Kennedy, he found "deep meaning in relationships which were often trivial" and "believed that any man-woman relationship . . . created an enduring bond."[7]

After he became president, the gossip circulating at the White House indicated that while serving as a senator on Capitol Hill, Lyndon could not leave the pretty girls alone. He supposedly had fathered one illegitimate child and gotten a second girl pregnant. It's difficult to say with certainty just how many illegitimate offspring might exist. One filed a paternity suit against Johnson's widow in 1987.

Lyndon often entertained company at his 413-acre ranch in Texas and pressured guests, especially pretty female ones, to stay overnight. One time he made certain remarks openly to a pretty young female guest in front of his wife and other guests that contained obvious double entendres indicating what he had planned for the evening. She left in a hurry. Another attractive female aide stayed over at the Johnson ranch only to find herself awakened in the middle of the night in her darkened room by Lyndon's flashlight and his voice. "Move over. This is your president," he said.[8] It's not clear whether she yielded to this presidential order.

At White House dance parties, Lyndon would often kiss so many of the women present that he would have lipstick all over his face. He usually greeted a woman with the hackneyed line "You remind me of my mother!" He would often try to cut some pretty little filly from the herd and corral her in a corner of the room. Next, he would begin a discussion and then suggest they continue it in another room away from all the noise. In *The Dark Side of Lyndon Baines Johnson*, author Joachim Joesten characterized Lyndon as a "full-fledged hypomaniac" and "the crafty seducer with six nimble hands who could persuade a woman to surrender her favors in the course of a long conversation confined to obscure words. No woman, even a lady, can discern his intentions until the critical moment."[9]

☆ ☆ ☆

Lady Bird knew about Lyndon's philandering but purportedly did not let it bother her. Once, after Lyndon's death, when a television producer asked her what she thought of her husband's philandering, she responded, "You have to understand, my husband loved people. All people. And half the people in the world are women. You don't think I could have kept my husband away from half the people?"[10] After a brief pause she added, "If all those ladies had some good points that I didn't have, I hope I had the good sense to learn a bit from it."

On another occasion, Lady Bird also admitted to a reporter that Lyndon "got a lot of solace and happiness and inspiration from women" and that Lyndon was "a flirt and a ladies' man."[11] Lady Bird seemed to accept and justify this side of Lyndon, preferring instead to focus on his better qualities. She did not appear overly distraught or unhappy with this existence, either. She was regularly seen tucked into bed with Lyndon by the White House staff. Lyndon and Lady Bird treated each other in a warm and affectionate manner. He would often reach out and grab her to give her a big kiss.

☆ ☆ ☆

Lyndon had a thirty-year relationship with Alice Glass, the mistress and later common-law wife of Texas millionaire Charles E. Marsh. Marsh published newspapers in numerous U.S. cities, including the *Austin American Statesman*. He liked Lyndon, took him on as a protégé of sorts, and provided him a large amount of favorable newspaper coverage and financial support during his political campaigns. Lyndon first met Alice in 1937 at Longlea, Marsh's thousand-acre estate near Culpepper, Virginia. She lived there with Marsh and their two children.

Alice was described as a beautiful, slender woman with bright blue eyes, creamy white skin, and waist-length strawberry blond hair. She was elegant, idealistic, very independent, and a liberated woman way ahead of the times.

Lyndon's love affair with Alice probably did not began until late in 1938 or early in 1939. According to Alice, they would meet secretly in Marsh's apartment at the Mayflower Hotel on Connecticut Avenue in

Washington or in a suite at the Allies Inn. Alice confided to her sister, Mary Louise Glass, and her cousin, Alice Hopkins, that she had begun an affair with Lyndon in 1938. She later claimed that this was the "most serious love affair of her life." According to Mary Louise, Alice was "absolutely mad" for Lyndon. Alice admitted that she and Lyndon had discussed marriage and that he had promised to obtain a divorce, marry her, and become a corporate lobbyist. If Lyndon had divorced Lady Bird, it certainly would have ended his hopes of being elected to high office, since the electorate was very unforgiving of such actions in that era. Lyndon may have impulsively promised Alice he would get a divorce but probably never seriously considered it. Gaining political power was always his first priority.

He would often visit Longlea from nearby Washington, ostensibly to gather advice and financial support from Marsh; while there, he spent much time alone with Alice. Occasionally he would take Lady Bird with him, but she seemed ill at ease and out of place, so most weekends he just left her at home in their little apartment in Washington.

Lyndon was more than twenty years younger than Marsh and much closer to Alice's age. They both were idealists and shared common political interests. Lyndon used his connections and political know-how to help Alice achieve some of her goals. She helped him refine his image and taught him some of the softer political skills, like dressing well and demonstrating proper manners. This affair was different from those Lyndon had with other women. Lyndon and Alice had fallen in love. Unlike his other trysts, he did not brag about this one, which may have indicated the degree of respect he felt for Alice. Or perhaps it showed that he was cautious and afraid of incurring Marsh's wrath if the affair was ever discovered.

At first, Marsh was not aware of the intimate relationship. Later, he must have discovered their deception, because he accused Lyndon of "shacking up" with Alice and ordered Lyndon to leave his house. However, when Lyndon returned later that same evening, Marsh acted as if none of these events had occurred.[12]

After Alice realized that politics was Lyndon's one great love, she gave up hopes of ever marrying him and finally consented to marry Marsh, who had been asking her to do so for some time. In 1941, however, when Lyndon asked her to accompany him on a combination military assign-

ment–campaign trip to California, she went along. According to her sister, she returned from the trip thoroughly disgusted with Lyndon, realizing he was not the pure idealist she thought him to be. But she was
"still powerfully attracted to him sexually." By mid-1942, Lyndon and
Alice resumed their affair. He began spending many of his weekends at
Longlea again, leaving Lady Bird at home.

Their affair ended in the mid-1960s, when they came to a strong disagreement over the Vietnam War. Lyndon supported the war and the
battle against communism. Alice opposed it. She even burned the love
letters he had written her in protest over his stand on the war. Alice continued corresponding with him and always addressed her letters to "Dearest Lyndon." Her surviving letters reveal a warm friendship but give no
indication that there was ever a love affair.

Several regular guests at Longlea believed that Lady Bird must have
known that Lyndon and Alice were having an affair, since he would regularly go to Longlea without her on weekends; she could have easily determined that Charles Marsh would not be there, either.

☆ ☆ ☆

In 1987, Madeleine Brown claimed she had been Lyndon Johnson's
mistress for a period lasting twenty-one years. The affair began in 1948
and ended in 1969. Madeleine was twenty-three years old when she first
met Lyndon. He was forty and a congressman at the time. She had a
cherubic face, cute turned-up nose, and red hair. She also had long, slender legs and a slim, womanly figure. Madeleine was described as eager,
vivacious, and wild. She was working as a radio advertising buyer for a
Dallas ad agency. Naturally, the job brought her into contact with rich
and privileged Texans at various social affairs. She was invited to attend
a reception at the Austin-based radio station KTBC. Jesse Kellam, the
station manager, introduced Madeleine to Lyndon. Kellam invited her
to attend a second KTBC reception three weeks later at the Driskill
Hotel in Austin.

Madeleine says that Lyndon "looked at me like I was an ice cream cone
on a hot day." After a brief conversation, Lynson said, "Well, I'll see you
up in my apartment." They had sex that afternoon. She described Lyndon's lovemaking style as "rough," "a little kinky," and "commanding."[13]

Afterward, Lyndon warned her that their affair must be kept secret and advised her by saying, "You see nothing, you hear nothing, you say nothing."

Kellam would call Madeleine to set up liaisons between Lyndon and her, usually at the Driskill Hotel in Austin, but also in Houston, San Antonio, and Dallas. Their sexual encounters lasted anywhere from fifteen minutes to three hours, with thirty minutes being the norm. One time when Lyndon was rushed for time he hugged Madeleine and said, "Honey, I can give you fifteen minutes of my valuable time." Madeleine became unhappy when she learned she was not Lyndon's only lover, and after dropping a hint about this disturbing news, he would just say, "Today's today, tomorrow's tomorrow."

Madeleine also claimed to have given birth to Lyndon's illegitimate son, whom she named Steven Brown.[14] "I was his mistress, but actually I was his other family. We were just the hidden family that Steve and I never been [sic] shared publicly with him," Madeleine said.[15] When Lyndon found out she was pregnant in 1950, he flew into a rage and yelled, "How could you be such a dumb Dora?" After he finally calmed down, he assured Madeleine that he would provide for her and the child. A doctor listed Madeleine's estranged husband as the father on the child's birth certificate, but Madeleine said that Lyndon was the real father. In 1987, Steven Brown, then thirty-six, filed a $10.5 million lawsuit against Lady Bird Johnson, claiming he had been "deprived of his birthright" and wanted to change his last name to Johnson, "the way it ought to be." If proved true, Steven might have inherited a sizable portion of Johnson's estate. However, Steven lost a battle with lymphatic cancer and has since died. Steven was over six feet tall and had a profile and hairline that resembled Lyndon's.

Madeleine claimed her relationship with Lyndon was "purely physical" and contends that neither Lady Bird nor the other family members knew about it. But she thinks Lady Bird may have suspected some hanky-panky was going on between Lyndon and her in the 1960s. Madeleine could not produce any evidence that she and Lyndon had been lovers. But she did claim to possess a letter (a facsimile of which is displayed here) written in 1973 by Jerome T. Ragsdale, a Texas attorney, who has since passed away, that promised he would "continue with the financial arrangements that Lyndon provided for you and Steve throughout the

JEROME T. RAGSDALE
ATTORNEY AND COUNSELOR AT LAW
1807 MERCANTILE BANK BUILDING
DALLAS, TEXAS 75201
May 18, 1973

Mrs. Madeleine Brown
218 South Windomere Avenue
Dallas, Texas

Dear Madeleine:

Thanks so much for breaking your plans and meeting with Jess and me
in Houston last week. I sincerely hope we did not inconvenience
you in any way.

Those of us that were close to Lyndon are saddened by his recent
death. It is fortunate that he died at the ranch; he would have
wanted it that way. It is unfortunate, however, that he died so
bitter and tormented.

As we discussed in Houston, you have my personal assurance that I will
continue with the financial arrangements that Lyndon provided for you
and Steve throughout the past. I know you were very concerned about
this and I simply wanted to relieve your mind.

As always, if you need additional funds for you and Steve's living
expenses, please do not hesitate to call me. Of course, I will
continue to make weekly home visits to verify you and Steve's welfare.

Sincerely yours,

Jerome T. Ragsdale

JTR:mm

Enc.

past." However, the payments did eventually stop two years after she received the notification from Ragsdale. Madeleine believes the letter is
proof that she and Lyndon were lovers. If authentic, it would certainly
seem to indicate that Lyndon provided financially for this woman and
her son. In the letter Ragsdale also offered Madeleine "additional funds
for you [sic] and Steve's living expenses." Clearly, according to this
lawyer, the money Lyndon provided was for their "living expenses,"

which seems very odd if this promise was continued payment for a business transaction. Since close friends of the Johnsons have said that they have never heard of Madeleine Brown or her son, it is quite possible that Lyndon's final secret was a mistress and a son.

Madeleine claimed that Lyndon paid to have her "set up in a two-bedroom home with a live-in maid, unlimited charge cards, and a new car every two years." The home was purchased for $15,000 by Ragsdale.[16]

While growing up, Steven was always anxious because he did not know who his father was. He suspected it might be this kind lawyer, Jerome Ragsdale. Ragsdale would take Steven to ball games and would act as his surrogate father when Steven needed one for some important event at school. Although initially angry at his mother for hiding the truth about his paternity, Steven concluded that neither she nor Lyndon had much choice in this matter. He knew that there was some hidden secret concerning his mother and Lyndon Johnson, whom he would often see when his mother took him to Johnson political rallies, and even claims to have seen Lyndon take his mother into his arms and walk together up a stairway in San Antonio's Menger Hotel. Steven even claims that one time Lyndon patted him on the head and told him that one day he would be in the White House. This was the closest Johnson ever came to acknowledging his paternity to the young man.

Madeleine's last visit with Johnson came in 1969. They met secretly at the Shamrock Hotel in Houston. Madeleine hardly recognized Lyndon, since he was overweight, haggard, and sickly looking. He had come to mend a fence. They talked for two hours, and Madeleine cried intermittently. They had a real conversation for the very first time. Although she tried to convince him to acknowledge to Steven that he was his real father, Lyndon was unwilling to consider it because of Lady Bird and his two girls.

Today Madeleine still has fond memories of Lyndon Johnson. In 1992 she said, "He was always warm and cordial to all us ladies. He was definitely a ladies' man, but he had such strength about him and he was totally fascinating."[17] In February 1992 the *Washington Post* reported that Madeleine still loved LBJ and thought about him "all the time." Also in 1992, *A Current Affair* reported that "Madeleine Brown's scandal was one of the worst-kept secrets in Texas" and that she was "long regarded in many circles as LBJ's mistress."

PRESIDENTIAL SEX

☆ ☆ ☆

In addition to the two mistresses described above, Lyndon also had sex with numerous White House secretaries while he was president. Lyndon personally handpicked his secretaries; the number-one qualification was appearance. They had to be gorgeous. He once said, "I can't help it. I put a high mark on beauty. I can't stand an ugly woman around or a fat one who looks like a cow that's gonna set on her own udder."[18] If another of his staffers had a pretty secretary that struck his fancy, Lyndon would make her his. One example was a beautiful black woman named Geraldine "Gerry" Whittington. She originally worked in the office of Lyndon's aide, Ted Reardon, but after Johnson met Gerry, he became fond of her and had her promoted to his private secretary.

Lady Bird respected Lyndon's privacy and his need for freedom, but she also watched the woman around him with an eagle eye. She would step in the moment she sensed any trouble brewing. One attractive blond secretary who developed a significant degree of intimacy with Lyndon and other family members was quickly cut off after a rumor circulated indicating she was caught sitting in Lyndon's lap. The secretary insisted she had simply tripped over the rug when approaching the president's desk but never explained what she was doing on the wrong side of his desk in the first place.

One journalist who knew Johnson since the beginning of his congressional days likened Lyndon to the king in the movie Anna and the King of Siam. He had one head wife, Lady Bird, plus many other "babes."[19] The other babes in Johnson's harem were often found in the White House secretarial pool. Johnson's male aides quietly referred to his pool of secretaries as "the harem." Lyndon's press secretary, George Reedy, said, "He may have been just a country boy from the central hills of Texas, but he had the instincts of a Turkish sultan in Istanbul."[20]

Lyndon would make a pass at one of the White House secretaries, and if she allowed him to bed her, she would be made one of his private secretaries or assistants so that he could have regular access to her. He personally hired at least eight gorgeous young secretaries and was sleeping with all but three of them.[21]

In fact, one unnamed Secret Service man said that Lyndon became furious and blamed the Secret Service after "Lady Bird had caught him

194

screwing a secretary in the Oval Office." According to the agent, Lyndon said, "You should have done something." The agent replied, "We don't do that. That's your problem." Lyndon ordered the Secret Service to install an alarm system in the Oval Office with a buzzer placed near the elevator from the private family quarters on the second floor that led to the Oval Office. The Secret Service agents were given instructions to push the buzzer to warn him whenever "we saw Lady Bird heading for the elevator or stairs. . . ." A bell would ring in the Oval Office to give Lyndon enough time to avoid another embarrassing interruption.

The president did not restrict the location of his lovemaking with his secretaries to the White House. According to Robert M. MacMillan and D. Patrick O'Donnell, a steward and flight engineer, respectively, aboard *Air Force One,* Lyndon had sex with pretty secretaries while locked up for hours in the stateroom aboard the presidential plane, sometimes with Lady Bird aboard. He also entertained often on the presidential yacht *Sequoia* and always had an ample supply of pretty young secretaries and aides aboard. It is safe to assume that he used this location for casual sex as well.

The president did not restrict his lovemaking to women in the White House secretarial pool. According to Bill Gulley, a White House aide, Lyndon would spot pretty girls outside the White House in the crowds and send one of his aides to make a proposition on his behalf.[22] He also received regular visits from one female reporter on the staff of the former *Washington Star.* Lyndon would invite her into the Oval Office, close and lock the door, and have sex with her. After an hour or so she would leave.

Next to John F. Kennedy, Lyndon Johnson likely enjoyed the most active extramarital sex life of any American president.

☆ ☆ ☆

Lyndon suffered his first heart attack in 1955. After this crisis, Lady Bird watched over his diet and reminded him to limit his consumption of alcohol to moderate levels to preserve his health for as long as possible. He suffered a major heart attack again in 1972 and died in January 1973.

13

BILL CLINTON

The Only Sitting President Sued for Sexual Misconduct

☆

Bill Clinton is the first sitting president ever to be sued for any type of sexual misbehavior. In February 1994, Paula Corbin Jones claimed publicly that Bill had harassed her sexually nearly three years earlier at a hotel in Little Rock when he was still governor of Arkansas. Jones has contended that Clinton requested she perform oral sex. Clinton's lawyer contended the incident did not occur. This is the most recent, and perhaps most serious, allegation involving sex that Clinton has had to confront. But there have been many others in the past.

Bill Clinton was born William Jefferson Blythe IV shortly after the end of World War II. His father, William Blythe, and mother, Virginia Cassidy, had met a few years earlier at a hospital in Shreveport, Louisiana, where Virginia was studying to be a nurse. William Blythe, a car salesman from Texas, was visiting Shreveport with a friend. William and Virginia fell in love and married soon afterward. The young couple's plans to start a family had to be delayed, since William enlisted in the military for three years during the war.

After the war, the young veteran returned to the States and found a job selling steel for a company headquartered in Chicago. Since William

Bill Clinton
Forty-second President of the United States (1992–)

Biographical Information

Born: August 19, 1946
Wife: Hillary Victoria Rodham
Children: One girl

Extramarital Affairs

Suspected Sexual Partners:	Dates:	Locations:
Deborah Mathis	1970s	Little Rock, Ark.
Elizabeth Ward	1981	Little Rock
Susie Whiteacre	before 1990	Little Rock
Lencola Sullivan	1980	Little Rock; New York City
Gennifer Flowers	1977–1989	Little Rock; Dallas
Sally Perdue	1983	Little Rock
Connie Hamzy	1984	Little Rock
Bobbie Ann Williams	1984	Hot Springs, Ark.; Little Rock
Paula Corbin Jones	1991	Little Rock

Alleged Illegitimate Child: Danny Williams

spent most of his time on the road, Virginia and her husband agreed that she should move in with her parents in Hope, Arkansas. In late 1945 or early in 1946, Virginia realized that she was expecting the couple's first child. The Blythes soon became excited about the imminent birth of their first youngster. But William died when his car slid off Highway 61 late one evening near Sikeston, Missouri, a few months before his son was born. Bill Clinton would never meet his biological father.

While Virginia worked in the local hospital as a nurse-anesthetist, Bill was left in the care of his maternal grandparents. They were devout southern Baptists who believed in the value of religion and education. Bill's grandfather taught him to read at a young age and impressed upon him traditional Christian values and the importance of obtaining a good education.

Virginia Blythe married Roger Clinton in 1950, and the family moved to Hot Springs, Arkansas, in 1953. Roger owned a Buick dealership, and Virginia worked in the local hospital. In 1956, Virginia gave birth to her second son, and they named him Roger Clinton Jr., after his father. Roger Clinton Sr. adopted Bill Blythe, and at age fifteen, Bill Blythe legally changed his last name to Clinton.

Bill Clinton attended a parochial elementary school and was a good student. He earned straight A's on one report card in all academic subjects but also received a single "D" for conduct. Bill's teacher gave him the low grade to get his attention. He was so smart and competitive that he would not give the other students a chance to answer any of her questions. Bill soon calmed down and gave his classmates the opportunity to participate. But this schism between Bill's personal success and his private conduct would become a pattern in his life, repeating itself over and over again.

Roger Clinton and Virginia had a stormy and sometimes violent relationship. Roger was an alcoholic with a bad temper. He often beat Virginia and her two sons. Roger and Virginia quarreled frequently, separated, but reconciled quickly until their next fight caused another split. Bill found himself in the difficult position of protecting his mother and younger brother from Roger Clinton's beatings. Because he was the oldest child, Bill acted like the head of the home, watching over his younger brother while his mother and stepfather were at work.

Just ten years old, Bill became fascinated with the political process when he watched the Democratic National Convention in 1956 on the family's first television set. His hero, John Kennedy, battled Estes Kefauver for the vice-presidential nomination that year but lost. Kennedy fought his way back in 1960, however, to capture the Democratic party's nomination for the presidency. In 1963, after being elected as a delegate to Boys Nation, Bill visited Washington to meet John Kennedy personally and shake his hand. Bill then decided on a career in politics.

In high school Bill was elected president of the junior class and was a leader in the high school band. He played the tenor saxophone and formed a jazz trio with two other friends that became known as the Three Blind Mice. He was president of the Key Club (similar to the Kiwanis civic group), a member of the National Honor Society, and a National Merit Scholarship semifinalist. He graduated fourth in his senior class. After high school Bill matriculated at Georgetown University in the fall of 1964 to pursue a bachelor of arts degree in international government studies. Clinton financed his education by working numerous part-time jobs, including one as an aide for Sen. J. William Fulbright of Arkansas, the chairman of the powerful Senate Foreign Relations Committee.

After completing his undergraduate work, Bill applied for a Rhodes scholarship, was accepted, and was soon at Oxford University in England, where he remained for two years. He spent some time in the beautiful seaport known as Chelsea and would later name his only daughter after this lovely town. Once, while attending a lecture at Oxford given by a feminist, Germaine Greer, who was wearing a tight, sexy, rawhide skirt and lecturing about the reasons dumber men perform better in bed, Clinton approached Greer after her talk and said something like "If you ever abandoned your aversion to intelligent men, I'd be happy to help you out."[1]

Bill Clinton is a handsome man with thick wavy hair, twinkling eyes, and a sensitive mouth. His voice is calm and reassuring. He is vulnerable and often displays his emotions in public. He has been described as idealistic, tolerant, and inspirational, as well as self-indulgent, undisciplined, and imprudent.

Bill returned to the United States in 1971 and attended Yale Law School, where he first met a young law student named Hillary Victoria Rodham. Hillary was born in Chicago on October 27, 1947, to Hugh Rodham and Dorothy Howell Rodham. Hillary graduated from Wellesley College and then matriculated at Yale Law School, from which both Bill and she graduated in 1973. After graduation, Bill returned to Arkansas and took a professorship at the University of Arkansas Law School at Fayetteville. Hillary ended up working for the House Judiciary Committee. Bill loved Hillary and hoped that she would eventually come to Arkansas to be with him, but he was also afraid she would not be happy there.

In college, Hillary looked like a typical female college student of the 1960s. She had straight, stringy hair of moderate length that she pushed back behind her ears. She wore no makeup and a pair of huge, thick-rimmed glasses that gave her an unappealing but formidable intellectual look. As a young wife, she sported a shag haircut or big bushy curls. As a politician's wife she softened her look. She shed her heavy-framed glasses in favor of contact lenses, began wearing makeup, and wore her hair in a variety of stylish cuts.

Hillary was described as very intelligent, forceful, and articulate, but also as cold, intimidating, and unpopular. Some observers said that her ambition rivaled, or even exceeded, Bill's.

In 1974, Bill decided to run for a congressional seat in Arkansas' Third District. Although Bill was only twenty-seven years old, he was challenging a fifty-four-year-old incumbent Republican who was considered unbeatable. He came close to winning the election, garnering 48.5 percent of the popular vote, but was unable to unseat the incumbent. The newspapers called him the "Boy Wonder." During the campaign Hillary Rodham joined Bill on the faculty of the University of Arkansas Law School. Since Bill was in the midst of his first political campaign, Hillary volunteered to help and became his unofficial campaign manager. While Hillary managed his campaign, Bill continued to sleep with one of his congressional campaign workers.[2] Even after Bill and Hillary eventually married, rumors circulated indicating that Bill continued to womanize and frequent "sleazy clubs."

In August 1975, Bill bought a house that Hillary had casually mentioned she found attractive, and he asked her to marry him. She yielded to his proposal, and they were married at this house two months later, on October 11, 1975. Like many couples, Bill and Hillary experienced difficulties in their marriage. They have both indicated that they wanted their marriage to succeed and have worked hard at keeping it intact. For example, they jointly underwent counseling to deal with their marital difficulties.[3] Some alleged that Bill and Hillary had a marriage of convenience, or even an open marriage in which both parties knowingly tolerated each other's marital infidelity. However, both of the Clinton's have vigorously denied publicly that this was ever the case. Their marriage has been nonetheless difficult.

The Clintons' sex life may have been a contributing factor. A Clinton security guard once overheard a portion of a private quarrel between Hillary and Bill during which the guard heard Hillary say, "Bill, I need to be fucked more than twice a year." One of Bill Clinton's alleged mistresses claims that he told her that Hillary did not enjoy sex with him, that she was not playful in bed and insisted they make love only in the missionary position.[4]

Betsey Wright, Bill's campaign manager and longtime friend, confirmed that there had been a breach of adultery in their relationship when in an interview she used the following words to explain their marital difficulties: "It's not that they sit around and tolerate each other running around. It takes really hard work to heal the wounds in a relationship following infidelity."[5] Wright did not specify whether it was Bill or Hillary who had cheated. Most would assume she was referring to Bill. It is possible that both of them were unfaithful.

In 1976, Bill Clinton campaigned and won his first election—for attorney general of Arkansas. Hillary accepted a job at the Rose law firm, and the Clinton's moved to Little Rock. Bill was now on track to win the governor's election in two years, and in 1978 he defeated his Republican challenger handily, with 64.4 percent of the popular vote. Bill Clinton, at thirty-two, became the youngest governor in the nation. But his sweet political victory was short-lived. Two years later, he lost his first reelection campaign. His loss was tempered with some good news, however, since Hillary gave birth to their only child, Chelsea Victoria Clinton, earlier in February of that same year. In 1982, Bill was reelected governor, an office he retained until he ran for president ten years later. He had become the first governor of Arkansas to suffer defeat and then regain office.

It was during the time of his first heady political victory and the subsequent political defeat that Bill Clinton temporarily lost his way. Friends and associates say that after the people of Arkansas did not return him to the governor's mansion he became depressed and entered a period of semiseclusion.[6] He took a job with a law firm in Little Rock and seemed to become bitter over what he perceived as unfair treatment by the Arkansas electorate. It was during this period, too, that Bill Clinton's sexual behavior may have become irresponsible or even reckless. Rumors began to circulate that he was involved in one or more extramarital affairs. Although rumors of such indiscretions continued to circulate among members of the local press corp throughout Clinton's tenure as governor, it was not until ten years later, in 1992, that the national press formally linked Bill's name romantically to those of several women. Two years earlier, the local Arkansas press began to publish stories about Clinton's womanizing, but finding no evidence, the reporters quickly ended their written speculation.

In 1988, Bill Clinton met with his former top aide, Betsey Wright, to discuss a presidential campaign that year. Wright was very concerned about "the undercurrent," or "the question," that was certain to surface in any presidential campaign. How would Bill handle questions about rumors of extramarital affairs. According to *Washington Post* reporter and Clinton biographer David Maraniss, who won a Pulitzer Prize for his coverage of Clinton in 1992, Wright sat down with Clinton, made a list of all the women Bill had slept with and the places where these trysts occurred, and then went through them one by one to determine if the women would talk during a presidential bid and ruin Bill's hopes of winning the election. According to Maraniss, Wright confronted Clinton after she "was convinced that some state troopers were soliciting women for him and he for them."[7] When their discussion ended, Betsey recommended that Clinton postpone his tentative plan to run that year out of consideration for his wife and daughter. After the Maraniss book was published, Wright was questioned about her remarks and said, "I think David Maraniss misunderstood what I told him about the troopers."[8] Wright did not deny that she had a discussion with Bill Clinton about his extramarital affairs in 1988.

In mid-October 1990, Larry Nichols, a disgruntled ex-employee of the state of Arkansas, was fired by Bill Clinton after evidence surfaced indicating that Nichols had run up a huge telephone bill during 1988 while using state telephones to raise funds for the Nicaraguan Contras. On October 25, 1990, Nichols, who claimed he was innocent and fired unjustly, decided to file a $3.05 million lawsuit in Little Rock's U.S. District Court against Governor Clinton to get his old job back. In the lawsuit he cited libel and defamation of character and accused Clinton of misconduct in office, claiming that Bill had used a secret state slush fund containing 200 million taxpayer dollars to entertain six women with whom he was having extramarital affairs. Nichols named five women in his lawsuit and identified a sixth one only as a member of Bill's staff who "became pregnant and had an abortion" after having sex with Clinton. Years later, Nichols admitted he named the women in the lawsuit based on rumor and innuendo and that he was out to destroy Bill Clinton.[9] It's clear that Nichols' allegations could hardly be considered objective.

Although the Arkansas press briefly reported the lawsuit in the local newspapers, the five women were not named, and Bill managed to keep reports about his infidelity out of the newspapers for two weeks after the press learned about the Nichols lawsuit, until just after the November elections. At that time, John Plegge, a circuit judge Clinton appointed, sealed the legal papers for fourteen days.[10] The five women named in the Larry Nichols lawsuit were Deborah Mathis, Elizabeth Ward, Susie Whiteacre, Lencola Sullivan, and Gennifer Flowers. One reporter for the *Arkansas Democrat,* John Robert Starr, claimed in a subsequent press report to have contacted all five women and said that each one denied any involvement with Clinton. But Gennifer Flowers has stated that Starr did not talk with her and made no attempt to contact her at all.[11] Local reporters contacted the women in the lawsuit and, finding nothing of consequence, dropped the matter.

But in 1992 the rules would prove to be very different. After Bill Clinton announced his candidacy for the presidency, members of the national press swarmed like locusts all over Little Rock, devouring information and looking for anything of substance to report. They quickly discovered the Larry Nichols lawsuit, and soon their reports were making the headlines of national newspapers. A supermarket tabloid, the *Star,* was the first to reveal some of the details of Clinton's alleged extramarital affairs with the five women named in Nichols's lawsuit on January 13, 1992. Two weeks later, the *Star* published an exposé of Clinton's relationship with Gennifer Flowers, one of the five women named in the lawsuit.

☆ ☆ ☆

Deborah Mathis was a young reporter for the *Arkansas Gazette.* According to Larry Nichols, Deborah and Bill began an affair when she was in her thirties. Deborah was also a friend of another woman named in Nichols's lawsuit, Gennifer Flowers. Both women worked as reporters for KARK-TV during the late 1970s. Flowers could not confirm whether Mathis had been involved in an affair with Clinton but remembers that Bill told her to "watch out for Deborah, since she had a big mouth."[12]

Gennifer said that Deborah talked about sex all the time and mercilessly teased the male reporters who worked at KARK and who were trying to sleep with all of the women in the newsroom.

☆ ☆ ☆

Elizabeth Ward, a former beauty queen and Miss Arkansas, was also crowned the winner of the Miss America Pageant in 1981. Although Nichols gave few details of her affair with Clinton in his lawsuit, in sworn testimony he claimed that after Bill met this twenty-one-year-old beauty queen, their relationship escalated into a "shameless, red hot entente."[13] Nichols further claimed that Elizabeth was forced to leave Arkansas "because her affair with Clinton got too hot to handle."[14] When Ward appeared in *Playboy* in May 1992, Clinton's handlers quickly released a written statement issued by Ward herself that denied she had ever been involved with Bill Clinton romantically.

☆ ☆ ☆

Susie Whiteacre, the governor's press secretary, was identified as one of Clinton's lovers in Nichols's lawsuit. Nichols alleged that Bill used the Arkansas State Police to provide transportation for several surreptitious rendezvous with Susie. Susie called Nichols a liar, and her lawyer stated that the allegations made about her in the lawsuit were false.[15]

☆ ☆ ☆

In September 1980, Governor Clinton had the honor of greeting Miss Arkansas, Lencola Sullivan, a twenty-something African-American beauty queen who was returning to Arkansas from Atlantic City for a jubilant reception after taking fourth place in the Miss America Pageant. Bill greeted her publicly with a dozen roses but later also met her privately and soon began an extramarital affair that same month.[16]

After returning to Little Rock, Lencola took a job at KARK-TV, the same place where Deborah Mathis and Gennifer Flowers were working. If what Nichols and Flowers claim is true about the timing of the extramarital affairs, then Bill was sleeping with Lencola at the same time he was having an affair with Gennifer Flowers. It is likely that his alleged affair with Deborah Mathis had already ended sometime earlier in 1980, before he began the affair with Sullivan.

When Clinton learned that word of his relationship with Sullivan would soon leak out, Lencola was quickly rushed out of Little Rock to New York City without a job or even a place to stay. But she was also safely out of the reach of local reporters. However, the affair didn't end then. Nichols stated in his lawsuit: "The governor used state funds on three separate occasions to travel to New York to see Lencola."[17]

☆ ☆ ☆

Gennifer Flowers was also identified by name in the lawsuit. Nichols said that her affair with Bill Clinton took place in Gennifer's apartment. John Kaufman, manager of the Quapaw Tower, Flowers's apartment building in Little Rock, confirmed that Bill was having an affair with Gennifer. He said that Clinton visited Flowers in her apartment on ten to twenty occasions, for anywhere from one to four hours at a time, and always left his car parked in the unloading zone in front of the building.

At the time their affair began, Gennifer Flowers was an attractive, well-endowed woman with green eyes, dark brown hair, and a pleasant smile. Since that time she has dyed her hair blond, and some have said she resembles Hillary Clinton.

In her book *Gennifer Flowers: Passion and Betrayal*, Flowers disclosed many of the intimate details of her alleged twelve-year affair with Bill Clinton. This is Flowers's version of the affair:

Gennifer, twenty-seven, met Bill Clinton when she was assigned by KARK to interview the young attorney general at the local airport after he had returned from a business trip. According to Flowers, Clinton's first word to her were "Where did they get you?" Gennifer said that he looked at her in a seductive manner. On subsequent press encounters, Bill would single her out from the group of reporters, show her favoritism, give her special attention and information, and "seduce her with his eyes" as he spoke with her.

Almost at once Flowers felt the sexual vibes, energy, and tension that existed between them. After bantering for several weeks, Bill confided, "I don't know about you, but I can't stand this anymore. I just have to see you. Would you give me your phone number?"[18] Although Gennifer was ambivalent about seeing a married man, she nonetheless did it and soon found herself sleeping with Bill Clinton. During their first private meeting in Gennifer's apartment, Bill was very sensitive and a perfect gentleman. He even gave her a "sweet and gentle" good-night kiss before he left. Flowers said, "He played me like a violin that night." Although she thought he was just a sweet and loving man, later, after evaluating the situation, Gennifer decided that Bill was a master seducer and simply calculated that if he had attempted to "jump her bones" on their first date, she would have been reluctant to sleep with him.

It was during his second visit to Gennifer's apartment that they first made love. Soon after she had closed the door, Bill grabbed her and started kissing her passionately. They struggled frenetically to rip each other's clothes off and stumbled toward Flower's big four-poster bed. It was like the scene in *Fatal Attraction* where the young lawyer and his oversexed temptress just couldn't wait to consummate their newfound lust. Little did Bill realize then that Gennifer would become his near-fatal attraction. She would threaten his lifelong dream of becoming president.

Gennifer indicated that Bill was a sensitive lover and was very eager to please her even though he was "not particularly well-endowed." They made love multiple times over a two- to three-hour period, with only short breaks in between. Bill impressed Gennifer with his physical stamina. He was insatiable. She is convinced that he could have gone on making love indefinitely but almost never spent the entire night with her because he had to go home to his wife. Gennifer said that it was the "greatest sex" she ever had. Bill left his T-shirt behind so that Gennifer could have his scent nearby. She found herself falling in love with Bill. And Bill told her he loved her, too. He said, "This was the best sex he ever had."[19] Thus began an affair which she alleges lasted for twelve years.

Afterward, Gennifer had trouble keeping her mind on her reporter's job. When she would meet Bill in public, she began thinking about "how his hands felt as they caressed *her* naked skin," she said. Bill and Gennifer continued to meet each other privately either in her apartment or in a hotel (especially the Excelsior Hotel in little Rock) for sex two to three times a week during the first several months of their affair. Gennifer said they made love "all over the apartment," including in the kitchen, shower, and on the floor as well as in her bedroom.[20]

During sex Bill never offered to use a condom, and Gennifer never asked him to. She believed Bill was having sex with her exclusively during this time and thought she only had to worry about birth control. After their affair ended and news of his other sexual encounters came to light, Gennifer became concerned that he might have exposed her to some form of sexually transmitted disease, was tested for AIDS, and was found to be negative. Bill also introduced Gennifer to oral sex.[21] She said oral sex seemed very natural to Bill, and he really seemed to enjoy this form of sexual expression. There was no risk of an unwanted pregnancy, too, if they engaged in this type of sexual activity.

By December 1977, however, Flowers realized her period was late and went to a doctor to confirm her suspicion that she was pregnant. She was devastated and wondered how Bill would take the news. After telling him, she was relieved that he showed deep concern for her but also disappointed that he did not even discuss the possibility of leaving his wife for her. She realized she could only be Bill's mistress. Reluctantly, Gennifer was willing to accept her fate. Flowers contacted a local abortionist, whom she had interviewed on one of her reporting assignments, and went to the clinic and aborted Bill Clinton's baby. Bill paid for the abortion.

Bill became so brazen during the affair that he invited Gennifer to sing at the governor's mansion at a social function before a football game. Although Gennifer knew she would be entering a "danger zone," she was ready to do battle with Hillary should they happen to meet. Gennifer claims that Bill tried to convince her to have sex with him inside the men's room of the governor's mansion while she was on a break from entertaining. Gennifer had just stepped out of the women's rest room, and Bill grabbed her and started to kiss her passionately. Bill tried to maneuver her into the men's bathroom, and although she wanted to have sex with him, her judgment told her it was very foolish, so she refused. Gennifer told Bill she thought it was too risky, but he didn't care. Clinton felt he could get away with just about anything. No one saw them together caressing outside the men's room that day.

Gennifer said that since they spent so much time together, it was only natural that they developed pet names for each other and for their "private parts." Bill affectionately called Gennifer Pookie, and she called him Baby or Darling. Gennifer named her vagina Precious, and Bill referred to his penis as Willard, for "Willy," since he always liked that name. Bill referred to Gennifer's two breasts as "the girls." And Gennifer referred to Bill's testicles as "the boys." When they talked by phone, Gennifer would know that Bill was not alone if he started the conversation by asking, "How are the girls?" She would reply, "How're the boys?" When they couldn't be together, Gennifer said Bill wanted to engage in a form of vicarious phone sex. They would both masturbate while talking dirty to each other. Gennifer admits that she usually only pretended to masturbate, because she was not turned on by phone sex, as was Bill. She said it got to the point where Bill wanted to have phone sex every time he called, but after making excuses, she told him it wasn't the same for her, and they stopped doing it.

Bill encouraged Gennifer to fantasize about having sex with him when they were apart. Every time Bill passed a furniture store with a bedroom set in the window, he would fantasize about making love to Gennifer in the store window. Another one of Bill's sexual fantasies was to have sex with Gennifer on top of his desk or on the carpeting in the governor's office, with all of his staff working right outside the closed door.

Gennifer decided to surprise Bill and fulfill his sexual fantasy one day by showing up at his office wearing her fur coat with nothing on underneath but the lingerie Bill favored. Months earlier, Gennifer had surprised Bill when he came to visit at her apartment one evening. When he arrived, she was wearing a fur coat. She flung open the coat and was wearing nothing underneath but a white bustier, stockings, a furry white garter, and high heels. Bill grabbed at her and pawed at the garter as he quickly maneuvered her onto her four-poster for another evening of lovemaking. But Gennifer never made it into the governor's office wearing this outfit. She met Bill on the stairs as he was leaving his office. When he saw the fur coat, he knew instantly why she had come. Gennifer could see the look of disappointment on Bill's face, but it was too late to change his plans. She did surprise him with this same outfit, though, at another time, when he was staying at a local hotel.

Gennifer said that Bill would often buy her sexy lingerie as a gift. The state troopers who were assigned to guard Clinton confirmed that he would often slip them cash to purchase gifts of lingerie for his various girlfriends from the Victoria's Secret store in Little Rock. One time Bill asked Gennifer to wear a short skirt with no underwear and sit opposite him, crossing and uncrossing her legs like the character actress Sharon Stone portrayed in the movie *Basic Instinct*. Gennifer said that this occurred before the movie was released and gave Bill credit for the idea after reading about it in a magazine. According to Flowers, Bill was very innovative and constantly looking for new ways to heighten their sexual pleasure. He suggested that he drip water from melting ice on her naked body to arouse her before making love. Gennifer said they "reached a climax beyond anything we'd ever experienced together."

On another occasion, Bill returned from the kitchen with an assortment of condiments. He slowly squeezed a bear-shaped plastic bottle, and the honey dripped all over Gennifer's naked body.[22] Next, he gave her a sensual massage, rubbing the honey all over her face, neck, shoulders, breasts, and the rest of her body. She was blindfolded and had to guess which condiment he would rub on her body next. He poured a little juice in her mouth until it overflowed and ran down all over her nude body. She loved it! Soon they were both so excited they had to consummate this erotic experience in Pookie's big four-poster double bed. She pulled Bill down on top of her, and they made passionate love.

Over time, Bill's suggestions got wilder. He suggested that Gennifer drip hot wax from a candle all over his body as a prelude to lovemaking, but she got scared and refused. But she did agree to spank Bill during their foreplay, and he enjoyed it. On another occasion he suggested that he tie Gennifer to her bed. When she refused, he asked if she would tie him to the bed. Gennifer thought it was a great idea. She teased and taunted him until he couldn't stand it any longer, and then they made love. They both enjoyed it so much that they tried it several more times. Bill also once asked her to use a vibrator on him. Like John Kennedy, his hero and predecessor, Bill even suggested that he set up a *ménage-à-trois* encounter among himself, Gennifer, and another girl. She refused, finding it "repugnant" and "too kinky." He apologized and never suggested it again.

Gennifer also claimed that Bill smoked marijuana on numerous occasions when he came to her apartment. She added: "He did inhale." She also said he confided in her that he had used cocaine, although she admits he never used it in her presence.

On one occasion Bill interrupted their lovemaking when he jumped out of bed and began to cry and shake uncontrollably. Gennifer tried to get him to tell her what was the matter, but he stood there as if in a trance, refusing to speak. Eventually, she helped calm him down and convinced him return to bed for more lovemaking. Afterward, Flowers reflected on what might have caused Bill's unexplained behavior. Perhaps he had been overcome with grief because he was committing adultery. Clearly, Bill believed adultery was wrong, for he once told Trooper Patterson that he had researched the topic of oral sex in the Bible and decided that "oral sex isn't considered adultery." This may explain his preference for this form of sex. Perhaps it is also why Clinton introduced Flowers to oral sex and allegedly performed it with so many other women. He could justify it in his own mind because he was convinced the Bible didn't consider oral sex adultery.

In 1989, after twelve years together, Gennifer Flowers ended her affair with Bill Clinton. She had met a man named Finis Shelnutt, thought there was a chance for happiness with him, and wanting to be more than a married man's mistress, decided it was time to end the affair. After making love to Bill one last time, she held him close to her on her couch and explained that she had found someone special that she cared for deeply. Bill was quiet and speechless. Tears streamed down his face. Gennifer wept, too. After composing himself, Bill told her he understood and wanted her to do what she needed to do. But he added, "If you ever change your mind and you ever want me to come back, all you have to do is call me."[23]

After news of the Larry Nichols lawsuit was printed in the local newspapers in 1990 and Gennifer was named as one of Bill Clinton's lovers, she began to panic. Reporters began calling and leaving messages for her at work and on the answering machine in her apartment. They also began to wait outside the hotels where she sang in the evening to supplement her income, hoping to obtain an interview. The hotel managers were spooked, and one did not renew a booking she had been expecting. Gennifer began to worry about the long-term effect the publicity would have on her singing career and on the state job that Bill helped her obtain.

When she asked Bill about the reports of his affairs with the other women named in Nichols's lawsuit, he innocently explained away all of the accusations about each of the women except those about Deborah Mathis. His silence about Deborah made Gennifer believe that Bill did have an affair with Mathis. Gennifer worried that she needed to protect herself and began to audiotape her telephone conversations with Bill Clinton without his knowledge. Friends that knew about her affair with Bill had been encouraging her to tape their conversations for some time in case anything went wrong. So in December 1990, and in again in 1991 and 1992, she called Bill and used her tape machine to silently record several of their conversations. Bill suspected nothing. The tapes would lend credence to her allegations of an extramarital affair and certainly proved that she and Clinton were more than casual acquaintances.

A radio station in Little Rock, KBIS-AM, obtained a copy of the lawsuit and read it on the air. When Gennifer told Bill about this, he suggested that she contact her lawyer and have him write a letter to the disk jockey threatening a lawsuit if he did not stop broadcasting such accusations. The broadcasts ceased. Years later, Bill Clinton's handlers cited the letter to demonstrate that Flowers kept changing her story. They tried to convince the American public that Flowers had changed her story for money. Perhaps she did. Since Flowers had accepted a large payment to tell her story, this certainly is one way the events could be interpreted.

Soon after Bill announced his candidacy for the presidency of the United States on the steps of the Old Statehouse in Little Rock in October 1991, Gennifer claims Ron Fuller, an Arkansas legislator with the Republican party, who was working with the George Bush reelection campaign, phoned her. Fuller said he had some "friends in the Republican party" that would give her "$50,000 and a job in California" if she would just admit publicly that she had an affair with Bill Clinton. Gennifer refused, for she considered her personal relationship with Bill was nobody else's business. She also did not want to be used for political purposes. Fuller, of course, denied that he ever made any such offer. When Gennifer told Bill about Fuller's phone call, she claims he asked her to sign an affidavit indicating that the Republican party made her this offer so he could use it to embarrass them if they tried to pull any other dirty tricks. Gennifer was apprehensive about signing a legal document and demurred until Bill forgot about the idea.

On January 13, 1992, a supermarket tabloid, the *Star*, appeared on the newsstands. The feature story (dated January 28, 1992) accused Bill Clinton of affairs with five women. The headline and first few sentences read:

Former Aide Charges in Court: Dem Front-Runner Had Affair With Miss America.
Bill Clinton, the Democrat's leading candidate for the White House had a hot affair with a former Miss America and at least four other women. These are stunning charges made in a lawsuit against the married Arkansas governor that could scuttle his presidential ambitions.[24]

Clinton labeled these press accounts "rehashed lies."

Before the *Star* published the story, its managing editor, Dick Kaplan, obtained Gennifer Flower's unlisted phone number and left the following recording on her answering machine: "I think you should know we are going to print an article about what we know of your relationship with Bill Clinton, and we would like to talk to you about it. We also have photographs of you."[25]

Gennifer contacted her attorney, Blake Hendrix, who called Dick Kaplan and, after speaking with him, advised Gennifer to go to New York to meet Kaplan. After reviewing advanced copies of the article, she realized she could not prevent the *Star* from publishing the story. Much of the information came from the Nichols lawsuit, which was now a matter of public record. Believing she had no alternative, Gennifer agreed to corroborate the story if they would pay her enough money to leave Arkansas and hide out until the fallout had dissipated.

Two weeks later, in the February 4, 1992, edition of the *Star,* a more detailed account of Gennifer Flowers's affair with the former governor was published. A few weeks before the story appeared, there were rumors that Flowers would talk to the press. Trooper Patterson overheard Clinton refer to Flowers as a "fucking slut" and say, "What does that whore think she's doing to me?"[26] The Clinton handlers were panicked when they heard that Flowers was about to go public. Since they felt the story would come out eventually, they developed a strategy to steer Flowers toward a trashy tabloid magazine. The Clinton handlers were relieved to discover that the *Star* was working on the story and, through the use of local contacts in Little Rock, helped to arrange a meeting between *Star* reporter Steve Edward and Gennifer Flowers. In fact, when Clinton confidante Dee Dee Myers heard that the *Star* would publish Flower's story, she said: "Who the hell pays mind to what that trashy supermarket tabloid prints! Let them run it . . . we'll tell them that it's all garbage."[27]

The second *Star* article came out when Clinton was campaigning in New Hampshire. He denied the charges, saying, "The allegations in the *Star* are not true." Hillary also came to her husband's aid to quickly transfer the attention from her husband's scandalous behavior to the accuser's motives when she said to Jane Fullerton, a reporter for the *Arkansas Democrat-Gazette*:

> It's really unfortunate that political opponents of Bill's . . . didn't make charges against him. The people of Arkansas didn't believe them. All of the people [the women named as having had illicit relationships with Clinton], including that woman [Flowers], have denied this many, many times. I'm not going to speculate on her motive. We know she was paid.[28]

In this press interview Hillary then claimed that Flowers's motive was money. When the *Star* questioned Clinton about charges that he conspired with Flowers to cover up their affair and advised her to lie if she was asked by reporters about their alleged twelve-year relationship, Bill denied Gennifer's claims by saying, "The allegations are not true. She's obviously taken money to change her story."[29]

In fact, Flowers did take a lot of money. The *Star* paid her a six-figure fee (somewhere between $100,000 and $150,000) to corroborate their story. This fact certainly created the appearance that Flowers's main interest was money. However, she maintains that the *Star* intended to publish their story with or without her, and at that time she quickly decided that one of her goals should be financial security. Therefore, she agreed to an interview. Although the financial motive certainly taints' Flowers's testimony, it does not invalidate it. Her mother, Mary, corroborated her story, and Gennifer's roommate, Lauren Kirk, stated, "There can be no doubt that she and Bill Clinton had sex with one another."[30]

The Clintons appeared on the television program *60 minutes* in January 1992, directly after the Super Bowl. They knew millions of Americans would be watching TV and wanted to project the image of a loving couple who admitted to trouble once in their marriage but to confirm now that their marriage was solid and secure. When asked if he knew Gennifer Flowers, Clinton labeled her just "a friendly acquaintance." During this interview Hillary explained why she had decided to come

on national television and sit beside her husband, who had just been accused by his alleged mistress of having a twelve-year affair with her.
Hillary said:

> I'm not sitting here because I'm some little woman standing by my man,
> like Tammy Wynette. I'm sitting here because I love him and I respect
> him and I honor what he's been through and what we've been through
> together. And you know, if that's not enough for people, then heck, don't
> vote for him.[31]

Her comments may have convinced many Americans that if she had forgiven Bill for "causing pain" in their marriage, then so could the voters.
The jab toward Tammy Wynette offended Wynette deeply, and Hillary
issued a halfhearted apology, saying, " I didn't mean to hurt Tammy as
a person. I happen to enjoy country music."[32] The Clintons were successful at convincing the American public they were a wholesome and
happy couple with a solid marriage. But to those closest to them for ten
years, their security guards in Arkansas, the Clinton's marriage was more
like a political partnership or business arrangement. During the now-famous 60 Minutes interview, when CBS newsman Steve Kroft referred to
the Clintons' marriage as an "arrangement," Bill Clinton reacted sharply
and said: "Wait a minute. You're looking at two people who love each
other. This is not an arrangement or an understanding. This is a marriage."[33]

Gennifer watched the 60 Minutes interview propped up in bed with
the flu. She felt betrayed after Bill Clinton appeared to deny their twelve-
year affair and make her out to be liar. She felt "devastated" and "hit
rock bottom." Did Bill Clinton really deny he had an affair in front of
millions of Americans on 60 Minutes? Let's look at the crucial point in
the interview and see what he actually said.

> STEVE KROFT: She [Gennifer Flowers] is alleging and has described in
> some detail in a supermarket tabloid what she calls a twelve-year affair
> with you.
> BILL CLINTON: That allegation is false.
> STEVE KROFT: I am assuming from your answer that you're categorically
> denying that you ever had an affair with Gennifer Flowers.
> BILL CLINTON: I've said that before, and so has she.

It would appear on the surface that Clinton denied the charges of an affair with Flowers, but he did not actually make any denial when you look closely at his responses to Steve Kroft's statements. When asked if he had a twelve-year affair with Flowers, Clinton said the allegation was false. This may have been because the affair lasted a little bit less than, or longer than, twelve years, giving Clinton the right to claim that the allegation was not true. When asked if his response meant he was categorically denying he ever had an affair with Flowers, Clinton responded, "I've said that before . . . ," implying that he had categorically denied this charge at some time in the past. So he did not actually deny the affair in front of the millions of Americans watching 60 Minutes that Sunday evening. But Clinton did manage to shift the focus away from his own denial to Flowers's denial of the affair by the second part of his response, ". . . and so has she." Clinton was probably referring to the letter Flowers's lawyer sent to the Arkansas radio station that threatened a lawsuit if he continued broadcasting information in the Nichols lawsuit about Flowers. According to Flowers, Clinton advised her to send that letter to help him cover his tracks.

Immediately after the show ended, the Star contacted Gennifer and said that she had to hold a press conference to answer questions and establish her credibility. The next day, she was riding in a limousine to the Waldorf-Astoria Hotel in New York to face the press. Gennifer read a prepared statement, played an excerpt from one of her taped phone conversations with Bill Clinton, and answered questions.

Flowers has continued to capitalize on her notoriety and give interviews to magazines and television reporters that have brought in some hefty payments. She was interviewed by Maureen O'Boyle of the television tabloid magazine A Current Affair. Another interview was published in Spectrum Weekly magazine. She even dressed up like Marilyn Monroe and sang a campy rendition of "Happy Birthday, Mr. President" for television's Comedy Central, mimicking Monroe's performance at President Kennedy's gala birthday celebration thirty years earlier.

In the summer of 1992, Gennifer Flowers agreed to do a Penthouse photo exposé and interview; it was published in the December issue that year. Flowers claims she did the interview because she had assurances from the magazine's publisher, Bob Guccione, that she would finally have

BILL CLINTON

an opportunity to tell her side of the story. Guccione estimated she could possibly earn $5–10 million for her story and photo layout. Since it was consistent with her goals of strong publicity for personal and financial security, Flowers agreed. However, there was a stipulation: Flowers would have the right to approve the final written copy before the article was published. This was never done. Instead, Bill Clinton was given an advance copy of the article and the opportunity to deny Flowers's version of the facts. Although Flowers was angry and considered a lawsuit against *Penthouse,* she knew that it would be tied up for years in the courts and decided it was not worth the effort.

In May 1994, Gennifer offered a sixty-minute audiocassette tape of her conversations with Bill Clinton, a transcript of the conversations so it would be easier for the listeners to follow along, and a booklet entitled *Setting the Record Straight.* You could even order this information by dialing a toll-free 800 number. She also claimed to have a letter from Bill Clinton that would answer once and for all the question of whether they ever had an affair.

Whatever her motives, there can be little doubt that there is a significant amount of evidence to corroborate Flowers's story. Four Arkansas state troopers came forward with stories that supported her allegations. For example, the troopers confirmed that they took hundred of calls from her for Clinton. If Hillary was home at the governor's mansion when she called, they had been instructed to buzz the governor on the intercom. Bill would come down to the security guardhouse to use a private outside telephone line so that he could talk to Gennifer without fear that Hillary might accidentally pick up the phone and catch him chatting with his mistress.[34] The troopers also stated that they regularly took Clinton to Flowers's apartment. Even though Clinton told them he was visiting a state official in the same apartment building, they knew what he was doing. Like Lyndon B. Johnson, Bill Clinton liked to brag about his sexual prowess. The troopers also confirmed Gennifer's allegation that Bill Clinton used his influence to obtain employment for her; they overheard him call Bill Gaddy, the director of the Arkansas Employment Security Division, and ask him to find her a state job.

☆ ☆ ☆

Although Hillary Clinton thought it unfortunate that Bill's political opponents would make accusations against her husband for political and financial gain, she did not hesitate to sling similar charges toward her husband's Republican rival, George Bush. In the May 1992 issue of *Vanity Fair*, contributing editor Gail Sheehy quoted Hillary under the following headline:

Mrs. Clinton Spreads Rumor About Bush's Girlfriend
Hillary Goes Tabloid
I had tea with Anne Cox Chambers and she's sittin' there in her sunroom saying, "You know I just don't understand why they think they can get away with this—everybody knows about George Bush." And then Chambers launches into this long description of, you know, Bush and his carrying on, all of which is apparently well known in Washington. But I'm convinced part of it is that the Establishment—regardless of party— sticks together. They're gonna circle the wagons on Jennifer [Fitzgerald] and all these other people.[35]

Hillary was referring to a rumor that had plagued the Bush campaign in 1988, and now she was bringing it to the forefront of the news again. This comment was probably a clever political strategy on her part. It certainly shifted some of the media's emphasis about her own husband's character to the sexual behavior of his Republican opponent. Then again, she could have just been speaking out of frustration because of all of the attacks that her family had experienced.

Whatever Hillary's motive, the press latched on to this statement, and three months later, in August 1992, the *New York Post*, a daily newspaper, published an article about Bush's alleged one-night stand with a woman named Jennifer Fitzgerald. Jennifer with a "J," as she soon became known, was a top Bush aide when he became vice president in 1980. She accompanied him to the Nuclear Disarmament Talks in Geneva in 1984. She was fifty-one years old at the time and bore an astonishing resemblance to the president's wife, Barbara.

The *Post* story was prompted by a footnote in a book that had just been published by Susan Trento called *The Power House*. Trento's husband, Joe, when working as a CNN reporter, had interviewed U.S. ambassador Louis Fields in 1986. Fields, who died in 1988, had allegedly told Joe Trento that "he had arranged for Mr. Bush and Ms. Fitzgerald to use a guest house during an official visit that Mr. Bush made to the talks in 1984."[36] Fields also said, "It became very clear to me that the vice president and Ms. Fitzgerald were romantically involved. It made me very uncomfortable," but "he did not say he had firsthand knowledge of an affair" between Bush and Fitzgerald. Joe Trento recorded the interview with Fields on his tape recorder but did not produce the tapes for voice corroboration at the time his wife's book reopened the question. *Newsweek* magazine listened to audiotapes of the Fields interview but considered the remarks "ambiguous."

After the *Post* article was released, during a live news conference in Kennebunkport, Maine, CNN correspondent Mary Tillotson asked President Bush, with Prime Minister Yitzhak Rabin of Israel standing by his side, about the *Post's* reports of his alleged affair. Bush replied angrily:

> I'm not going to take any sleazy questions like that from CNN. I am very disappointed that you would ask such a question of me, and I will not respond to it. I haven't responded in the past and I think it's an outrage![37]
>
> In this kind of screwy climate that we're in, why, I expect it. But, I don't like it and I'm not going to respond other than to say it's a lie.[38]

Bush spokesman Marlin Fitzwater said that Mary Tillotson "will never work around the White House again."

Jennifer Fitzgerald denied the rumors to then *Gannett News Service* reporter Ann Devroy some time in the early 1980s, when it first surfaced. Fitzgerald was last reported to be working as a deputy chief of protocol at the State Department.

Previously, both the *Washington Post* and the *Los Angeles Times* investigated the rumor but could not find any corroborating evidence. In the July-August 1992 edition of *Spy* magazine, Joe Conason published an article charging Bush with multiple "extramarital dalliances" and said a mysterious reporter, identified only as "Ms. X," had claimed she "had an affair with Bush while he was running for president in 1980."[39]

☆ ☆ ☆

On December 20, 1993, the stories of two Arkansas state troopers, Larry Patterson and Roger Perry, were released. They alleged that two of their official duties included helping to facilitate and then cover up then governor Bill Clinton's extramarital affairs during the period from the late 1980s until just before President-elect Clinton left for Washington in January 1993. In an interview with David Brock that was published in the conservative magazine the *American Spectator*, Brock described what the troopers meant when they said that their official duties included facilitating Clinton's extramarital affairs:

> This meant that, on the state payroll and using state time, vehicles, and resources, they were instructed by Clinton on a regular basis to approach women and to solicit their telephone numbers for the governor; to drive him in state vehicles to rendezvous points and guard him during sexual encounters; to secure hotel rooms and other meeting places for sex; to lend Clinton their state cars so he could slip away and visit women unnoticed; to deliver gifts from Clinton to various women (some of whom, like Flowers, also had state jobs); and to help Clinton cover up his activities by keeping tabs on Hillary's whereabouts and lying to Hillary about her husband's whereabouts.[40]

The troopers said Clinton had about six "steady girlfriends whom he saw two or three times a week."[41] Brock said that the troopers confided in him the names of these woman and that he contacted them personally. All of the women either denied involvement with Clinton or responded with "no comment" to his queries.

The troopers also alleged that Bill would entertain women at all hours of the night. Like Lyndon Johnson, Bill had a system worked out with the state troopers; they would call him if Hillary returned to the governor's mansion unexpectedly to prevent him from getting caught in the act.[42] And like former President John F. Kennedy, Bill Clinton liked the chase more than the kill. Gennifer Flowers believed this about Bill when she wrote, "I think Bill was addicted to the chase, not the sex act itself, but the actual conquering of all those women."[43]

Two other troopers corroborated these accusations but did not wish to be named in the initial press reports. (The names of the two troopers who wished to remain anonymous eventually became known. They were Danny Ferguson and Ronnie Anderson.) When asked why they waited until December 1993 to come out with their shocking accusations, Perry, aged forty-three, said that he believed that Clinton's sexual conduct was a "matter of national security" and that he did not come forward sooner because he did not believe Clinton would be elected president. Later, Perry added: "The American people should know the true color of the man. He is reckless. He likes flirting with disaster."[44] Immediately, Bruce Lindsey, a White House aide and Clinton confidant, issued a statement saying: "The allegations are ridiculous." But he did not deny they were true.

The next day, just before Christmas, on December 21, 1993, during an interview with an AP reporter at the White House, Hillary was asked about the state troopers' allegations that they had helped Bill conceal his extramarital affairs and then lied to protect him. Hillary branded the allegations "outrageous," but she did not deny them. Look carefully at her words:

> I find it not an accident that every time he [Bill Clinton] is on the verge of fulfilling his commitment to the American people and they respond . . . out comes yet a new round of these outrageous, terrible stories that people plant for political and financial reasons. For me, it's pretty sad that we're still subjected to these kinds of attacks for political and financial gain from people, and that it is sad—especially here in the Christmas season—people for their own purposes would be attacking my family.[45]

Hillary did not describe the trooper's reports as untrue but as "outrageous, terrible stories." She sought to shift the focus from the actual charges to the motives of those who would bring them.

In December 1993 a reporter confronted Clinton about his extramarital affairs when he was still governor of Arkansas after several members of his security detail admitted to the press that they helped arrange sexual encounters for Clinton and were offered federal jobs to prevent them from going public with their stories. Clinton stammered for ten seconds or more, then he responded:

> I have nothing else to say. . . . We . . . we did, if, the, the, I, I the stories are just as they have been said. They're outrageous and they're not so." Then recovering a bit, he added, "We have not done anything wrong. The allegations on abuse of the state or the federal positions I have they're just not true.[46]

Raymond L. "Buddy" Young, who headed Clinton's security contingent for ten years, was given a job as a regional director with the Federal Emergency Management Agency (FEMA), with an annual salary of between $92,300 and $120,000 after Clinton was elected president. Both Roger Perry and Larry Patterson agreed that Clinton, or one of his emissaries, had offered them federal jobs in return for their silence.

In December 1993, another state trooper, Danny Ferguson, in an audiotaped interview with several *Los Angeles Times* reporters, said Clinton had asked him whether he was interested in one of two federal jobs, either as a regional head of the FEMA or as a U.S. marshal. Soon after Ferguson made these remarks, Betsey Wright, Clinton's former top aide, now working as a political consultant in a Washington-based firm, "volunteered" to visit Little Rock to "urge State Trooper Danny Ferguson to back away from his statement that Mr. Clinton offered federal jobs to discourage them from speaking out about his actions as governor."[47]

The schism between Bill Clinton's personal success and private conduct was growing wider. In January 1994 a joint *Washington Post*–ABC News poll gave Clinton a favorable rating of 60 percent, but a week earlier a *Wall Street Journal*–ABC New poll indicated that "only 33 percent of Americans gave him good marks for his ethical and moral values, down from 50 percent a year ago."

In the April-May edition of the *American Spectator*, another Arkansas state trooper, L. D. Brown, who guarded the Clintons from late 1982 until 1985, further corroborated the accounts of the four troopers who came forward in December 1993. He, too, claimed that on state time and using state cars, he transported Bill Clinton to, and guarded him during, "extramarital trysts." Brown estimated he solicited over a hundred sexual partners for Clinton and helped hide his extramarital activities from Hillary.

In 1984, Brown accompanied Clinton when he attended an Arkansas-SMU football game in Irving, Texas. After the game, Clinton went to a strip joint near the stadium and was shoving money in the dancer's G-strings. Brown also recalled another trip when he accompanied Clinton to a disco in Boca Raton, Florida. He solicited a girl for Clinton and watched from a distance of ninety feet as she performed oral sex on Bill in a parked car.

It is doubtful that all five of the state troopers are lying, but all did have a falling out with Clinton and had an ax to grind.

☆ ☆ ☆

In July 1992, Sally Perdue, a beauty queen and former Miss Arkansas, admitted to the studio audience of the *Sally Jesse Raphael* show, that she had an affair with Bill Clinton nearly ten years earlier. Perdue first met Clinton in 1973, when she was a journalist with Little Rock's Public Broadcast Service (PBS) television station. Despite a mutual attraction, Sally and Bill did not become involved romantically until August 1983 when she invited the governor to her condominium in Little Rock to enlist his aid for the creation of a railroad historical society. Sally said they slept together that first night and began an affair that she described as "fun and games." She said Bill's driver would drop him off, and he would sneak in through a back entrance to her condo to have sex with her for one to three hours at time. He would never stay all night. Like Gennifer Flowers, Perdue also claimed that Bill Clinton smoked marijuana when he had sex with her because he claimed it "enhanced his sexual pleasure."[48]

Sally admitted that she knew Bill was married, and she took full responsibility for the affair; it did not bother her that he was a married man, since she considered their three-month relationship an "affair of the moment." The affair ended after Bill was critical of her plans to run for mayor of Pine Bluff, Arkansas, telling her she would get killed in the primary election. Although the *Sally Jesse Raphael* show was taped before a live audience, the programming was never aired; a rerun was substituted just before airtime.

There is some trouble with the facts associated with Perdue's account of their affair. She claimed to have met Bill in 1973 when she was a reporter spending much time around the legislators in the Arkansas state senate. In 1973, however, Bill was teaching law in Fayetteville and would not have been spending much time in the senate. These two events are not necessarily in conflict, though, since she could have met Bill on a chance visit he made to the statehouse, even though he did not spend a large amount of time there.

But Ambrose Evans-Pritchard, the Washington, D.C., correspondent for London's *Sunday Telegraph*, published an interview with Perdue in his paper in January 1994 in which Perdue, now fifty-five, alleged that a Clinton intermediary from the Democratic party offered her a "job in exchange for her silence during the 1992 campaign." She also said that the intermediary warned her that "he couldn't guarantee what would happen to my pretty little legs" if she turned down his offer.[49]

Arkansas state trooper L. D. Brown, told the *American Spectator* that Bill Clinton mentioned to him that he "had an affair, a liaison" with Sally Perdue.[50]

☆ ☆ ☆

Connie Hamzy, a groupie who allegedly had sex with hundreds of rock-and-roll musicians, also described a bizarre sexual encounter with Bill Clinton that supposedly took place on August 31, 1984. According to Connie, she was sunning herself in a skimpy bikini beside the swimming pool at the Riverton Hilton Hotel in Little Rock when Bill sent one of his aides to request a meeting with her. Connie said she could not meet the governor in her "teensy-weensy purple bikini," but the governor's aide just laughed and said, "I'm sure that's fine with him," then, "That's why he wants to meet you."

After following the aide into the hotel, Bill dismissed his aides so that he and Connie could be alone. According to Connie, Bill said, "You looked so good lying out there by the pool that I just had to meet you. You really made my day."[51] Then he added, "I'd love to get with you. Where can we go?"[52] Although Connie suggested that Bill have one of his aides book a room for the two of them under an assumed named, he said he didn't have time, so they quickly walked down the hall fondling each other while looking for an empty room where they could have sex. Either most of the doors were locked or there were people inside the rooms, so they did not find a place to consummate their encounter. Bill allegedly kissed Connie and said goodbye after promising to try to return later.

Bill Clinton's handlers described the brief encounter with Connie Hamzy very differently. His press secretary issued the following rebuttal to Connie's account of their meeting which had been published in *Penthouse* magazine:

> The allegations published in *Penthouse* are baseless and malicious lies. As three witnesses traveling with the governor on the date in question

have stated, Ms. Hamzy introduced herself to the governor and accosted him in the lobby of the North Little Rock Hilton as he was leaving a lunch time speaking engagement. Governor Clinton rebuffed the advance and promptly left the hotel.[53]

One of Bill's traveling companions that day was legislator Jimmie Don McKissack, who claimed Connie had pulled down her bikini top, propositioned the governor, and then reached for his groin while Bill turned red from embarrassment. But when Connie heard that Bill had claimed she had initiated their meeting, she responded: "That's just ridiculous. First of all, I didn't even know he was in the hotel. Besides, I'm a rock groupie. Politicians are not my thing. But I have to admit, I was willing to do him when he asked me."[54]

☆ ☆ ☆

In 1984, Bill may have had a sexual escapade with a trio of prostitutes in Little Rock's "Hooker's Row." Bobbie Ann Williams, then a twenty-four-year-old prostitute, worked the corner of Seventeenth and Main streets. Williams said that she was paid $200 to perform oral sex on Clinton and that she she arranged for an orgy after Clinton offered to pay each of the participants $400 apiece. Williams also alleged that she had late-night sex with Clinton at the Holiday Inn in Little Rock on numerous occasions and that Clinton was the father of her light-complexioned, ten-year-old mulatto son, Danny.[55]

☆ ☆ ☆

State trooper Larry G. Patterson, once a member of Governor Clinton's security detail, claimed that Bill Clinton had other long-term mistresses, including "a staffer in Clinton's office, an Arkansas lawyer Clinton appointed to a judgeship, the wife of a prominent judge, a local reporter, an employee at Arkansas Power and Light (AP&L) . . . and the cosmetic sales clerk at the Little Rock department store."

Patterson signed an affidavit stating that he drove Clinton to the parking lot of Booker Elementary School, where Bill's daughter, Chelsea, went to school, to rendezvous with a "sales clerk from a local department store." Next, Patterson claimed: "I could see Clinton get into the front seat and then the lady's head go into his lap. They stayed in the car for 30 to 40 minutes."[56]

On another occasion, the department store clerk drove her yellow-and-black Datsun (or Nissan) pickup truck to the parking lot of the governor mansion, and Bill got inside. Trooper Patterson claimed that he used one of the mansion's security cameras to watch this woman perform oral sex on Clinton on his twenty-seven-inch monitor in the guard house. While Patterson watched the governor and the clerk, he noticed another vehicle approaching their truck. It was Chelsea's baby-sitter, Melissa Jolley. Patterson intercepted Jolley and quickly made up a story about some security problem on the grounds and sent her to her destination by another route. After Clinton was finished having sex, he jogged over to the guardhouse and asked, "Did she see us? Did she see us?" When the trooper explained how he diverted her away from the truck, Clinton responded with "Atta boy."

Another one of Clinton's girlfriends continued to see him right up until he left Little Rock for Washington on January 16, 1993. She would meet him along his jogging route, pick him up in her car, and then later would drop him back off on his route. Although Bill claimed to have jogged several miles, Trooper Perry told him, "Governor, you better see a doctor. There's something wrong with your sweat glands." After this, Bill began stopping in the troopers' bathroom to "splash water on his face and shirt" before returning to the governor's mansion to give the impression he had worked up a sweat after jogging for several miles.[57]

Douglas Frantz and William Rempel, two reporters with the *Los Angeles Times,* wrote that Governor Clinton had called one of his girlfriends, who worked for Arkansas Power and Light, fifty-nine times over a two-year period, calling her elelven times on July 16, 1989, and in August 1989 spent ninety-four minutes on the phone with her after midnight.[58] Roger Perry stated that President-elect Clinton sneaked this woman into the governor's mansion on at least three separate occasions—one time at 5:15 A.M. One trooper escorted her through the basement of the governor's mansion into the game room, where Bill was already waiting for her. He instructed the trooper to stand guard outside the game-room door and warn him if Hillary should awake and come looking for him.[59] When confronted about her actions by reporters from the *Los Angeles Times,* the woman claimed she had done nothing wrong and denied having sex with Clinton.

☆ ☆ ☆

Paula Corbin Jones also had a steamy tale to tell about Bill Clinton. In February 1994, Jones made her charges public at a press conference in Washington, held during a meeting of the Conservative Political Action Conference. Little Rock lawyer and Clinton adversary Cliff Jackson brought her to the conference.[60]

Although Paula maintains that she did not have sex with Clinton, she decided to come forward and charge him with "severe emotional distress, deprivation of civil rights, and defamation of character" and sue him for $700,000 after Danny Ferguson implied in both the *Los Angeles Times* and *American Spectator* articles that she had sex with the governor after being summoned to his room in Little Rock's Excelsior Hotel on May 8, 1991. Then twenty-four years old, she allegedly told Ferguson that she was "available to be Clinton's regular girlfriend" if he wanted her. Jones maintains that she did not speak to Ferguson after leaving Clinton's room.

Clinton had asked Ferguson to arrange for a room so that he and Paula could meet privately after telling Ferguson that Paula had "that come-hither look." Ferguson told the hotel that Clinton was expecting a call from the White House so that they would allow Clinton temporary use of the room. Although Ferguson did not know what went on inside the room, he says that he stood guard outside the door until Paula emerged.

According to Paula, Ferguson summoned her from her post behind a registration table in the hotel during the Third Annual Governor's Quality Management Conference to discuss the duties and responsibilities of a better state job for which she had applied. Trusting Clinton, Paula made her way into Clinton's suite, where they chatted until Bill began to make unwanted sexual advances. It's difficult to believe that Jones thought only that Clinton wanted to discuss job prospects, since she testified in her lawsuit that Ferguson said, "The governor said you make his knees knock," and then returned a few minutes later with a slip of paper containing the number of Clinton's hotel room.

Ferguson escorted her to Clinton's room, and she went inside alone. After a few minutes of idle chatter, Clinton told Paula, "I love the way your hair flows down your back," and, "I love your curves." According to Jones, Bill first held her hand and began to loosen his tie. He tried to pull Paula closer to him, but she backed away from him. Clinton then tried to move closer to Paula. She pulled back a second and third time, after which Bill allegedly tried to slide his hand along her leg, and up her thigh, and under her culottes while trying to kiss her on the neck at the same time. Paula pushed him away, stood up, and demanded to know what he was doing. Then Bill unzipped his fly, dropped his pants and underwear, and asked her to "kiss it," referring to his erect penis. Paula refused his request, told him she wasn't that type of girl, and said she had to go. Then Bill supposedly said, "Well, I don't want to make you do anything you don't want to do," while fondling his penis as he spoke. Next, Bill stood up, zipped up his pants, and before she left, said, "You are smart. Let's keep this between ourselves." Paula told reporters from the *Washington Post*, "I'll never forget the look on his face. His face was just red, beet red."[61]

Paula claims she can prove her allegations, since "there were distinguishing characteristics in Clinton's genital area." After leaving the governor's private room only fifteen to twenty minutes after she had entered it, she fled back to her post and told a coworker, Pamela Blackard, that the governor had just made several unwanted sexual advances toward her which she rebuffed. Paula told her longtime friend Debra Ballentine about the traumatic meeting later that same day. She also told her mother and two sisters what had happened. Paula's younger sister said that Paula seemed traumatized by the experience.

But her older sister, Charlotte Brown, said Paula seemed rather "flattered" and amused by the events and confided that "whichever way it went, it smelled of money." This testimony created the perception that Paula was only interested in financial gain. However, Charlotte's story may be tainted. Her husband ran a honky-tonk nightclub that Clinton frequented on numerous occasions, and he may have influenced his wife's story to help protect the governor and ensure his continued patronage.

Paula has offered to donate any money received from the lawsuit to charity to prove that she is more interested in "restoring her reputation" than in profiting from her alleged encounter with Bill Clinton.[62] However, others are quick to remark that she stands to earn far more from book, television, and movie rights even if she gives the proceeds from the lawsuit to charity. If what Paula's brother-in-law, Mark Brown, says is true, her reputation will need a lot of restoring. Brown was quoted in *National Affairs* in May 1994:

> She went with one man (to a duck-calling and gumbo cook-off) and when she got there, she spotted another one. She goes right up to him, puts her leg right between the legs of the other man and rubs herself up and down on him. It hurts me Paula has done this. She stated earlier that she was going to give the money to charity. Bullshit. Is the money the book brings in going to charity or the movie or any of that crap? Shit no. Paula's always loved money. Promiscuity? Good gosh. Her mother is fixing to get the shock of her life when Paula's life comes out. She went out and had herself a good time. I've seen her at the Red Lobster pinch men on the ass. . . .[63]

Jones sued the president for severe emotional distress" and "deprivation of her civil rights." She was prevented from suing him for sexual harassment because Arkansas state law requires this to be done within six months of the alleged incident and too much time had passed. This was the first time a sitting president had been sued for sexual misconduct.

Clinton's lawyer, Robert Bennett, denied in a press conference that the encounter ever took place and said that the president has "no recollection of ever meeting Jones, though he couldn't rule it out."[64] After seeing the *Jones v. Clinton* lawsuit, Bennett went on to say: "The President adamantly denies the vicious and mean-spirited allegations in the complaint. Quite simply the incident did not occur. . . . This is about money and book contracts, and radio and television appearances."[65] Notice, Bennett did not refute all the charges. Perhaps the president only denied those allegations he considered vicious and mean-spirited which were not true.

On December 28, 1994, a U.S. district judge, Susan Webber Wright, of Little Rock, ruled that a *Jones v. Clinton* trial must be postponed until after the president leaves office. But the judge agreed that pretrial discovery, including questioning of Clinton and other potential witnesses, can proceed. Clinton's lawyers said they would appeal the ruling.

Judge Wright agreed with Clinton's lawyers that a sitting president has immunity from trial while in office. Since Wright agreed that the president and other witnesses could be questioned, Jones's lawyer, Mark Cammarata, said that he intended to examine all of the state troopers assigned to protect Clinton to determine "if there's a pattern of conduct here."

So Paula Jones's suit will have to wait until at least 1997, or 2001 if Clinton gets elected to another four-year term, to go to trial. It is unlikely that the legal issues involved will be resolved before the president faces reelection in 1996. Any information uncovered by Jones's lawyers would be a matter of public record, and if damaging information is found, it will very likely be used to damage Clinton's hopes of being reelected.

☆ ☆ ☆

There can be little doubt that Hillary knew about Bill's philandering. Once, when Hillary awoke at 2:00 A.M., she discovered that Bill was missing from their bed. When she called his security detail to find out where he was, the trooper told her that Bill had gone for a drive. Hillary became incensed and said, "That sorry damn son of a bitch!" When one of the troopers tracked Bill down and told him about Hillary's remark, he distinctly remembers Bill's lamenting, "Oh, God! God! God! What did you tell her?" Bill jumped in his car, sped back to the governor's mansion, jumped out, leaving the car door open, ran inside, and found Hillary waiting for him in the kitchen. A fight ensued, complete with screaming and profanity. The next morning, Trooper Perry found a kitchen-cabinet door all but torn off its hinges and broken debris spread all over the kitchen floor.[66]

On another occasion, Hillary watched Bill flirt with an attractive woman at a political function until she had had enough and finally said, "Come on, Bill, put your dick up. You can't fuck her here." On Bill Clinton's last day in Little Rock in 1993, before leaving for Washington, he arranged for Trooper Patterson to pick up the wife of the judge with whom he had been having an affair as a type of farewell when he left the Little Rock airport. When Hillary saw Patterson arrive with the woman, she said to the trooper, "What the fuck do you think you're doing? I know who that whore is. I know what she's doing here. Get her out of here."

The president-elect was standing nearby and didn't respond when the trooper looked at him. Clinton shrugged his shoulders, so Patterson drove the woman into town and dropped her off at the Holiday Inn in central Little Rock.

Gennifer Flower claims that she and Bill discussed whether Hillary knew about their affair, and both assumed she did. Flowers said she was not sure, though, until one time when she met Hillary at a social function where Flowers was singing. Bill was talking to Gennifer when Hillary walked up to them. The cold, indifferent treatment she received from Hillary convinced her that Hillary knew that Flowers was sleeping with her husband. Gennifer also claimed that one evening, shortly after Bill hung up the telephone after having a conversation with her, Hillary walked into the room and asked Bill, "How's Gennifer?" Bill sheepishly responded, "Just fine." Perhaps Hillary was trying to let Bill know she was well aware of his relationship with Flowers.

According to Clinton biographer David Maraniss, one time after Hillary discovered one of Bill's affairs, she told him she intended to sleep around just to get back at him.[67] Five Arkansas state troopers who guarded the Clintons allege that Hillary had an affair with Vince Foster, a fellow law partner and friend of the Clintons. Foster committed suicide in July 1993 after revelations of the Clinton's financial dealings and Whitewater were beginning to come to light. One of the troopers, L. D. Brown, claimed that Bill knew about the affair.[68]

Bill Clinton is one of the most sexually active political figures to become president. It is not clear whether this activity has been curbed since he rose to the highest elected office in the land. One thing is clear, if this promiscuous sexual activity continues, it will very likely come to light in the years ahead.

14

AFTERWORD

Here are some lessons we as Americans and our future U.S. presidents might learn from the sexual behavior of their predecessors.

☆ **A presidential candidate is made of flesh and blood, like any other man.**

Although we expect our presidents to be above all of the problems faced by average Americans, we find instead that our leaders are very human and not very different from the rest of us. Some have troubled marriages and extramarital affairs. They lie about their actions to cover up past embarrassing behavior. So far no ex-president has divorced his wife, but some probably live on in unhappy marriages, like many Americans. We discovered that some presidents used drugs, frequented prostitutes, and engaged in sexual behavior that many of us would consider deviant. Presidents Kennedy and Clinton experimented with pot and may have used cocaine. Both of these presidents also allegedly frequented prostitutes and had sex with two or more women at a time. Presidents father illegitimate children whom they sometimes support financially and sometimes abandon.

☆ **Presidential extramarital affairs and sexual scandal are not new phenomena.**

We learned that throughout our nation's history selected presidents were involved in extramarital affairs and other types of scandalous sexual behavior. And it is very likely this type of behavior will continue to occur. In fact, sexual prurience is increasing in frequency among our presidents. Only three of the first fourteen presidents were involved in any sexual scandals. Four of the next fourteen presidents were involved in a sex scandal. And eight of the last fourteen presidents were involved in some type of sexual scandal. If this trend continues, many, if not all, of our next group of fourteen presidents will be philanderers. As a voter, you will have many opportunities to determine whether the president's sexual behavior is an issue of concern to you or whether the political issues of the day are of far greater importance.

☆ **The electorate is usually stunned by these revelations.**

Since the presidents have always tried to hide from the voters any sexual behavior that might be considered scandalous, their sexual dalliances are not widely known to most voters. Many younger voters may not know the history of the sexual behavior of past presidents. As a result, they are stunned when they discover that their president, whom many consider to be a moral exemplar, has been involved in some sort of sexual scandal. As one astute political observer once commented, "One hundred percent of the voters are against sin." As long as presidents continue to hide their sexual philandering and voters consider this type of behavior sinful or significant, the outcome of future presidential primary and general elections will be determined in large part by the candidates' sexual behavior or misbehavior.

☆ ☆ ☆

And now, a few lessons for future presidents and presidential candidates.

☆ **The president's sexual behavior has always been used as a weapon during political campaigns.**

Stories about presidential sex and sexual scandals have rocked the nation throughout its history, disturbing many voters and threatening the success of presidential campaigns. It seems likely that rumor and innuendo will continue to be used as weapons during political campaigns. A

AFTERWORD

third of the voters interviewed by a *Life* magazine poll in 1984 said they would not have voted for John F. Kennedy in 1960 if they had known about his philandering. If this news had leaked out before the elections, Richard Nixon would likely have been elected president, and the whole course of American history would have been different. Gary Hart might well have become president in 1988 if a sexual scandal had not ruined his presidential primary campaign.

Future presidential candidates must know that any sexual indiscretion will most likely be discovered and revealed during the primary elections and before the general elections in November. This will be facilitated by their opponents, who will test the waters to determine the attitudes of each generation of voters toward presidential philandering. Many political commentators suggest that the president's sexual behavior is none of the voters' business and should not be an issue. Others posit that the president is the moral leader of the nation and, consequently, his sexual behavior should be scrutinized by the electorate. Regardless of what commentators think, the voters will always decide whether a candidate's sexual behavior is a pertinent campaign issue.

Unless several generations of voters consistently reject a candidate's sexual behavior as a campaign issue, much as they did during the elections of 1828 and 1884, when they knowingly elected as president a known adulterer, Andrew Jackson, and an alleged fornicator, Grover Cleveland, the opposition campaigns will not abandon such an issue but will continue to promote it onto the front pages of the nation's newspapers. Therefore, aspiring future presidents should realize that any past sexual indiscretions will likely be revealed to voters and should decide ahead of time whether they personally and their families can withstand the scrutiny.

☆ **A president's affairs will eventually be exposed to the general public (very likely during his lifetime).**

George Washington's love letter, written to one woman while engaged to another, has been published for all to read. Thomas Jefferson's affairs have been spread across the headlines of the nation's newspapers and ridiculed in poetry and verse. Andrew Jackson's marriage to a bigamist was resurrected and revealed during his first presidential election campaign. Revelations of Grover Cleveland's tryst with Maria C. Halpin and the birth of Cleveland's illegitimate son were lampooned in political cartoons and in the popular song "Ma! Ma! Where's My Pa?" which was composed and sung frequently during Cleveland's first presidential-election campaign. Woodrow Wilson personally wrote a gushy, embarrassing press release about his upcoming marriage to his soon-to-be second wife, Edith Bolling Galt, that had to be heavily censored by members of the press, many of whom may have suspected that Wilson was already sleeping with his fiancée.

Some presidents managed to keep their indiscretions secret until after their deaths, but they were revealed eventually. James Garfield managed to hide his sexual behavior with Rebecca J. Selleck and Mrs. Lucia Gilbert Calhoun until after his death. Franklin Roosevelt's affairs were kept hidden from the public with much assistance by the press (much as his paralysis from polio was concealed). But news of his affair with Lucy Mercer Rutherfurd was eventually reported in 1946.

Dwight Eisenhower's love affair was exposed after his death by Harry Truman during an interview with Truman's biographer, when Harry admitted that Eisenhower wrote a letter stating his intention to divorce his wife, Mamie, and to marry his wartime driver, Kay Summersby. Warren G. Harding's mistress, Nan Britton, revealed the details of their affair shortly after Harding's death, since the support Harding has been supplying her was suddenly cut off. Harding's family members turned a deaf ear to her plight, so she wrote a book to provide financial support for her daughter. The mistresses of John F. Kennedy and Lyndon B. Johnson told reporters about the details of their love affairs with these two presidents.

During the 1990s we have witnessed a new trend developing. Members of the press are no longer willing to look the other way when it comes to presidential philandering. They reported openly about presidential contender Gary Hart's philandering during the Democratic primary campaign in 1987 and ended his chances for election. The press reported rumors of George Bush's alleged one-night stand and Bill Clinton's alleged affairs with numerous women while they were both running for president and continued to write about Clinton's dalliances even after he was elected. Bill Clinton was the first president to be sued for sexual harassment and may face a pending lawsuit after his term of office expires in 1997 if he is not re-elected for another four-year term in 1996.

☆ **A president's mistress will very likely write a kiss-and-tell book exposing the details of the affair to the public.**

Nearly all of the mistresses of modern presidents have written books exposing the details of their affairs. Here is a list of the books in reverse chronological order:

Gennifer Flowers: Passion and Betrayal by Gennifer Flowers, alleged mistress of President Bill Clinton

Texas in the Morning: My Secret Life With LBJ by Madeleine Brown, alleged mistress of President Lyndon Johnson

My Story by Judith Campbell Exner, alleged mistress of John F. Kennedy

Past Forgetting; My Love Affair With Dwight D. Eisenhower by Kay Summersby, Dwight D. Eisenhower's World War II driver and alleged mistress

The President's Daughter by Nan Britton, alleged mistress of Warren G. Harding

The Story of Mrs. Peck by Mary Allen Hulbert Peck, alleged mistress of Woodrow Wilson

Tell the Truth; or, The Story of a Working Woman's Wrongs by the James G. Blaine campaign, with assistance from Maria C. Halpin, alleged mistress of Grover Cleveland

The alleged mistresses of six of the last seven presidents wrote about their extramarital affairs. Only Franklin Roosevelt escaped such embarrassing revelations. However, members of his family did talk about what they knew of his affair with Lucy Mercer (and several other women); consequently, these revelations were published.

☆ **Sexual relations sometimes lead to unwanted pregnancy.**

Like most Americans, U.S. presidents may not always realize the con- sequences of their promiscuous behavior sometimes leads to an unwanted or unplanned pregnancy. Thomas Jefferson was said to be the father of several mulatto children of his slave girl Sally Hemings. Grover Cleveland allegedly fathered an unwanted child whom his mistress named Oscar Folsom Cleveland, leaving little doubt as to his parentage. John Kennedy allegedly fathered an illegitimate child by his girlfriend Inga Arvad. Lyndon Johnson allegedly fathered Steven Brown, the son of Madeleine Brown, his alleged mistress. Gennifer Flowers says Bill Clinton impregnated her and she had an abortion. A prostitute also claims Bill Clinton fathered her son.

Interestingly enough, Dwight D. Eisenhower and Warren G. Harding told their mistresses that they wanted to have a child by them. In Eisenhower's case it was probably not possible. But Harding became very troubled after learning he was soon to become a father for the first time and even suggested that this matter could easily be taken care of, implying that his mistress, Nan Britton, could get an illegal abortion.

☆ **The mores of the American voters tend to swing along a pendulum ranging from outrage to forgiveness.**

What are the mores of the American voters concerning the sexual behavior of our presidents, and how have they changed over the last two hundred years?

In some foreign countries the populace views the sexual exploits of their national leaders very differently than we do in America. For example, in France, when a former French president had an automobile accident while driving home in the early hours of the morning, the electorate assumed he must have been returning from a liaison with his mistress, and his popularity rose in the opinion polls. According to *U.S. News & World Report* newsman Fred Coleman, "The French regard press reporting of political sex scandals in America as prudish, in Britain as excessive."[1]

In Britain, sexual shenanigans are regularly reported on the front pages of the respectable newspapers as well as the tabloids. The difference is that in America the president usually denies the press reports, tries to characterize his mistress as a bimbo, and continues on about his business, whereas in Britain the public official usually resigns from office after he is caught. British journalist Peter Hitchens, who writes for England's *Daily Express* said:

> Fleet Street has never been known for restraint when it comes to tawdry fare. "We take a joyous delight in other people's sexual problems in England. If a British prime minister had been accused with this much evidence, he would've had to resign."[2]

In America, we tend to hold our presidents (and presidential contenders) to higher standards of sexual conduct. One commentator has said that we expect our presidential candidates to be "purer than the (Roman Catholic) pope." Some political observers consider Americans prudish when it comes to matters of sexual conduct and consider this unfortunate and unfair. They point out that if American voters had known beforehand about the philandering of inspiring presidents like Franklin D. Roosevelt and John F. Kennedy, these two men may not have been elected at all. These observers may be correct in their assumptions, but we will never know for sure. The American voters have shown themselves to be tolerant and very forgiving on the two occasions when shocking sexual scandals occurred during two different presidents' first presidential election campaigns.

Voters elected Andrew Jackson in 1828 even though he married a bigamist. The voters also elected Grover Cleveland in 1884 even after revelations about his love affair with Maria Crofts Halpin were made known. Democratic contender Gary Hart ended his 1988 presidential campaign in disgrace after his affair with Donna Rice was exposed; he saw his popularity dropping in the polls and was afraid voters would not elect a known philanderer to the highest office in the land. But Hart may have been wrong. Bill Clinton was elected president in 1992 despite strong suspicion that he was lying about his alleged affairs with Gennifer Flowers and several other women. The voters elected this alleged pot-smoking, draft-dodging, womanizing Democratic candidate over the incumbent Republican president who was a decorated war veteran and family man with strong traditional values.

Some political observers urge presidential contenders to be frank and open about their previous affairs to allow voters to make their decisions based on the campaign issues they consider important rather than on whether the candidate appears to be lying or telling the truth about his past sexual behavior. Most candidates avoid this option, probably considering it political suicide.

The best advice I can give to future, aspiring U.S. presidential candidates is to live their lives in a manner that is above reproach, for where there is no fire, there can be no smoke—and no smoking gun.

APPENDIX A

Quick Reference Guide to the Sexual Behavior of Selected U.S. Presidents

President	Mistress	Prostitutes	Fornication*	Adultery†	White House Staff	Illegitimate Children	Homosexuality	Group Sex	Unusual death of lover
George Washington				❤?					
Thomas Jefferson	❤		❤	❤		❤			
Andrew Jackson	❤								
James Buchanan							❤		❤
James Garfield	❤		❤	❤					
Grover Cleveland	❤	❤?	❤			❤			
Woodrow Wilson	❤		❤‡	❤					
Warren Harding	❤	❤	❤	❤		❤			
Franklin D. Roosevelt	❤		❤						
Dwight D. Eisenhower	❤		❤						
John F. Kennedy	❤	❤	❤	❤	❤	❤		❤	❤
Lyndon B. Johnson	❤		❤	❤	❤	❤			
Bill Clinton	❤	❤	❤	❤		❤		❤	

*Fornication means sex with an unmarried woman
†Adultery means sex with a married woman
‡Wilson may have had sex with his fiancee

241

APPENDIX B

Answers to Presidential Sexual Behavior Quiz

1. Warren G. Harding
2. Andrew Jackson
3. George Washington
4. Thomas Jefferson
5. Bill Clinton
6. John F. Kennedy
7. James Buchanan (Anne Coleman) and John F. Kennedy (Mary Pinchot Meyer)
8. John F. Kennedy
9. Thomas Jefferson, Grover Cleveland, John F. Kennedy, Lyndon B. Johnson, and Bill Clinton
10. Lyndon B. Johnson
11. John F. Kennedy and Lyndon B. Johnson
12. Thomas Jefferson
13. Franklin D. Roosevelt
14. Lyndon B. Johnson
15. John F. Kennedy and Lyndon B. Johnson
16. James Buchanan
17. Bill Clinton
18. Andrew Jackson
19. Dwight D. Eisenhower
20. Grover Cleveland
21. Franklin D. Roosevelt

ANSWERS TO PRESIDENTIAL SEXUAL BEHAVIOR QUIZ

22. John F. Kennedy
23. Warren G. Harding
24. John F. Kennedy and Bill Clinton
25. John F. Kennedy

Notes

Chapter 1: George Washington

1. Richard N. Smith, *Patriarch: George Washington and the New American Nation* (Boston: Houghton Mifflin, 1993), 197.

2. Thomas Fleming, *First in Their Hearts: A Biography of George Washington* (New York: Walker, 1984).

3. George W. Nordham, *George Washington's Women: Mary, Martha, Sally, and 146 Others* (Philadelphia: Dorrance, 1977), 5–6.

4. Ibid., 6.

5. Wilson M. Cary, *Sally Cary: A Long Hidden Romance of Washington's Life* (New York: DeVinne Press, 1916), 36–38.

6. Ibid., 40.

7. Irma Hunt, *Dearest Madame: The President's Mistresses* (New York: McGraw-Hill, 1978), 39.

8. Cary, *Sally Cary*, 54–55.

Chapter 2: Thomas Jefferson

1. Thomas Walker letter, Library of Congress, 27117–21.

2. Fawn M. Brodie, *Thomas Jefferson: An Intimate History* (New York: Norton, 1974), 81.

3. William Burwell memoir, Ms., Library of Congress.

4. Thomas Walker letter, Library of Congress, 27117–21.

5. *American Citizen*, July 24, 1805.

6. Brodie, *Jefferson*, 65.

7. Irma Hunt, *Dearest Madame: The President's Mistresses* (New York, McGraw-Hill, 1978), 39; Richard Shenkman, *Legends, Lies, and Cherished Myths of American History* (New York: Harper & Row, 1988), 30.

8. Brodie, *Jefferson*, 298.

9. Hunt, *Dearest Madame*, 56.

10. Shelley Ross, *Fall From Grace: Sex, Scandal, and Corruption in American Politics From 1702 to the Present.* (New York: Ballantine, 1988), 35.

11. Brodie, *Jefferson* 654–667.

NOTES

Chapter 3: Andrew Jackson

1. James Marquis, *The Life of Andrew Jackson* (Indianapolis: Bobbs-Merrill, 1938), 383.
2. Shelley Ross, *Fall From Grace: Sex, Scandal, and Corruption in American Politics From 1702 to the Present* (New York: Ballantine, 1988), 58.
3. Ben Truman, *The Field of Honor* (1884), 283.

Chapter 4: James Buchanan

1. David R. Collins, *James Buchanan: 15th President of the United States* (New York: Garrett Educational Corp., 1990), 30.
2. Philip S. Klein, *President James Buchanan* (Norwalk, Conn.: Easton Press, 1962), 31–32.
3. George T. Curtis, *Life of James Buchanan: Fifteenth President of the United States* (New York: Harper & Brothers, 1883), 18–19.
4. Curtis, *Buchanan*, 18–19.
5. William DeGregorio, *The Complete Book of U.S. Presidents* (New York, Dembner Books, 1984), 222.
6. Elbert B. Smith, *The Presidency of James Buchanan* (Lawrence: University of Kansas Press, 1975), 13.
7. Letter from Aaron V. Brown to Mrs. James K. Polk, January 14, 1844, *Polk Papers*, Library of Congress.
8. Shelley Ross, *Fall From Grace: Sex, Scandal, and Corruption in American Politics From 1702 to the Present* (New York, Ballantine, 1988), 89.

Chapter 5: James Garfield

1. Margaret Leech and Harry J. Brown, *The Garfield Orbit* (New York, Harper & Row, 1978), 41.
2. Ibid., 43.
3. Ibid., 43.
4. Ibid., 52.
5. Ibid., 66.
6. Ibid., 68.
7. Ibid., 71–72.
8. Ibid., 72.
9. Ibid., 75.
10. Ibid., 75.
11. Ibid., 89.
12. Allan Peskin, *Garfield* (Ohio: Kent State University Press, 1987), 75.
13. Leech and Brown, *Garfield* 194–195.
14. Shelley Ross, *Fall From Grace: Sex, Scandal, and Corruption in American Politics From 1702 to the Present* (New York: Ballantine Books, 1988), 117.

NOTES

Chapter 6: Grover Cleveland

1. Irving Wallace and Amy Wallace, *The Intimate Sex Lives of Famous People* (New York: Delacorte, 1976), 322.
2. Webb Garrison, *Behind the Headlines: American History's Schemes, Scandals and Escapades* (Harrisburg, Penn.: Stackpole Books, 1983), 51.
3. William DeGregorio, *The Complete Book of U.S. Presidents* (New York: Dembner Books, 1984), 351.
4. Rexford G. Tugwell, *Grover Cleveland* (London: Collier-Macmillan, 1968), 92–93.
5. Richard E. Welch Jr., *The Presidencies of Grover Cleveland* (Lawrence, University of Kansas Press, 1988), 38–39.

Chapter 7: Woodrow Wilson

1. Mary Allen Hulbert, *The Story of Mrs. Peck* (New York: Minton Balch, 1933), 86.
2. Ibid., 170.
3. Shelley Ross, *Fall From Grace: Sex, Scandal, and Corruption in American Politics From 1702 to the Present* (New York: Ballantine Books, 1988), 150.
4. August Heckscher, *Woodrow Wilson* (New York: Scribners, 1991), 185.
5. Ibid., 187.
6. Ibid., 187.
7. Hulbert, *Mrs. Peck*, x.
8. Arthur C. Walworth, *Woodrow Wilson: American Prophet* (New York: Longmans, Green, 1958), 417.
9. Heckscher, *Wilson*, 350
10. Tom Shachtman, *Edith & Woodrow: A Presidential Romance* (New York: G. P. Putnam's Sons, 1981), 110.
11. Ibid., 112–13.
12. Ibid., 115.
13. Ross, *Fall From Grace*, 153–54.
14. Ibid., 154–55.
15. Traphes Bryant and Frances Spatz Leighton, *Dog Days at the White House* (New York: Macmillan), 1975), 35.
16. Arthur C. Walworth, *Woodrow Wilson* (New York: Norton, 1978), 431.
17. Ibid., 432–33.

Chapter 8: Warren Harding

1. Charles L. Mee, *The Ohio Gang: The World of Warren G. Harding* (New York: Evans, 1981), 48.
2. Irma Hunt, *Dearest Madame: The President's Mistresses* (New York: McGraw-Hill, 1978), 142.

3. Francis Russel, *The Shadow of Blooming Grove: Warren G. Harding in His Times* (New York: McGraw-Hill, 1968), 84.

4. Ibid., 169.

5. Mee, *Ohio Gang*, 63.

6. Shelley Ross, *Fall From Grace: Sex, Scandal, and Corruption in American Politics From 1702 to the Present* (New York: Ballantine, 1988), 165.

7. Ibid., 165.

8. Russel, *Blooming Grove*, 249.

9. Nan Britton, *The President's Daughter* (New York: Elizabeth Ann Guild, 1927), 25–26.

10. Ibid., 32–33.

11. Ibid., 44.

12. Ross, *Fall From Grace*, 164.

13. Britton, *President's Daughter*, 135.

14. Ibid., 172–73.

15. Ibid., 240.

Chapter 9: Franklin D. Roosevelt

1. Ted Morgan, *FDR: A Biography* (New York: Simon & Schuster, 1985), 202.

2. Eleanor Roosevelt, *This I Remember* (New York: Harper & Brothers, 1949), 348–49.

3. Morgan, *FDR*, 203.

4. Geoffrey C. Ward, *A First-Class Temperament: The Emergence of Franklin Roosevelt* (New York: Harper & Row, 1989), 680.

5. Irving Wallace and Amy Wallace, *The Intimate Sex Lives of Famous People* (New York: Delacorte, 1976), 327.

6. Morgan, *FDR*, 204.

7. Ward, *Roosevelt*, 412.

8. Irma Hunt, *Dearest Madame: The President's Mistresses* (New York, McGraw-Hill, 1978), 177.

9. Shelley Ross, *Fall From Grace: Sex, Scandal, and Corruption in American Politics From 1702 to the Present* (New York: Ballantine, 1988), 175.

10. Ibid., 175.

11. Wallace, *Famous People*, 324.

12. Wallace, *Famous People*, 324; Ross, *Fall From Grace*, 175.

Chapter 10: Dwight D. Eisenhower

1. Irving Wallace and Amy Wallace, *The Intimate Sex Lives of Famous People* (New York, Delacorte, 1976), 330.

2. Kay Summersby Morgan, *Past Forgetting: My Love Affair With Dwight D. Eisenhower* (New York: Simon & Schuster, 1976), 200.

NOTES

3. Stephen E. Ambrose, *Eisenhower: Volume One-Soldier General of the Army President-Elect 1890–1952* (New York, Simon & Schuster, 1983), 224.
4. Ibid., 190.
5. Ibid., 224.
6. Morgan, *Eisenhower*, 146–47.
7. Ibid., 151–52.
8. Ibid., 194–95.
9. Ibid., 268–70.
10. Ibid., 279.
11. Merle Miller, *Plain Speaking: An Oral Biography of Harry S. Truman* (New York: Berkley, 1974), 340.

Chapter 11: John F. Kennedy

1. Maxwell Meyersohn, *Memorable Quotations of John F. Kennedy* (New York: Crowell), 1985.
2. Taki, "High Life: Broad-minded," *Spectator*, 1 February 1992: 41.
3. For those of you unfamiliar with the term "ménage à trois," it refers to sex among three persons, usually one man and two women. Translated literally it means *household of three. Webster's New International Dictionary*, 3rd ed., defines *ménage à trois* as an arrangement in which three persons (such as a married couple and the lover of one of the couple) share sexual relations, especially while they are living together."
4. "Sex and the Presidency," *Life*, August 1987: 71.
5. Irma Hunt, Dearest Madame: *The President's Mistresses* (New York, McGraw-Hill, 1978), 243.
6. David Kramer, "The Kennedy Complex: Why They Womanize," *McCall's*, August 91: 44–45.
7. C. David Heymann, *A Woman Named Jackie* (New York: Lyle Stuart:, 1989), 109.
8. Poon is a crude but common navy term used to describe a part of a woman's sexual anatomy and is also used to describe philandering.
9. Tempest Storm, with Bill Boyd, *Tempest Storm: The Lady Is a Vamp.* (Atlanta: Peachtree, 1987,) 159.
10. James N. Giglio, *The Presidency of John F. Kennedy* (Lawrence: University of Kansas Press, 1991), 268.
11. "Jackie—Oh, What a Cheat," *Examiner*, 28 March 1995: 15.
12. Ronald Kessler, *Inside the White House: The Hidden Lives of the Modern Presidents and the Secrets of the World's Most Powerful Institution* (New York: Pocket Books, 1995), 2, 35.
13. Judith Exner and Ovid Demans, *Judith Exner: My Story* (New York: Grove Press, 1977), 86.

NOTES

14. Ibid.
15. "J.F.K. and the Mobsters' Moll," *Time* 29 December 1975: 10.
16. John H. Davis, *The Kennedys: Dynasty and Disaster 1848–1983* (New York: McGraw-Hill, 1984), 616–17.
17. Hunt, *Dearest Madame,* 245.
18. Heymann, *Jackie,* 246.
19. Ibid.
20. Peter H. Brown and Patte B. Barham, *Marilyn: The Last Take* (New York: Penguin, 1992), 71; Heymann, *Jackie,* 287.
21. Brown and Barham, *Marilyn,* 152.
22. Kessler, *White House,* 2.
23. Nigel Hamilton, *JFK: Reckless Youth* (New York: Random House, 1992),
24. Mary B. Gallagher and Frances S. Leighton, *My Life With Jacqueline Kennedy* (New York: McKay, 1969), 115.
25. Davis, *Kennedys,* 159.

Chapter 12: Lyndon B. Johnson

1. Doris K. Goodwin, *Lyndon Johnson and the American Dream* (New York: St. Martin's Press, 1991), 56.
2. Ibid., 57.
3. Ronnie Dugger, *The Politician: The Life and Times of Lyndon Johnson—The Drive for Power From the Frontier to Master of the Senate* (New York: Norton, 1982), 178.
4. Robert A. Caro, *The Years of Lyndon Johnson: The Path to Power* (New York: Knopf, 1982), 485.
5. Traphes Bryant and Frances Spatz Leighton, *Dog Days at the White House* (New York: Macmillan, 1975), 196.
6. Robert Dallek, *Lone Star Rising: Lyndon Johnson and His Times, 1908–1960* (New York: Oxford University Press, 1991), 189.
7. George Reedy, *Lyndon B. Johnson: A Memoir* (New York: Andrews and Mc-Neel, 1982), 32.
8. Shelley Ross, *Fall From Grace: Sex, Scandal, and Corruption in American Politics From 1702 to the Present* (New York: Ballantine, 1988), 209.
9. Joachim Joesten, *The Dark Side of Lyndon Baines Johnson* (London: Dawnay, 1968), 16.
10. Dallek, *Lone Star,* 191.
11. Bryant and Leighton, *Dog Days,* 37.
12. Dallek, *Lone Star,* 190.
13. Montgomery Brower, "Was LBJ's Final Secret a Son?" *People Weekly,* 3 August 1987: 32–33.
14. Ibid., 31.

15. Leslie Fagan, "LBJ's Mistress," New York, A *Current Affair*, February 24, 1992.
16. Brower, "Final Secret," 34.
17. Fagan, "LBJ's Mistress."
18. Bryant and Leighton, *Dog Days*, 108.
19. Dallek, *Lone Star*, 189.
20. Reedy, *Johnson*, 36.
21. Ronald Kessler, *Inside the White House: The Hidden Lives of the Modern Presidents and the Secrets of the World's Most Powerful Institution* (New York: Pocket Books, 1995), 13.
22. Ibid., 13.

Chapter 13: William J. Clinton

1. Matthew Cooper, "Running From the Start," *Washington Post Book World*, 12 February 1995: 9.
2. Ibid., 1.
3. George Carpozi Jr., *Clinton Confidential: The Climb to Power—The Unauthorized Biography of Bill and Hillary Clinton* (Del Mar, Calif.: Emery Dalton Books, 1995), 223.
4. Gennifer Flowers, with Jacquelyn Dapper, *Gennifer Flowers: Passion and Betrayal* (Del Mar, Calif.: Emery Dalton Books, 1995), 42.
5. Carpozi, *Confidential*, 223.
6. Charles F. Allen and J. Portis, *The Comeback Kid: The Life and Career of Bill Clinton* (New York: Carol, 1992), 71.
7. Gleick, Elizabeth, "Making Book on Clinton," *Time*, 13 February 1995: 27.
8. Ibid., 27.
9. Allen, *Comeback Kid*, 189.
10. Carpozi, *Confidential*, 279.
11. Flowers, *Passion*, 99, 109.
12. Ibid., 29.
13. Carpozi, *Confidential*, 221.
14. Ibid., 222.
15. Ibid., 225.
16. Ibid., 119–21.
17. Ibid., 121.
18. Flowers, *Passion*, 2.
19. Carpozi, *Confidential*, 197.
20. Ibid., 100.
21. Ibid., 100.
22. Flowers, *Passion*, 74.
23. Ibid., 82.

24. "FORMER AIDE CHARGES IN COURT: DEM FRONT-RUNNER HAD AFFAIR WITH MISS AMERICA," *Star*, January 28 1992; 1.

25. Flowers, *Passion*, 101.

26. David Brock, "His Cheatin' Heart," *American Spectator*, December 20, 1993 (reprinted January 1994), 30.

27. Carpozi, *Confidential*, 320.

28. Jim Moore, with Rick Ihde, *Clinton: Young Man in a Hurry* (Fort Worth: Summit Group, 1992), 190.

29. Benedetto Nagourney and Richard and Lewis Davis, "Clinton Forced to Deny Report on Affair—Again," *USA Today*, 24 January 92: 11A.

30. Brock, "Cheatin' Heart," 19.

31. Moore and Ihde, *Young Man*, 190.

32. Ibid., 190–91.

33. Allen, *Comeback Kid*, 192.

34. Ronald Kessler, *Inside the White House: The Hidden lives of the Modern Presidents and the Secrets of the World's Most Powerful Institution* (New York: Pocket Books, 1995), 239.

35. Carpozi, *Confidential*, 361–62.

36. "The 1992 Campaign: Bush Angrily Denies a Report of an Affair," *New York Times*, 12 August 1992: A14.

37. Carpozi, *Confidential*, 362.

38. *New York Times*, "1992 Campaign," A14.

39. Jon Swan, Jennifer, *CJR*, November/December 1992: 36.

40. Brock, "Cheatin' Heart," 21.

41. Kessler, *White House*, 240.

42. Brock, "Cheatin' Heart," 27.

43. Flowers, *Passion*, 77.

44. Howard Schneider, "Arkansas Troopers Spark Media Blitz," *Washington Post*, 22 December 93: A16.

45. Ruth Marcus, "First Lady Lashes Out at Allegations," *Washington Post*, 22 December 1993: A1, 16.

46. Frank J. Murry, "President Stops Short of Denying Stories of Trysts" *Washington Times*, 23 December 93: A1, A13.

47. Ibid.

48. Daniel Wattenberg, "Love and Hate in Arkansas: L. D. Brown's Story," *American Spectator*, April-May 1994.

49. Howard Kurtz, "Brits Keep Tabs on Clinton Sex Life; London Papers Trumpet Tawdry Allegations About the President," *Washington Post*, 3 May 94: B1.

50. Wattenberg, *Love and Hate*, 5.

51. Carpozi, *Confidential*, 226.

52. Allen, *Comeback Kid*, 146.

53. Ibid., 165.

54. Carpozi, *Confidential*, 226–27.

55. Ibid., 175–80
56. Diamond, Edwin, "Gennifer, Part II," *New York*, 17 January 1994: 16–17.
57. Kessler, *White House*, 242.
58. Diamond, "Gennifer," 16.
59. Kessler, *White House*, 242.
60. Richard Lacayo, "Jones v. the President," *Time*, 16 May 1994: 45.
61. "Clinton Hires Attorney to Fend Off Sex Suit," *Capital*, 5 May 1994: A2.
62. "Money Always on Mind of Presidential Accuser," *Capital*, 5 May 1994.
63. M. Hosenball, G. Carroll, and B. Cohn, "No Laughing Matter," *National Affairs*, 16 May 1994: 22–24.
64. Ibid., 22.
65. Lacayo, "Jones," 45.
66. Kessler, *White House*, 241.
67. Cooper, *Running*, 9.
68. Wattenberg, *Love and Hate*, 7.

Chapter 14: Lessons Learned

1. Fred Coleman, "Vive la Difference!," *U.S. News & World Report*, 14 November 1994.
2. Howard Kurtz, "Brits Keep Tabs on Clinton Sex Life; London Papers Trumpet Tawdry Allegations About the President," *Washington Post*, 3 May 94: B1.

Select Bibliography

Chapter 1: George Washington

Cary, Wilson M. *Sally Cary: A Long Hidden Romance of Washington's Life*. New York: De Vinne Press, 1916.

Fleming, Thomas. *First in Their Hearts: A Biography of George Washington*. New York: Walker, 1984.

Nordham, George W. *George Washington's Women: Mary, Martha, Sally, and 146 Others*. Philadelphia: Dorrance, 1977.

Shenkman, Richard. *Legends, Lies, and Cherished Myths of American History*. New York: Harper & Row, 1988.

Smith, Richard N. *Patriarch: George Washington and the New American Nation*. Boston: Houghton Mifflin, 1993.

Chapter 2: Thomas Jefferson

Brodie, Fawn M. *Thomas Jefferson: An Intimate History*. New York: Norton, 1974.

Buchanan, Patrick J. "Washington: The Town Without Pity." *Capital*. 18 January 1993: Section A.

Mapp, Alf J., Jr. *Thomas Jefferson Passionate Pilgrim: The Presidency, the Founding of the University, and the Private Battle*. Lanham, Md.: Madison Books, 1991.

Meltzer, Milton. *Thomas Jefferson: The Revolutionary Aristocrat*. New York: Franklin Watts, 1991.

Shenkman, Richard. *Legends, Lies, and Cherished Myths of American History*. New York: Harper & Row, 1988.

Wallace, Irving, and Amy Wallace. *The Intimate Sex Lives of Famous People*. New York: Delacorte Press, 1976.

Chapter 3: Andrew Jackson

Anthony, Carl S. "Battle of Better Halves." *Washington Post*. 23 August 1992: F1, F5.

Cole, Donald B. *The Presidency of Andrew Jackson*. Lawrence: University of Kansas Press, 1993.

Marquis, James. *The Life of Andrew Jackson*. Indianapolis: Bobbs-Merrill, 1938.

Moody, Sid. "Sex, Politics Nothing New, Despite Tabloid Headlines." *Capital*. 5 December 1993: F12.

Remini, Robert V. *Andrew Jackson and the Course of American Freedom, 1822–1832*. New York: Harper & Row, 1981.
Shenkman, Richard. *Legends, Lies, and Cherished Myths of American History*. New York: Harper & Row, 1988.

Chapter 4: James Buchanan

Cahalan, Sally S. *James Buchanan and His Family at Wheatland*. Lancaster, Penn.: James Buchanan Foundation, 1988.
Collins, David R. *James Buchanan: Fifteenth President of the United States*. New York: Garrett Educational Corp., 1990.
Curtis, George T. *Life of James Buchanan: Fifteenth President of the United States*. New York: Harper & Brothers, 1883.
Hoyt, Edwin P. *James Buchanan*. Chicago: Reilly & Lee, 1966.
Klein, Philip S. *President James Buchanan*. Norwalk, Conn.: Easton Press, 1962.
Smith, Elbert B. *The Presidency of James Buchanan*. Lawrence: University of Kansas Press, 1975.
Whitney, David C. *The American Presidents*. Garden City, N.Y.: Doubleday, 1978.

Chapter 5: James Garfield

Anthony, Carl Sferrazza. "Romance in the White House." *Washington Post*. 8 February 1987: G4, G7.
Doenecke, Justus D. *The Presidencies of James A. Garfield & Chester A. Arthur*. Lawrence: Regents Press of Kansas, 1981.
Leech, Margaret, and Harry J. Brown. *The Garfield Orbit*. New York: Harper & Row, 1978.
Peskin, Allan. *Garfield*. Ohio, Kent State University Press, 1987.
Taylor, John M. *Garfield of Ohio: The Available Man*. New York: Norton, 1970.

Chapter 6: Grover Cleveland

Garrison, Webb. *Behind the Headlines: American History's Schemes, Scandals and Escapades*. Harrisburg, Penn.: Stackpole Books, 1983.
Hoyt, Edwin P. *Grover Cleveland*. Chicago: Reilly & Lee, 1962.
Tugwell, Rexford G. *Grover Cleveland*. London: Collier-Macmillan Ltd., 1968.
Wallace, Irving, and Amy Wallace, *The Intimate Sex Lives of Famous People*. New York: Delacorte, 1976.
Welch, Richard E., Jr. *The Presidencies of Grover Cleveland*. Lawrence: University of Kansas, 1988.

Chapter 7: Warren G. Harding

Britton, Nan. *The President's Daughter*. New York: Elizabeth Ann Guild, 1927.
Dubrow, Marsha. "All the President's Women." *Punch*. 26 February 1992: 26–28.

Mee, Charles L. *The Ohio Gang: The World of Warren G. Harding.* New York: Evans, 1981.

Moody, Sid. "Sex, Politics Nothing New, Despite Tabloid Headlines." *Capital.* 5 December 1993: F12.

Russel, Francis. *The Shadow of Blooming Grove: Warren G. Harding in His Times.* New York: McGraw-Hill, 1968.

Shenkman, Richard. *Legends, Lies, and Cherished Myths of American History.* New York: Harper & Row, 1988.

Sinclair, Andrew. *The Available Man: The Life Behind the Masks of Warren Gamaliel Harding.* New York: Macmillan, 1965.

Wallace, Irving, and Amy Wallace. *The Intimate Sex Lives of Famous People.* New York: Delacorte, 1976.

Chapter 8: Woodrow Wilson

Anthony, Carl Sferrazza. "Romance in the White House." *Washington Post.* 8 February 1987: G4, G7.

Bryant, Traphes, and Frances Spatz Leighton. *Dog Days at the White House.* New York: Macmillan, 1975.

Heckscher, August. *Woodrow Wilson.* New York: Scribners, 1991.

Hulbert, Mary Allen. *The Story of Mrs. Peck.* New York: Minton Balch, 1933.

McAdoo, Eleanor W. *The Priceless Gift: The Love Letters of Woodrow Wilson and Ellen Axson Wilson.* New York: McGraw-Hill, 1962.

Shachtman, Tom. *Edith and Woodrow: A Presidential Romance.* New York: G. P. Putnam's Sons, 1981.

Tribble, Edwin. *A President in Love: The Courtship Letters of Woodrow Wilson and Edith Bolling Galt.* Boston: Houghton Mifflin, 1981.

Walworth, Arthur C. *Woodrow Wilson: American Prophet.* New York: Longmans, 1958.

———.*Woodrow Wilson.* New York: Norton, 1978.

Wilson, Edith Bolling. *My Memoir.* Indianapolis: Bobbs-Merrill, 1938.

Chapter 9: Franklin D. Roosevelt

Bryant, Traphes, and Frances Spatz Leighton. *Dog Days at the White House.* New York: Macmillan, 1975.

Collier, Peter, and David Horowitz. *The Roosevelts: An American Saga.* New York: Simon & Schuster, 1994.

"FDR Secret Recordings Revealed." *Facts on File World New Digest.* January 1982: 20G1.

Goodwin, Doris Kearns. *No Ordinary Time: Franklin and Eleanor Roosevelt—The Homefront in World War II.* New York: Simon & Schuster, 1994.

Miller, William "Fishbait," and Francis Spatz Leighton. *Fishbait: The Memoirs of the Congressional Doorkeeper.* Englewood Cliffs, N.J.: Prentice-Hall, 1977.

Miller, Nathan. *FDR: An Intimate History.* New York: Doubleday, 1983.

Morgan, Ted. *FDR: A Biography.* New York: Simon & Schuster, 1985.

Roosevelt, Eleanor. *This I Remember.* New York: Harper Brothers. 1949.

Ross, Shelley. *Fall From Grace: Sex, Scandal, and Corruption in American Politics From 1702 to the Present.* New York: Ballantine, 1988.

Wallace, Irving, and Amy Wallace. *The Intimate Sex Lives of Famous People.* New York: Delacorte Press, 1976.

Ward, Geoffrey C. *A First-Class Temperament: The Emergence of Franklin Roosevelt.* New York: Harper & Row, 1989.

Wills, Garry. "How Pure Must Our Candidates Be?" *American Heritage.* May-June 1988: 84–89.

Chapter 10: Dwight D. Eisenhower

Ambrose, Stephen E. *Eisenhower: Volume One—Soldier General of the Army President-Elect 1890–1952.* New York: Simon and Schuster, 1983.

Bryant, Traphes, and Frances Spatz Leighton. *Dog Days at the White House.* New York: Macmillan, 1975.

Miller, Merle. *Plain Speaking: An Oral Biography of Harry S. Truman.* New York: Berkley, 1974.

Morgan, Kay Summersby. *Past Forgetting: My Love Affair With Dwight D. Eisenhower.* New York: Simon & Schuster, 1976.

Pach, Chester J. *The Presidency of Dwight Eisenhower.* Lawrence: University of Kansas Press, 1991.

Wallace, Irving, and Amy Wallace. *The Intimate Sex Lives of Famous People.* New York: Delacorte, 1976.

Chapter 11: John F. Kennedy

Brady, James. "Angie Dickinson." *Parade.* 4 April 1993: 29.

Brown. Peter H., and Patte B. Barham. *Marilyn: The Last Take.* New York: Penguin, 1992.

Bryant, Traphes, and Frances Spatz Leighton. *Dog Days at the White House.* New York: Macmillan, 1975.

Collier, Peter, and David Horowitz. *The Kennedys: An American Drama.* New York: Summit Books, 1984.

Davis, John H. *The Kennedys: Dynasty and Disaster 1848–1983.* New York: McGraw-Hill, 1984.

Exner, Judith, and Ovid Demaris. *Judith Exner: My Story.* New York: Grove Press, 1977.

Gallagher, Mary B., and Frances S. Leighton. *My Life With Jacqueline Kennedy.* New York: McKay, 1969.

Giglio, James N. *The Presidency of John F. Kennedy.* Lawrence: University of Kansas Press, 1991.

BIBLIOGRAPHY

Hamilton, Nigel. *JFK: Reckless Youth.* New York: Random House, 1992.

Heymann, C. David. *A Woman Named Jackie.* New York: Lyle Stuart, 1989.

"Jack Does Penetrate the Kennedy Myths." *Capital.* 17 November 93: F1.

"Jack Kennedy's Other Women." *Time.* 29 December 1975: 11–12.

"Jack Kennedy's Private Side: Mixing Sex and Politics." *Newsweek.* 8 June 1981: 22.

"J.F.K. and the Mobsters' Moll." *Time.* 29 December 1975: 10–11.

Kelley, Kitty. "'The Dark Side of Camelot." *People.* 29 February 1988: 106–14.

Kramer, David. "The Kennedy Complex: Why They Womanize." *McCall's.* August 91: 44.

Lawford, May, and Buddy Galon. *"Bitch!": The Autobiography of Lady Lawford.* Brookline Village, Mass.: Branden, 1986.

Martin, Ralph G. *A Hero for Our Time: An Intimate Story of the Kennedy Years.* New York: Macmillan, 1983.

Miller, William "Fishbait," and Francis Spatz Leighton. *Fishbait: The Memoirs of the Congressional Doorkeeper.* Englewood Cliffs, N.J.: Prentice-Hall, 1977.

Meyersohn, Maxwell. *Memorable Quotations of John F. Kennedy.* New York: Crowell, 1985.

Reeves, Thomas C. *A Question of Character: A Life of John F. Kennedy.* New York: Free Press, 1991.

Reuben, David. *Everything You've Always Wanted to Know About Sex*: * But Were Afraid to Ask.* New York: Bantam, 1969.

"Sex and the Presidency." *Life.* August 1987: 70–75.

Sidney, Hugh. "Upstairs at the White House." *Time.* 18 May 1987: 20.

Spada, James. *Peter Lawford: The Man Who Kept the Secrets.* New York: Bantam, 1991.

Storm, Tempest, with Bill Boyd. *Tempest Storm: The Lady Is A Vamp.* Atlanta: Peachtree, 1987.

Strait, Raymond. *Here They Are: Jayne Mansfield.* New York: Shapolsky, 1992.

Taki. "High Life: Broad-minded." *Spectator.* 1 February 1992: 40–41.

Thompson, Nelson. *The Dark Side of Camelot.* Chicago: Playboy Press, 1976.

Wallace, Irving, and Amy Wallace. *The Intimate Sex Lives of Famous People.* New York: Delacorte, 1976.

Wilson, Earl. *Show Business Laid Bare.* New York: Putnam, 1974.

Chapter 12: Lyndon B. Johnson

Brower, Montgomery. "Was LBJ's Final Secret a Son?" *People.* 3 August 1987: 30–35.

Bryant, Traphes, and Frances Spatz Leighton. *Dog Days at the White House.* New York: Macmillan, 1975.

Caro, Robert A. *The Years of Lyndon Johnson: The Path to Power.* New York: Knopf, 1982.

———.*The Years of Lyndon Johnson: Means of Ascent.* New York: Knopf, 1990.

259

BIBLIOGRAPHY

Conkin, Paul W. *Big Daddy From the Pedernales*. Boston: Twayne, 1986.

Dallek, Robert. *Lone Star Rising: Lyndon Johnson and His Times 1908–1960*. New York: Oxford University Press, 1991.

Dugger, Ronnie. *The Politician: The Life and Times of Lyndon Johnson—The Drive for Power From the Frontier to Master of the Senate*. New York: Norton, 1982.

Fagan, Leslie. "LBJ's Mistress." New York. *A Current Affair*. February 24, 1992.

Goodwin, Doris K. *Lyndon Johnson and the American Dream*. New York: St. Martin's Press, 1991.

Harwood, Richard, and Haynes Johnson. *Lyndon*. New York: Praeger, 1973.

Joesten, Joachim. *The Dark Side of Lyndon Baines Johnson*. London: Dawnay, 1968.

Kessler, Ronald. *Inside the White House: The Hidden Lives of the Modern Presidents and the Secrets of the World's Most Powerful Institution*. New York: Pocket Books, 1995.

"LBJ's 'Mistress' Signs With Contemporary." *Publishers Weekly*. 16 October 1987: 42–43.

Miller, William "Fishbait," and Francis Spatz Leighton. *Fishbait: The Memoirs of the Congressional Doorkeeper*. New Jersey: Prentice-Hall, 1977.

Mooney, Booth. *LBJ: An Irreverent Chronicle*. New York: Crowell, 1976.

Muslin, Hyman L., and Thomas H. Jobe. *Lyndon Johnson: The Tragic Self*. New York: Insight Books, 1991.

Reedy, George. *Lyndon B. Johnson: A Memoir*. New York: Andrews and McNeel, 1982.

Shenkman, Richard. *Legends, Lies, and Cherished Myths of American History*. New York: Harper & Row, 1988.

Sidney, Hugh. "Upstairs at the White House." *Time*. 18 May 1987: 20.

Chapter 13: Bill Clinton

Allen, Charles F., and J. Portis. *The Comeback Kid: The Life and Career of Bill Clinton*. New York: Carol, 1992.

"Arkansas Police Allege Clinton Sexual Liaisons." *Washington Post*, 20 December 1993.

Brock, David. "His Cheatin' Heart." *American Spectator*. December 20, 1993, reprinted January 1994.

———. "Book Reveals What Makes Clinton Tick." *Capital*. 5 February 95: A.

Buckman, Robert. " 'Troopergate' Attorney Defends Role in Allegations Against President Clinton." *Editor & Publisher*. 14 May 19945: 15-.

Carpozi, George, Jr. *Clinton Confidential: The Climb to Power—The Unauthorized Biography of Bill and Hillary Clinton*. Del Mar, Calif.: Emery Dalton Books, 1995.

"Clinton Hires Attorney to Fend Off Sex Suit." *Capital*. 5 May 1994: A2.

Cooper, Matthew. "Running From the Start." *Washington Post Book World*. 12 February 1995: 1

BIBLIOGRAPHY

Diamond, Edwin. "Gennifer, Part II." *New York.* 17 January 1994: 16–17.

Flowers, Gennifer, with Jacquelyn Dapper. *Gennifer Flowers: Passion and Betrayal.* Del Mar, Calif.: Emery Dalton Books, 1995.

"Former Aide Charges in Court: Dem Front-Runner Had Affair With Miss America." *Star.* January 28 1992; 1.

Gleick, Elizabeth. "Making Book on Clinton." *Time.* 13 February 1995: 27.

Hosenball, M., G. Carroll, and B. Cohn. "No Laughing Matter." *National Affairs.* 16 May 1994: 22–24,

Kessler, Ronald. *Inside the White House: The Hidden Lives of the Modern Presidents and the Secrets of the World's Most Powerful Institution.* New York: Pocket Books, 1995.

King, Norman. *Hillary: Her True Story.* New York: Birch Lane Press, 1993.

Kurtz, Howard. "Brits Keep Tabs on Clinton Sex Life; London Papers Trumpet Tawdry Allegations About the President." *Washington Post.* 3 May 94: B1.

Lacayo, Richard. "Jones V. the President." *Time.* 16 May 1994: 44–46.

Maraniss, David. *First in His Class.* New York; Simon & Schuster, 1995.

Marcus, Ruth. "First Lady Lashes Out at Allegations." *Washington Post.* 21 December 1993: A1, 16.

Mollins, Carol. "The 'Fornigate' Question." *MacLean's.* 21 February 1994: 27–28.

"Money Always on Mind of Presidential Accuser." *Capital.* 5 May 94.

Moore, Jim, with Rick Ihde. *Clinton: Young Man in a Hurry.* Fort Worth: Summit Group, 1992.

Murry, Frank J. "President Stops Short of Denying Stories of Trysts." *Washington Times.* 23 December 93: A1,13.

Nagourney, Benedetto, and Richard and Lewis Davis. "Clinton Forced to Deny Report on Affair—Again." *USA Today.* 24 January 92: 11A.

"The 1992 Campaign: Bush Angrily Denies a Report of an Affair." *New York Times.* 12 August 1992: A14.

Quinn, Sally. "Clinton's Hidden Handicap." *Washington Post.* 30 January 94: C1,4.

Radcliffe, Donnie. *Hillary Rodham Clinton: A First Lady for Our Time.* New York: Warner Books, 1993.

Scheer, Robert. "Lust in the White House." *Playboy.* May 1992, 39:5:39.

Schneider, Howard. "Arkansas Troopers Spark Media Blitz." *Washington Post.* 22 December 93: A16.

———. "Trooper to Break Silence on Paula Jones Lawsuit." *Washington Post.* 29 May 94: A4.

Stump, Joe, and Rex Nelson. "Ex-Clinton Aide Urged Trooper to Recant Claim." *Washington Times.* 25 December 1993: A1,8.

Swan, Jon. "Jennifer." *CJR,* November/December 1992: 36.

Wattenberg, Daniel. "Love and Hate in Arkansas: L. D. Brown's Story." *American Spectator.* April/May 1994.

BIBLIOGRAPHY

Chapter 14: Lessons Learned

Coleman, Fred. "Vive La Difference!" *U.S. News & World Report*. 14 November 1994.

General References

DeGregorio, William. *The Complete Book of U.S. Presidents*. New York: Dembner Books, 1984.

Hunt, Irma. *Dearest Madame: The President's Mistresses*. New York: McGraw-Hill, 1978.

Kohn, George C. *Encyclopedia of American Scandal*. New York; Facts on File, 1989.

Ross, Shelley. *Fall From Grace: Sex, Scandal, and Corruption in American Politics From 1702 to the Present*. New York: Ballantine, 1988.

"Sex and the Presidency." *Life*. August 1987: 70–75.

Index

INDEX

INDEX

George VI, 125
Glass, Alice, 188–90, 203–204
Glass, Mary Louise, 189
Giancana, Sam "Momo," 156, 160
Greer, Germaine, 200
Guccione, Bob, 216–17
Gulley, Bill, 195

Halpin, Maria Crofts, 58, 60–63
Hamzy, Connie, 198, 224–25
Harding, Abigail "Daisy," 91, 97
Harding, Florence, 85, 87, 90, 92–93, 95, 97, 103, 110
Harding, George Tyron, 86
Harding, Phoebe Dickerson, 86
Harding, Warren G., 85–104, 109, 138, 146, 236, 237–38
    and Nan Britton, 85–86, 88, 91–104
    and Carrie Phillips, 86, 88–91, 101
    illegitimate children, 85, 99–100
    and prostitutes, 87–88
Harrison, Benjamin, 65
Hart, Gary, 235–36, 239
Hedin, Sigrid, 134
Hemings, Elizabeth (Betty), 17
Hemings, James, 17
Hemings, Madison, 18–19
Hemings, Sally, 12, 17–21, 238
Hemphill, Margaret, 37
Hendrix, Blake, 213
Heymann, C. David, 162, 178
Hickok, Lorena, 117–18
Hill, Isaac, 28
Hitchens, Peter, 239
Hoover, J. Edgar, 117, 145, 156
Hopkins, Alice, 189
Hopkins, James, 35
Horan, James, 146
House, Colonel Edward M., 78, 80–81
Houston, Sam, 32
Hubbell, Mary Louisa, 44–46
Hubley, Grace, 36
Hughes, Charles Evans, 75
Hulbert, Allen S., 71
Hulbert, Thomas, 71
Hulbert, Mary, see Mary Peck
Humphrey, Hubert, 156
Husted, John, 142

Jack (documentary), 175
Jackson, Andrew, 27–32, 29–30, 39, 235–36, 239
    adulterer, 27, 31, 39
Jackson, Rachel Donelson (Robards), 27–28, 30–32, 235–36, 239
Jacobs, Eliza, 35–36
Jayne Mansfield and the American Fifties (Strait), 163

Jefferson, Lucy Elizabeth, 18
Jefferson, Maria "Polly," 18
Jefferson, Martha "Patsy," 17
Jefferson, Martha W. Skelton, 12, 17–22
Jefferson, Thomas, 11–26, 54, 235, 238
    and Maria Cosway, 12, 22–25
    and Angelica Schuyler Church, 12, 25
    and Sally Hemings, 12, 17–22
    and Dolley Madison, 12, 26
    and Betsey (Moore) Walker, 12–15
JFK (movie), 165
Joesten, Joachim, 187
Johnson, Claudia Alta Taylor "Lady Bird," 138, 182, 184, 188, 189, 190–91, 194–95
Johnson, Lyndon B., 138, 151, 179, 181–95, 217, 236–37
    and Madeleine Brown, 182, 190–95
    and Alice Glass, 182, 188–90
    sexual boasts, 186
    illegitimate children, 182, 191–93, 238
Johnson, Sam Ealy, Jr., 182–83
Jolley, Melissa, 226
Jones, Paula Corbin, 197–98, 227–30
Jones v. Clinton, 229

Kaplan, Dick, 213
Katers, the, 149
Kefauver, Estes, 141, 172, 199
Kellam, Jesse, 190–91
Kelley, Kitty, 160
Kennedy, Caroline, 150
Kennedys—Dynasty and Disaster, The (Davis), 179
Kennedy, Ethel, 171
Kennedy, Eunice, 171
Kennedy, Jacqueline Bouvier, 136, 138, 141, 142, 144, 148, 149, 150, 153, 162, 173, 174, 175, 176–77, 178
    affairs, 148
    premarital sex, 142
Kennedy, John Fitzgerald, 26, 30, 135–80, 195, 199, 210, 216, 220, 233, 235–37, 239
    and Inga Arvad, 136, 144–46
    and Suzy Chang, 136, 147
    and Judy Campbell, 137, 151–60, 165, 174
    and Jill Cowan, 136, 150–51
    and Angie Dickinson, 137–138, 164–65
    and Joan Lundberg, 136, 147–48
    and Jayne Mansfield, 137, 163–65, 174
    and Mary Pinchot Meyer, 137, 159–62
    and Marilyn Monroe, 137, 164–70, 174
    and Marie Novotny, 136, 147
    and Florence Prichett (Smith), 137, 151
    and Blaze Starr, 136, 146
    and Tempest Storm, 136, 146
    and Gene Tierney, 137, 162–63
    and Pamela Turnure, 136, 148–49

INDEX